POLITICAL PORTRAITS

POLITICAL PORTRAITS

BY

CHARLES WHIBLEY

KENNIKAT PRESS
Port Washington, N. Y./London

POLITICAL PORTRAITS

First published in 1917
Reissued in 1970 by Kennikat Press
Library of Congress Catalog Card No: 70-112821
ISBN 0-8046-1088-6

Manufactured by Taylor Publishing Company   Dallas, Texas

CONTENTS

THOMAS WOLSEY

MINISTER OF WAR

IT has always been the fond boast of the English that they 'muddle through,' however hard they are beset. The boast is not the boast of wisdom and courage. He, indeed, is foolish who would let his bravery outrun his prudence; and there is small merit in success which comes by accident. The truth is that the man who first made a virtue of carelessness deserved very ill of his country. Even if we praise the valour which refuses to acknowledge defeat, we must esteem yet more highly the foresight and design which make defeat impossible from the first. However, our vice and our boast find their origin in the very beginnings of our history. We have always thrown away wilfully our armies and our energies, and not always has a War Minister come in the nick of time to save us from the consequences of our folly.

One such Minister was Thomas Wolsey, a spiritual ancestor in the direct line of William Pitt, father and son, of Castlereagh, and of other stout contrivers of victory. Born to a great inheritance of wisdom, he was a natural Minister of State, as Shakespeare was a natural poet. The genius which God gave him he marvellously perfected, until he lived in treaties and thought in campaigns. The very limitations of his talent favoured his success. Friend as he was of scholars, prodigal founder as he proved himself of learned houses, he was not of the breed of Erasmus and More. A Churchman by profession, he was no profound theologian ; of the Reformation, which in his day tore Europe in pieces, he saw none other than the political aspect. But if his King and his country were touched, he was instant in defence as he was prudent in counsel. So there was a oneness in his character which made him irresistible to England's enemies. Endowed with such a weight of authority as scarce another has ever upheld, he was able by a word or a gesture to enforce his will upon the world. Moreover, as his biographer says, ' he had a special gift of natural eloquence, with a filed tongue to pro-nounce the same, that he was able to allure and per-suade all men to his purpose.' And happy indeed was the monarch who might lean upon his patriotism and experience !

When Henry VIII. came to the throne he wished nothing so ardently as to distinguish himself in the pageantries of war and peace. His flamboyant de-meanour, the gaiety of his aspect, were as far as the poles apart from the hard, penurious austerity of his father, whose hoarded wealth he was presently to squander with a lavish hand. The testimony of foreigners is unanimous in enthusiasm. To choose

one of many tributes, here is what the oft-cited
Giustinian, Venetian ambassador, reported of him to
the Seigniory : ' His Majesty,' says he, ' is twenty-
nine years old, and very handsome. Nature could
not have done more for him. He is much handsomer
than any other sovereign in Christendom ; a great
deal handsomer than the King of France ; very fair,
and his whole frame admirably proportioned. On
hearing that Francis I. wore a beard, he allowed his
own to grow ; and as it is reddish, he has now got a
beard that looks like gold. He is highly accomplished ;
a good musician ; composes well ; is a most capital
horseman ; a fine jouster ; speaks good French,
Latin, and Spanish ; is very religious ; hears three
masses daily when he hunts, and sometimes five on
other days. He hears the Office every day in the
Queen's Chamber : that is to say, vesper and com-
pline. He is very fond of hunting, and never takes
his diversion without tiring eight or ten horses, which
he causes to be stationed beforehand along the line
of country he means to take ; and when one is tired
he mounts another, and before he gets home they
are all exhausted. He is extremely fond of tennis,
at which game it is the prettiest thing to see him
play, his fair skin glowing through a shirt of the
finest texture.' The Venetian's panegyric was well
deserved. In brief, it seemed to an expectant Europe
that there was nothing which this paragon of all the
virtues could not accomplish, with the aid of the
wisest of living counsellors. Truly, ' my King and

I' might have inspired all their adversaries with a salutary fear.

And yet, at the outset, Henry and his adviser were compelled to set England right in the eyes of the Continent. Her own troubles had driven her from the councils of the great Powers. The Wars of the Roses had taken their toll not only of men but of repute, and upon the seventh Henry had fallen the dull duty of re-establishing the credit of his realm. Henry VIII., being rich and ambitious, lost little time in attempting to prove his prowess in the field. His first campaign was a dismal failure. In alliance with Ferdinand, his father-in-law, he devised an attack upon France. An expedition left England in May 1512 for Spain, and arrived a month later at Fuenter-rabia. Here disaster upon disaster overtook the English. They were ill-fed, and not housed at all. The Spanish suns burnt them; the Spanish rains brought pestilence upon them. Deprived of the beef and beer which were the staple of their diet, they had no stomach for the fight. Above all, they clamoured loudly for their beer, of which their normal allowance was but a poor gallon a head daily, and without which they refused to move hand or foot. ' And it please your Grace,' wrote Stile to the King, ' the greatest lack of victuals that is here is of beer, for your subjects had lever for to drink beer than wine or cider; for the hot wine doth harm them, and the cider doth cast them in disease and sickness.' Nor even had they been willing to fight were they given the opportunity. Ferdinand, after his wont, took refuge in intrigue and delay. And the English soldiers mutinied first, and afterwards went on strike for higher pay. Finally, they threw off all discipline, and sailed for home without orders. The humiliation of England and her King was complete. 'You see,' said the Emperor, 'Englishmen have so long abstained from war, they lack experience from disuse.'

Then it was that Wolsey changed in a flash the whole aspect of affairs. Though he held no higher office than that of King's Almoner, he took sole charge of the campaign which in the following year was fought in France, and proved that he possessed all the qualities of a Minister at War. 'Proceeding thus in fortune's blissfulness,' says Cavendish, Wolsey's biographer, 'it chanced the wars between France and England to be open, in so much as the King, being fully persuaded, and resolved, in his most royal person to invade his foreign enemies with a puissant army, to delay their hault brags, within their own territory: wherefore it was thought very necessary, that this royal enterprise should be speedily provided and plentifully furnished in every degree of things apt and convenient for the same; the expedition whereof the King's highness thought no man's wit so meet, for policy and painful travail, as his well-beloved almoner's was, to whom therefore he committed his whole affiance and trust therein. And he being nothing scrupulous in anything that the King would command him to do, although it seemed to other very

difficile, took upon him the whole charge and burden
of all this business, and proceeded so therein, that
he brought all things to a good pass and purpose in a
right decent order, as of all manner of victuals, provisions, and other necessaries, convenient for so noble
a voyage and puissant army.' Cavendish was no politician. He knew not why England and France was
at war. He did know that, when once war was
declared, the King could find no better man to think
and to do than his almoner, Wolsey.

With the expedition of 1512 as a warning before
his eyes, Wolsey set himself to create and equip a
new army. The rank and file, which refused to bear
the yoke of discipline in Spain, the officers who knew
not how to command, were replaced by men who
had learned to obey, by commanders who insisted
upon obedience. The conditions of the time made
his duties easier than they would be to-day. His
hand was not weakened by the memory of an ancient
and obsequious friendship with the enemy. It was
not his business to discover the path of popularity.
He was not asked to conciliate the rebel or to keep the
constituencies in good humour. In brief, he was an
autocrat. All the functions of Government were
concentrated in him and him alone. He was not a
member of a war committee; he was a whole war
committee in his own proper person.[1] Nothing was

---

[1] Those who would measure the full achievement of Wolsey
may be referred to Dr. Brewer's great history of Henry VIII.,
and to Mr. Ernest Law's essay, *England's First Great*

beyond the scope of his activity ; nothing was too low for the grasp of his intelligence. Whatever men he needed for the campaign were at his disposal. The pitiful divorce of the citizen from the soldier had not been made in Henry VIII.'s reign, and nothing was necessary but to issue Commissions of Array to the Sheriffs of the southern counties, ' to make proclamations for all males between sixty and sixteen to be in readiness at an hour's warning to resort to such place in the said county as shall be assigned.' The notice, short and sharp, was obeyed perforce, and Wolsey might boast that he sent across the Channel an army of 40,000 men, armed and provisioned—the largest force that ever England landed on the Continent before the year 1914. It is not easy to exaggerate the greatness of Wolsey's achievement. His system of transport fell very far below our modern standard, and the heavy loads put upon our ships were all the heavier, because the warfare of the sixteenth century was in one sense far more elaborate than the warfare of to-day. When the Tudors met their enemies in the field, war was a pageant. as well as a business. It was not enough for them to beat their enemies ; they must beat them in accord with the splendid tradition of chivalry. If Henry VIII. took the field as a soldier, he must be housed as a king. The tents in which he and his generals lived were

War Minister, in which the almoner of Henry VIII. is set vividly before us, and an appropriate moral is drawn from his career.

symbols of the royal magnificence, and for the glory
and honour of England no detail of display might be
omitted.   And while Wolsey was asked to remember
all the trappings of kingship, he forgot nothing that
was needed for the carriage and maintenance of a big
army.   With a careful foresight, malt, beans, oats,
oxen, and lambs were ordered in vast quantities to
be collected together at Calais, and so well were the
orders carried out, that ' 40,000 men were living in
the camp before Tournay in time of war,' Richard
Pace tells us, ' far more cheaply than they lived at
home in time of peace.'   And in all these preparations Wolsey played the first, the only part.   He
became learned in all the matters of commissariat.
He was busy, says Brewer, ' with beer, beef, and
biscuit, transports, foists, and empty casks.'   With a
full knowledge that the lack of beer in Spain had
caused a mutiny, he was resolved that no English
soldier should lack his gallon a day.   A campaign
thus well organised could have but one end.   Terou-
enne fell into the hands of the English on August 22 ;
Tournay's surrender followed a month later ;   and
Wolsey, having justified the King's confidence, held
and maintained for many a year his supremacy in the
council chamber.

Thus it was that the English army, well trained
and well equipped, fought with all the pomp and
gallantry ordained by the chivalrous spirit of the age.
The aspect and behaviour of the soldiers were the
wonder of foreign nations.   Here is the testimony

of one enthusiastic Italian : ' Choicer troops, in more
perfect order, have not been seen for years. Amongst
them are from 9000 to 10,000 heavy barbed cavalry,
and 8000 light horse; the infantry includes 14,000
archers, and there are 2000 mounted bowmen. . . .
Others have spears, halberts, and axes, and cannon
that would suffice to conquer Hell.' So much for their
equipment. Their conduct, if we may believe another
Italian, fell not below the high level of Henry v.'s,
of Cromwell's, or of Kitchener's men. ' They are
efficient troops,' we are told, ' well accoutred, not
barefooted like those of Italy, men who do not go to
rob, but to gain honour, and who march at their own
cost. They do not take wenches with them, and they
are not profane swearers, like our soldiers. Indeed,
there are few who fail to recite daily the office of Our
Lady's rosary.' So our soldiers, then as now, ' went
into battle as though they were going to a sport or
game,' and if they fought always with clean hands and
stout hearts, it was due above all to the inspiration
of Wolsey. The only blot upon the army was the
conduct of our German allies. Nothing could
check their ingrained love of rapine and sacrilege.
They proved themselves worthy ancestors of the
modern Huns, whom we know too well. The testimony of an amiable Spaniard cannot be gainsaid.
The Spaniard complains, as well he might, of ' their
arrogance, ruffianism, and beastliness, which made
them firebrands and a source of danger among
whomsoever they went.' And that nothing should be

missing in this prophetic condemnation, the Spaniard asserts that ' such is their greediness that any one of them is ready to run the risk of introducing the plague into the ranks of the army in which they are serving by recklessly entering a village or farmhouse known to be stricken with the disease, simply with the object of stealing a chicken.' Strange, indeed, is the immutability of the Germans, and no better comment can be found for them, as we know them, than the familiar words of Froissart : ' Maudits soient-ils, ce sont gens sans pitié et sans honneur.'

It was, then, the campaign of 1513 which assured the rapid rise of Wolsey. Honours and offices were showered upon him, and at each step he increased marvellously in splendour and esteem. He lived, as I have said, in an age of pageantry, and he outdid even the King his master in the magnificence of his state. He moved always as though upon parade. Poleaxes and golden candlesticks preceded him wherever he went. Cavendish, his simple biographer, has enumerated the yeomen, the cooks, the servants of his household, with a proper pride, and makes us wonder that the many-coloured trappings of Wolsey's life did not strangle life itself. The gorgeous tapestries of Hampton Court Palace, which were changed once a week ; the fine cloths of diaper ; the cupboards of plate, parcel-gilt ; the other cupboards of gilt plate, very sumptuous and of the newest fashions ; the lights of wax as big as torches ; the silver and gilt plate, which hung on the walls to give light to the chambers—all these marvels surpass the fancies of fairyland. Nor was there any lack at Hampton Court of masks, tourneys, of those sports which were a necessary part of the pomp of the Tudors. And Wolsey's own splendour and solemn cheer must not be mistaken for mere vainglory. They were but images of his inward ambition, the signs of his overweening and justified pride. Moreover, there was in them a basis of sound sense. Wolsey knew the English people as he knew the English King, and he saw plainly that he could govern them only by flattering their love of display. The mob might gird at his extravagance, the satirists might hurl their insults at ' the butcher's dog ' ; but Wolsey cared not. He was no butcher's dog, that he should walk in the path of humility. He believed that the highest honours to be won on earth, even the papacy itself, were within his grasp. Wherefore the magnificence of Hampton Court seemed to him a worthy means to a great end, and not the ' fantastical dream ' of Cavendish's imagining.

And Wolsey, for all his splendour, showed himself always the kindly champion of the poor. Giustinian, the panegyrist of Henry viii., has sketched Wolsey's portrait also in words. After praising his eloquence, his ability, and his energy ; after admitting that he alone transacted the business, which in Venice occupied all the magistracies, all the offices, and all the councils, he thus describes him : ' He is pensive, and has the reputation of being extremely just. He favours the people, especially the poor, hearing their suits and seeking to despatch them instantly. He also makes the lawyers plead gratis for paupers. He is in very great repute, seven times more so than if he were Pope.' That was one side of the omnipotent Wolsey. The other side is wonderful indeed, when we remember the arrogance of the King. 'Wolsey is the person,' Giustinian goes on, ' who rules both the King and the kingdom. On my first arrival in England he used to say, " His Majesty will do so and so " ; subsequently by degrees he went on forgetting himself, and began saying, " We shall do so and so " ; at this present he has reached such a pitch that he says, " I shall do so and so." '

At that pitch he stayed for some twenty years. Not only was he Minister of War, he was also Lord Chancellor and Lord of the Treasury. He held bishoprics, and wore a cardinal's hat at the same time that he governed the country. He was in full charge of foreign affairs, and since it was in them that he was most intimately at home, he made himself arbiter of the destinies of Europe. The most powerful man of his time, not only in England but in the world, he used his influence always like a patriot. His policy of domination was uniformly successful. If we remember what England was before his Great War of 1513, and recall the height to which he raised her, we can measure vaguely the worth of his achievement. In all his thoughts and in all his deeds he was the pious servant of England, and he had the power to serve her because he was one of those rare men who at the same time could take large views and not overlook the importance of details. Despite the detraction of the chronicles, and the envy of those who presently divided his offices among them, he remains unassailable in glory and devotion. When he fell, the hopes of England fell for a time with him. The King did not recover from his loss. Without Wolsey's guiding hand to sustain him, he lapsed into the middle-class Bluebeard of popular history, the monarch who saw no other way out from a distasteful marriage than murder.

That Wolsey should fall was inevitable. In the very heyday of his power he was but preparing the necessary last act of his own drama. That there were contributory causes of disaster is obvious. The part which he had played in the divorce, the hatred of Anne Boleyn, who could not forget or mitigate her resentment, helped in his undoing. Then there was the rise to power of new Ministers, and the King's inherited greed for the possessions of other men—two potent influences working against him. But it was chiefly the nemesis which lies in wait for the greatest of men that brought the Cardinal low. So high had he climbed, that no other summit remained within the scope of his vision. And seated upon the topmost pinnacle of fame, he could change neither his purpose nor his method. The young generation misunderstood his pomp and made light of his services. 'The King has gone beyond me,' he said in Shakespeare's play, in sad explanation of his ruin. And yet the ruin itself was not so sad as the manner of it. Cavendish has left us an imperishable picture of his master's last days. We see sketched with a simple hand the great Cardinal riding up Putney Hill on his mule, and dismounting to kneel in the mire, with bowed head, before Sir Harry Norris. 'I am sorry,' quoth he to Norris, 'that I have no condign token to send to the King. But if ye would at this my request present the King with this poor Fool, I trust His Highness would accept him well, for surely for a nobleman's pleasure he is worth a thousand pounds.' We see six tall yeomen sent to convey the Fool to the Court, for the poor Fool, constant in fidelity, refused except by force to leave his master. And so Wolsey came to his place at Esher, and found no peace there. For his enemies at Court feared him more after his fall than in his prosperity, because they thought that by the King's favour he might be readopted into authority. 'Therefore,' says Cavendish, 'they took this order among them in their matters, that daily they would send something or do something against him, wherein they thought they might give him a cause of heaviness or lamentation.' Thus one day they would persuade the King to dismiss some of his gentlemen, another day they would have him stripped of some of his promotions. But he was a brave and a wise man, and he bore their malice in patience.

The King, wavering always between fear and affection, knew not how to treat his ancient favourite. Once upon a time, when the Cardinal fell sick, he bade his physician, Dr. Butts, go in haste to Esher. Now Dr. Butts told the King that, if he would have the Cardinal to live he must despatch him straightway a comfortable message. ' Even so will I,' said the King, ' and by you.' And he sent him as a token of goodwill and favour a ring, which the Cardinal knew well, for himself had given it to the King, and which contained a ruby, whereon was engraved the King's visage, ' as lively counterfeit,' says Cavendish, ' as was possible to be devised.' But no favour went with the gift, and Wolsey, still beset by the restlessness of disease, must needs leave Esher at once. And so he began his wanderings, sojourning a while at Richmond, and then setting forth, when money had been found for the purpose, to visit his benefice of York. Wherever he went on his journey he was received with a kindly enthusiasm by the people. When he could, he recovered something of his old state and much of his ancient charity. Shorn of his honours and his wealth, he took pleasure in the one boon left him, the boon of liberty. To Cavendish, who wondered why he had confessed himself guilty in the *praemunire*, he replied that he would rather yield and confess the matter, ' committing the sole sum thereof, as he did, unto the King's clemency and mercy, and live at large, like a poor vicar, than to lie in prison with all the goods and honours that he had.' Yet was there no resting-place for the poor vicar's head. He travelled, it seems, to escape not from his enemies but from himself. From Peterborough to Southwell he wandered, from Southwell to Saxby, and then, about the feast of St. Michael, he took the road towards Cawood Castle, ' where he lay long after with much honour and love of the county, both of the worshipful and the simple.' So he, who yesterday had been the ruler of Europe, spent his days in religious observances and in humility of soul, still dreading and still conscious of an impending doom. The omens were bad, and omens meant a vast deal to his pious mind. After dinner upon All Hallows' Day, one Dr. Augustine, physician, ' having a boisterous gown of black velvet upon him,' overthrew a cross which stood in the corner, and which fell upon Dr. Bonner's head, that the blood ran down. ' Hath it drawn any blood ? ' asked the Cardinal. ' Yea, forsooth, my lord,' answered Cavendish, ' as it seemeth me.' To Wolsey it was a *malum omen*, for in the signification, which he presently gave it, he was the cross, and Augustine, who overthrew it, was he who should accuse him, which came to pass. So that when the Earl of Northumberland and Master Walshe were sent to arrest him on the false charge of high treason, they met one expecting the worst disaster which might befall him. Yet he kept his courage high, and would not obey the Earl's arrest, because the Earl refused to show his commission. ' I trow, gentleman,' said he to Walshe, ' ye be one of the King's privy chamber ; your name, I suppose, is

Walshe ; I am content to yield unto you, but not to my Lord of Northumberland without I see his commission.' And when Cavendish bade him be of good cheer, for he could surely clear himself of all the surmised accusations of his enemies, ' Yea,' quoth he, with the pride of one who had been Lord Chancellor and Archbishop, ' if I may come to mine answer, I fear no man alive ; for he liveth not upon the earth that shall look upon this face (pointing to his own face), shall be able to accuse me of any untruth.' And what wonder was it that, at the last dinner which he ate as a free man, there was not a dry eye among those who sat at table with him !

When on the morrow he took his departure, riding upon a mule, the people of the county to the number of three thousand bade him farewell, crying with a loud voice, ' God save your Grace.' And as they rode he asked Cavendish whither they led him that night, and when he was told to Pomfret, ' Alas,' said he, ' shall I go to the castle, and lie there, and die like a dog ? ' But it was not at the castle of sinister memories, but at the abbey that they lodged ; and so, still accompanied by thousands of sorrowing people, they came to Sheffield Park, and there abode several weeks, until Sir William Kingston, Constable of the Tower, arrived with a guard to conduct Wolsey to the King's Majesty. His friends hoped that Kingston's coming was a token of the King's favour towards him, who would now at last be heard in his own defence. But in the Cardinal's ears the mere name of Kingston had the sound of doom. The soothsayers had long ago predicted that at Kingston he would have his end, and though he had always avoided the passage through the town of that name, he saw that at last the prophecy was coming true. However, he was subject to fortune, as he said, and to fortune he submitted himself. And then disease suddenly overtook him, relieving him of prison and robbing the greedy King of his prey. When he reached Leicester Abbey he knew himself a dying man. 'Father Abbot,' said he, 'I am come hither to leave my bones among you.' And as the sickness increased and he found no hope of recovery, he summoned Sir William Kingston to him, and made the speech upon which Shakespeare has conferred a gracious immortality. 'Well, well, Master Kingston,' said he, 'I see the matter against me how it is framed; but if I had served God as diligently as I have done the King, He would not have given me over in my grey hairs.' Thereafter he would have Kingston commend him to the King, and warned him to be well advised what matter he put in the King's head, 'for,' said he, 'ye shall never put it out again.' And lastly, he urged the King's Majesty, through Kingston, to keep a vigilant eye upon the pernicious sect of Lutherans, and thus, having delivered his supreme message, he died, in accord with his prophecy, as the clock struck eight.

When Cavendish brought Henry VIII. the tidings of the death of his faithful servant, the King received the news with his wonted composure. He was shooting with the bow, and finished his sport before he listened to the tragic story which Cavendish had to tell. And then, having wished liefer than twenty thousand pounds that Wolsey had lived, he asked incontinently for some fifteen hundred pounds, which Wolsey had delivered sealed to a certain priest. When Cavendish had satisfied his avarice, the King demanded that this gear should be kept secret between them, and delivered that homily upon discretion which will be ever memorable. 'Three may keep counsel,' said he, 'if two be away; and if I thought that my cap knew my counsel, I would cast it into the fire and burn it.' Thus he passed to what he thought were weightier matters, recking not that he had lost the wisest, staunchest counsellor that ever stood by the side of an ambitious king; and if we read without distaste Cavendish's homily upon the mutability of vain honours and the brittle assurance of abundance, those commonplaces of truth which we expect at the end of a Greek tragedy, we may remember with gratitude that Wolsey, fulfilling his genius in many ways, was one among the greatest of our Ministers of War, and that he still remains to his humbler successors a shining example of lofty courage and tireless energy.

SHAKESPEARE

PATRIOT AND TORY

SHAKESPEARE, whose tercentenary we celebrated amid the alarums and excursions of
war, has paid the full penalty, as he has taken the
generous guerdon of his greatness. Standing alone
upon the topmost mountain of fame, he has been the
mark, since death took him, for the slings and arrows of
perverted fantasy. The 'humourists,' as Ben Jonson
might have called them, have used his works as the
whetstone of their derogating ingenuity. They are of
many kinds, these humourists, and of many whims.
We all know those painstaking critics who would pluck,
if they could, the garland from Shakespeare's brow
—who, having shaped in their mind some image of the
poet, declare irrelevantly that they find not the linea-
ments of their ideal in the actor of Stratford. Who
are they that they should select the delicate colour
of the poet's singing robes, or dare to weigh in their
common scales the poet's brain and heart ? Even if
history had not taught them that poetry, impartial as
death, knocks, if it choose, at the cottage door, they
cannot dispute or abolish the testimony of Shakespeare's friends and contemporaries. Was Ben Jonson,

then, part and parcel of a great conspiracy when he acclaimed the sweet Swan of Avon? Was he throwing dust in posterity's eyes when he recorded the Players' praise of Shakespeare, that ' in his writing (whatsoever he penn'd) he never blotted out a line,' and gave his own answer, ' would he had blotted a thousand!' Was he a gross impostor whose memory Ben Jonson honoured ' on this side idolatry as much as any,' and of whom he said, ' he was indeed honest, and of an open and free nature; had an excellent fancy; brave notions and gentle expressions; wherein he flowed with that facility that sometime it was necessary he should be stopp'd'? *Sufflaminandus erat* —that is the tribute which scholarship ever pays to inspiration; and for the rest, Ben Jonson has so clearly described the poet, whom we know, that not all the Inns of Court shall pervert him into a legal monster of their own imagining. That a lawyer should be a great poet is clearly impossible. That a poet's apprehensive mind should acquire, with other vocabularies, the jargon of the courts, is in accord with all the world's experience.

And then comes the witling, who for his own better advertisement proclaims aloud the inferiority of Shakespeare to the moderns, who complains that the author of *Hamlet* had not the mind of a parish councillor, and who misses in *Macbeth* and *Othello* the subtle psychology of *Rosmersholm*. The witling matters not; he is but the symptom of a recurring folly; and when once his motive of self-aggrandisement is revealed he should be sent instantly into a deserved oblivion. He does not come for the first time upon the earth, and we may be sure that he will be seen again, unless vanity and stupidity are overtaken by sudden death. Coleridge knew him, and gave his folly a final answer. ' The Englishman,' he wrote, ' who without reverence, a proud and affectionate reverence, can utter the name of William Shakespeare, stands disqualified for the office of critic. He wants one at least of the very senses, the language of which he is to employ, and will discourse at best but as a blind man while the whole harmonious creation of light and shade, with all its subtle interchange of deepening and dissolving colours, rises in silence to the silent *fiat* of the uprising Apollo.'

The desire of the critics, especially when the critics have themselves essayed the art of drama, comes from the same sort of reaction which persuaded the Athenians to ostracise Aristides. They are tired of hearing Shakespeare's praises sung. So they find him coarse or barbarous, deficient in ' psychology ' or clumsy in construction. One insult commonly thrown at him is that he knew not what he did, that he happened upon such mastery of speech and drama as was his by a kind of accident. But in the realm of art there are no accidents. It is absurd to imagine Shakespeare sitting down to the composition of *Henry IV*., let us say, and sketching the superb speeches of Falstaff without premeditation. If he never

blotted a line, how many thoughts, I wonder, did he
blot out from his mind ? He came to his writing,
' whatsoever he penn'd,' with the processes of invention complete, and nothing left for accomplishment
but the mere breathing of poetry upon paper. And
when his work was done he knew better than any
other living man that it was good. In truth, none of
his time exceeded him in judgment as none excelled
him in inspiration. Like the complete artist that he
was, he was conscious always of his work's beauty
and perfection. Even Jonson, who loved the lamp
more piously than did Shakespeare, and disdained
not inkhorn terms, gave credit, full and ample, to
his master's art :

> ' For though the Poet's matter Nature be,
>   His art doth give the fashion.'

Even Jonson found words of lofty praise for Shakespeare's ' well-tuned and true-filed lines,' and admitted that he was a poet made as well as born. But
later writers have grumbled because they have not
found in Shakespeare's works what he never purposed
to put there. ' The mere dreams of a pedantry that
arraigns the eagle because it has not the dimensions
of the swan ' !

And then comes along another critic, who asserts
that Shakespeare lacked invention, that he had
' impulse ' and not ' fine thought,' that he lagged
sadly behind Ibsen, the belauded poet of the north.
Dumas was not of this critic's opinion. Shake-

speare, said he, 'after the good God, had created the most,' and humbly I range myself on the side of Dumas. The critics who deny Shakespeare 'invention' keep that quality within the narrowest limits. For them it is the mere making up of a story out of the poet's head. There was no such person in real life as Hedda Gabler, they say in effect ; such a person as Falstaff was known to his compatriots ; therefore Ibsen invented and Shakespeare did not. Was ever such nonsense talked in the guise of criticism ? The term 'invention' may not thus be limited. A single happy phrase may show far more of it than the most elaborately complicated situation. And if, in following the Greek tragedians, Shakespeare chose for the material of his plays plots and persons familiar to all men, he made whatever he touched his own, he filled with the blood of life the puppets of the chronicles, and showed himself the greatest inventor that ever expressed the emotions of men and women in noble speech and coloured imagery.

And behind the confused critic stands the sad biographer, who in the act of publishing a solid work laments that we know little or nothing of Shakespeare, because what the newspapers might have said about him, had there been newspapers, has escaped us. So he attempts to fill up the inevitable blank with scraps of conjecture and snippets of old deeds. That much good may be achieved by the industrious hodman none will deny. Nothing that touches Shakespeare is indifferent to us, and there is a certain heroism in the struggle which would rescue him from the oblivion of death. But the dryasdust biographer should remember that the Shakespeare best worth discovery is already known to us more clearly than any of his age and kind. He did not keep a dog in his yard to write his plays for him. He wrote them himself, and it is in them that we shall find the true poet whom we seek. When the pedants are at fault, it is enough to turn to the plays, for in them Shakespeare has revealed what manner of man he was, and has packed for all time the true story of his life. With the poet's text at our elbow, need we regret that we cannot follow his movements from Stratford to London, from London back again to Stratford ? Remember Coleridge's lament : ' O that eternal bricker-up of Shakespeare ! Registers, memorandum books—and that Bill, Jack and Harry, Tom, Walter and Gregory, Charles, Dick and Jim lived at that house, but that nothing more is known of them,' and resolve not to lose the substance of the plays for the shadow of archæology. Shakespeare, in truth, should be the man we know best, because he has said more to us than others, and it is to the plays, not to the biographer, that we must put the question who and what he was.

In the first place, he was a great Englishman, born at England's heart. He had none of the ' yearning ' and ' passion of revolt ' which some associate to-day with the Iberian fringe. Matthew Arnold did his memory a great disservice when he called his ' openness and flexibility of spirit' not English. The very fact that it was Shakespeare's makes it English. How shall you form a definition of 'English' and omit Shakespeare's genius from the argument ? The truth is that wherever Shakespeare's fancy seemed to roam, to Athens or to Verona, or to the sea-coast of Bohemia, it was still active at Stratford or on the Cotswolds. The names of distant cities meant nothing to him. He did but take them out of the story-books and make them his own and England's. He cared not a jot for the false 'local colour' wherewith the actor-manager is wont to over-decorate his plays. 'The flowers of Warwickshire,' says Madden, 'blossom in every clime, and we encounter in the most unlikely places the familiar characters of rural life—under a pent-house in Messina, in the cottage of a Bohemian shepherd, and in the hall of an Italian noble.' Theseus hunts the country about Athens with English hounds, and even Prospero's spirits are of the true breed, for he sets them on ' by names well known in Gloucester-shire kennels.' Moreover, the characters of Shake-speare's plays are as purely English as the scene which environs them, or as the metaphor which glows in their speech. *Troilus and Cressida*, for instance, has little touch with Homer save in its names. You must not expect to find in Achilles and Ulysses, in Thersites and Pandarus of Troy, the chaste memory of a Grecian urn. Their origin is romantic ; they bear themselves as true Elizabethans upon the stage. They are the men that Shakespeare met and knew at

Paris garden or in the taverns of London, genuine contemporaries of English blood and bone. No pale reflection, they, of the classical dictionary. Bravely they ruffle it in galligaskins, and should they ever appear upon our stage again, as I would they might, let them be habited not as Greeks and Trojans, but as the careless venturers of Shakespeare's day.

And if the English countryside was always a cherished memory to him, Shakespeare was no less loyal in devotion to the London of his time. When in 1586 he left Stratford to seek his fortune, London was indeed worthy the worship of a constant lover. It was the moment of England's belated rebirth. The spirit of curiosity, which had already restored the Greek and Latin classics to Italy, and had enriched France with the wisdom of Rabelais, was at last revivifying the wise land of England. And the renaissance took its own shape and form when it came across the Channel. Not only did the English follow eagerly the things of the mind ; they expressed a new-found energy in warlike enterprises and dauntless adventures oversea. The London to which Shakespeare came was agog with the glory of Drake, who, having singed the Spaniard's beard, had come back laden with the spoils of Cadiz and the isles. Returned soldiers were talking with hushed voices of Sir Philip Sidney's valour and sacrifice on the field of Zutphen. The discovery of plots devised against the Queen's safety and the punishment of the rebels had strengthened the loyalty of the people. The English sailors were making that conquest of the sea which was to inspire the epic of Hakluyt. The heroic Davys was searching ' for a passage under the frozen zone, by the upper part of America, to East India.' Nor was Cavendish far behind his rival. ' At the same time, in another part of the world,' says Camden, ' Thomas Cavendish of Suffolk, who had two years before set sail from England with three ships, passing the Straits of Magellan, fired many petty towns of the Spaniards upon the coasts of Chili, Peru, and Nova Spagnia, took and pillaged nineteen merchant ships, and amongst them a very rich ship of the King's near California, and returned home this year (1587) by the Philippines, the Malaccas, the Cape of Good Hope, and St. Helen's Isle, with a rich booty and great glory, as being the second next after Magellan which sailed about the world.'

Then came the greatest year of all, 1588—*annus mirabilis* Camden calls it—which the German chronologers presaged would be the climacterical year of the world. ' The rumours of war,' says the chronicler, ' which were before but slight, began now to increase every day more and more ; and now not by uncertain fame, but by loud and joint voice of all men, it was noised abroad that a most invincible Armada was rigged and prepared in Spain against England, and that the foremost captains and expertest leaders and old soldiers were sent for out of Italy, Sicily, yea, and out of America, into Spain.' The Spaniard, like many an

enemy since, found reasons not a few why he could not
be cheated of victory—'that England was not fortified,
that it was unprovided of leaders, soldiers, horsemen,
and munitions, bare of wealth and friends, that there
were many in all parts of the realm addicted to the
Romish religion, who would presently join their
forces with his.' Thus was the old and new story of
weakness and dissension told by our foes, and pointed
with the same moral. But to those alive in London
the years of triumphing adventure brought a pride
in which there was no vainglory. It is easy to
imagine that Shakespeare's quick and buoyant temper
responded to the news of victory. In many a blind
ale-house by Thames' side he would drink with sailors
home from America or the Spanish Main, with the
salt spray still on their beards, and hear the yarns
they spun of their ancient captains, Cavendish and
Davys. Or he would watch the soldier as he turned
back his sleeve to show the wounds he had won in the
service of his country. So the pride of England was
kindled in his breast. So he became the ardent lover
of his land that we know him. It was not for him to
disdain what nowadays we call imperialism. He was
no 'intellectual,' that he should make the vague
brotherhood of man the cloak of cowardice. He sang
the glory and valour of his England with a passion
and a fervour which make us glad that in days of bitter
warfare we were called to celebrate his name and fame.
What happier time could we have found to sing his
praise than the year in which we were crushing a

viler, crueller foe than any whom Elizabeth, his Queen, was asked to drive from her shores?

The poet of England, he gave to the love of country, to patriotism as nowadays we call it, a voice which never shall be stilled. His histories are, and will ever be, the epic of our race. The great Marlborough confessed that he owed what he knew of England's past to Shakespeare—and how many of Marlborough's countrymen have echoed his confession! The splendid sequence of plays from *King John* to *Henry VIII*. has been the breviary of many a gallant captain and wise statesman. And while Shakespeare's pride in England never flags, he does not forget what she owes to the jocund fate which made her an island. His clairvoyant spirit easily discerned the power of the sea. He tires not in celebrating

> ' The natural bravery of our isle, which stands
> As Neptune's park, ribbed and paled in
> With rocks unscaleable and roaring waters,
> With sands that will not bear your enemies' boats,
> But suck them up to the topmast.'

Many are the happy phrases which he finds for England's insularity : ' our salt-water girdle,' ' our sea-walled garden '—these are but two of his conceits. But it is in the famous passage of *Richard II*. that he most loudly acclaims our white cliffs, and pays as lofty a tribute to his England as ever was paid to Athens, the violet-crowned :

> ' This royal throne of kings, this scepter'd isle,
> This earth of majesty, this seat of Mars,

This other Eden, demi-paradise;
This fortress built by Nature for herself
Against infection and the hand of war;
This happy breed of men, this little world,
This precious stone set in the silver sea,
Which serves it in the office of a wall
Or as a moat defensive to a house,
Against the envy of less happier lands;
This blessed plot, this earth, this realm, this England,
This nurse, this teeming womb of royal kings,
Fear'd by their breed and famous by their birth,
Renowned for their deeds as far from home,
For Christian service and true chivalry,
As is the sepulchre in stubborn Jewry
Of the world's ransom, blessed Mary's Son;
This land of such dear souls, this dear dear land,
Dear for her reputation through the world,
Is now leased out, I die pronouncing it,
Like to a tenement or pelting farm:
England, bound in with the triumphant sea,
Whose rocky shore beats back the envious siege
Of watery Neptune, is now bound in with shame,
With inky blots and rotten parchment bonds:
That England, that was wont to conquer others,
Hath made a shameful conquest of itself.'

We, too, in a lawyer-ridden land, know something of
'inky blots' and 'parchment bonds.' But it is characteristic of Shakespeare that his love of England did
not blind him to her faults. His praise is the better
worth hearing, because it discriminates. He knew
that even England, perplexed by evil counsellors and
untrue to herself, might suffer bitterly for her folly and

her faults. ‘This England never did, nor never shall,’ says the Bastard Falconbridge, who incarnates the national virtues of doglike fidelity and blunt courage,

> ‘ Lie at the proud feet of a conqueror
> But when it first did help to wound itself.’

Alas ! does it not still help to wound itself more deeply than ever in the past ?

It is in *Henry V*. that Shakespeare fashioned for us the true epic of England. The dramatic form sits very loosely upon it. It is epic in shape as in spirit. Splendid in eloquence, swift in narrative, it is a pæan sung in our country’s praise. Its noble lines sound in our ears like a trumpet-call, and it has lost not a jot of its force and energy by the passage of three hundred years. We have fought since an enemy who knows nothing of the chivalry which inspired the proud adversary of Henry v. Not with other adversaries can we make peace as we made peace with the French on the very field of Agincourt. But we have fought upon the same ground with a better cause, and Shakespeare’s spirit still strengthens our arms and animates our courage.

Though it is but a cockpit which is asked to ‘ hold the vasty fields of France,’ though ‘ the very casques that did affright the air at Agincourt ’ are crammed within a wooden O, the warlike Harry assumes in every line the port of Mars, and speaks across the centuries with a voice which patriotic Englishmen will always understand. Vividly does the chorus sketch the scenes, which we, too, witnessed at Germany's first attack :

> ' Now all the youth of England are on fire,
> And silken dalliance in the wardrobe lies :
> Now thrive the armourers, and honour's thought
> Reigns solely in the breast of every man :
> They sell the pasture now to buy the horse,
> Following the mirror of all Christian kings,
> With winged heels, as English Mercuries.'

On either day, we doubted our courage as little as we feared our destiny. On either day, the enemy sought with crafty policy to divert English purposes, and found willing instruments ready to his hands. On either day, there were secret leagues and traitorous unions, and Shakespeare divined the danger which lay in England's path :

> ' O England ! model to thy inward greatness,
> Like little body with a mighty heart,
> What mightst thou do, that honour would thee do,
> Were all thy children kind and natural !
> But see thy fault !   France hath in thee found out
> A nest of hollow bosoms, which he fills
> With treacherous crowns.'

Thus dishonour shamefully recurs.   In Shakespeare's time the nest of hollow bosoms was well filled, and we and the enemy alike have known where to find it since.

King Harry's own speeches might still hearten brave men fighting in the field.   He speaks a language which soldiers of all ages can echo and understand. 'And you, good yeomen,' he cries,

> 'Whose limbs were made in England, show us here
> The mettle of your pasture; let us swear
> That you are worth your breeding; which I doubt not;
> For there is none of you so mean and base,
> That hath not noble lustre in your eyes.
> I see you stand like greyhounds in the slips,
> Straining upon the start. The game's afoot:
> Follow your spirit, and upon this charge
> Cry "God for Harry, England, and Saint George!"'

And while the game was afoot, he would have his yeomen respect the laws of chivalrous warfare. He gives them express charge to compel nothing from the villages, to take nothing but paid for, to upbraid or abuse none of the enemy in disdainful language. For, said he with a wisdom which barbarians never learn, 'when levity and cruelty play for a king-dom, the gentler gamester is the soonest winner.' And, despite their King's lofty courage, the English were already forced to deplore the shirkers who hung back from the martial service of their country. 'O that we now had here,' says Westmoreland,

> 'But one ten thousand of these men in England
> That do no work to-day.'

So the armourers accomplish the knights, 'with busy hammers closing rivets up.' So the royal cap-tain walks from watch to watch, visits all his hosts,

> 'Bids them good morrow with a modest smile,
> And calls them brothers, friends, and countrymen,'

and at the last inspires his ' ruin'd band ' to victory
with the famous speech about St. Crispian's day.
He tells his men how those who live this day and see
old age, will feast their neighbours on its vigil, and
take pride in the wounds they got on Crispin's day;
how their names, familiar as household words, will
be freshly remembered in their flowing cups :

> ' We few, we happy few, we band of brothers ;
> For he to-day that sheds his blood with me
> Shall be my brother ; be he ne'er so vile,
> This day shall gentle his condition :
> And gentlemen in England now a-bed
> Shall think themselves accursed they were not here,
> And hold their manhoods cheap whiles any speaks
> That fought with us upon Saint Crispin's day ? '

Throughout the play the clear note of patriotism
is heard. There is not a scene of it that, in Coleridge's phrase, ' does not counteract that mock
cosmopolitanism which, under a positive term, really
implies nothing but a negation of, or indifference to,
the particular love of our country.' For Shakespeare,
as I have said, was above and before all things a lover
of England. With how bitter a contempt would he
have lashed those friends of every country but their
own, who nowadays unpack what they have of souls
to strangers, and believe that flat treason is a mark of
superiority ! And Shakespeare, being a patriot, was
a Tory also. He loved not those who disturbed
the peace of England. He believed firmly in the

established order, and in the great traditions of his native land. He was a firm supporter of Church and State. He did not whine about the unfit, nor see salvation in the careful nurture of the imbecile. He had as keen a scent for the demagogue as Aristophanes himself, and his Jack Cade may stand side by side as a companion portrait with the Cleon of *The Knights*. With a few strokes he has sketched the familiar miscreant who, in pretending to serve others, serves himself. ' There shall be in England seven halfpenny loaves sold for a penny,' says Cade ; ' the three-hooped pot shall have ten hoops ; and I will make it felony to drink small beer : all the realm shall be in common ; and in Cheapside shall my palfrey go to grass : and when I am king, as king I will be, . . . there shall be no money ; all shall eat and drink on my score ; and I will apparel them all in one livery, that they may agree like brothers, and worship me their lord.' The vainglory and false promises of this speech have not lost a jot of their truth and freshness. Many fiery demagogues have in our day spoken to the people with greater rancour and no less ignorance than Cade himself. ' Seven halfpenny loaves for a penny ' is near enough to ' ninepence for fourpence ' to show that the politician's generosity with other people's money is to-day as large, in word at least, as it was in Shakespeare's time. And nowhere does Shakespeare demonstrate more plainly that ' he was not for an age, but for all time,' than in this immortal sketch of

Jack Cade, whose raucous voice is still heard at the hustings in our twentieth century.

But it is in *Coriolanus* that Shakespeare gives his wisest exposition of political philosophy. Hazlitt said truly enough that he who read this play might ' save himself the trouble of reading Burke's *Reflections* or Paine's *Rights of Man*, or the debates in both Houses of Parliament since the French Revolution or our own.' That Shakespeare drew the character of Coriolanus with a sympathy of understanding is evident; it is evident also that he turned the wise pages of Plutarch wisely to his purpose. In a vividly dramatic form he has set before us the never-ending struggle between the few and the many, between government and anarchy, between law and licence. His hero is ' the chief enemy to the people,' ' a very clog to the commonalty.' Whatever he does he will do by his own strength. In vain does the people burn at his altar the incense of its flattery. Not in response to its will does he consent to fight or die for his country. Like a brave man of independent spirit he detests the doles which purchase the favour of the citizens. The lesson of Athens and her fall is not lost upon him. He knows precisely whither the worship of the incompetent, the loudly advertised cult of ' democratic control,' will carry the state :

> ' It is a purposed thing, and grows by plot,
>   To curb the will of the nobility ;
>   Suffer it, and live with such as cannot rule,
>   Nor ever will be rul'd.'

In these lines we may read the history of our modern times, and discover a clear premonition of the nerveless ineptitude still dogging every movement of those ministers, who, in abasing themselves before the people, have lost the power to rule.

In the struggle that follows, Coriolanus alone holds himself with dignity. It is not for him, who has never quailed before an enemy, to fear or to wheedle his fellow-citizens, who, to have peace at their own price, would gladly have killed him. The 'dull tribunes' are as fierce in his dispraise as the 'fusty plebeians'; they hate his honours with all the envy of their kind; as Menenius says, they 'knew neither him, themselves, nor anything.' Their sole ambition is 'for poor knaves' caps and legs.' Above all, Brutus and Sicinius loathe his grandeur, as tribunes have loathed the grandeur of heroes at all times, and exult in the certainty that his independence of spirit will undo him. 'I heard him swear,' says Brutus with smug satisfaction,

> 'Were he to stand for consul, never would he
> Appear i' the market-place, nor on him put
> The napless vesture of humility,
> Nor showing, as the manner is, his wounds
> To the people, beg their stinking breaths';

and then hastens to explain, though none but his friend Sicinius is in earshot, that 'it was his word.'

Thus Coriolanus, true to his word, would not bend the knee to 'the beast with many heads.' When he should have appeased it, he speaks it the truth, 'that

some certain of your brethren roar'd, and ran from
the noise of our own drums.' When he should have
asked, with flattering humbleness, the ' sweet voices '
of the citizens, he bids them ' wash their faces and
keep their teeth clean.' And Brutus and Sicinius, like
the stealthy party politicians that they were, make
the most of his candour. Their speeches have the
true sound of election-addresses. Coriolanus, as
Brutus hints, will take their liberties away, and make
them of no more voice than dogs. Sicinius reminds
his masters ' with what contempt he wore the humble
weed, how in his suit he scorn'd you.' Such as
Coriolanus was in the end, so he was in the beginning.
His first speech, the best test of his qualities, be-
labours the people after the right fashion :—

> ' What would you have, you curs,
> That like nor peace nor war ? the one affrights you,
> The other makes you proud. He that trusts to you,
> Where he should find you lions, finds you hares,
> Where foxes, geese : you are no surer, no,
> Than is the coal of fire upon the ice,
> Or hailstone in the sun. . . .
> Who deserves greatness
> Deserves your hate ; and your affections are
> A sick man's appetite, who desires most that
> Which would increase his evil. He that depends
> Upon your favours swims with fins of lead
> And hews down oaks with rushes.'

Even after the banishment of Coriolanus, the vaga-
bond exile, worse than ' the steep Tarpeian death,'

Shakespeare will not let the people off. He pursues
it with an irony of scorn. ' For my own part,' says
one citizen, ' when I said, banish him, I said, 'twas
pity.' To which another replies : ' And so did I ;
and, to say the truth, so did very many of us : that
we did, we did for the best ; and though we willingly
consented to his banishment, yet it was against our
will.' There in a few lines are expressed the eternal
folly and shame of democracy. Ever committed to
the worse cause, the people has not even the courage
of its own opinions.

Shakespeare, then, perceiving the permanent, unchanging elements of politics, was a wise Tory. He
cherished no superstition of universal brotherhood ;
he did not preach equality for a doctrine ; the liberty
to which he aspired was liberty of thought, not liberty
of the hustings. Everywhere he accepts or implies
the true gospel, and nowhere with greater clarity or
eloquence than in the famous speech of Ulysses.
That wily politician expounds in *Troilus and Cressida*
the truth to Agamemnon. He points out that 'degree
being vizarded, the unworthiest shows as fairly in
the mask,' that the heavens, the planets, and this
centre ' observe degree, priority and place,' that when
the planets wander to disorder all the worst marks
are seen of revolution. ' What plagues, and what
portents, what mutiny,' says he,

> ' What raging of the sea, shaking of earth,
>   Commotion in the winds, frights, changes, horrors,
>   Divert and crack, rend and deracinate

> The unity and married calm of states
> Quite from their fixture ! '

Might he not have written these prophetic lines
with his mind's eye upon France of the Terror or
upon modern Russia. And then he acclaims in a
grave and pompous passage the virtues of degree and
inequality :

> ' O, when degree is shaked,
> Which is the ladder to all high designs,
> The enterprise is sick ! How could communities,
> Degrees in schools and brotherhoods in cities,
> Peaceful commerce from dividable shores,
> The primogenitive and due of birth,
> Prerogative of age, crowns, sceptres, laurels,
> But by degree, stand in authentic place ?
> Take but degree away, untune that string,
> And, hark, what discord follows ! each thing meets
> In mere oppugnancy.'

Thus all things merge into appetite, ' an universal
wolf,' which ' last eats up himself.'

And Shakespeare, who despised those who truckled
to the people, knew how to treat all men with an equal
ease and justice. 'He was a handsome well shap't man :
very good company and of a very ready and pleasant
smooth wit.' So says Aubrey ; and Aubrey, though
he was a gossip, cherished always a pedant's love of
accuracy. He did not describe Shakespeare by guess-
work. Indeed he went to the best and surest source
of knowledge, and that source was William Beeston,
whose link with Shakespeare is near and unbroken.
For Christopher Beeston, William's father, was a friend

of Shakespeare, and the two men are mentioned to-gether in the will of Augustine Phillips of the King's Company. And Aubrey's description, which came, with one intervention only, from Christopher Beeston himself, bears upon it the marks of truth. 'A handsome well shap't man,'—that we very well believe was Shake-speare. No ugly broken casket ever carried so precious a jewel as was his genius. ' Very good company, and of a very ready and pleasant smooth wit.' How better should a friend depict one who always bore himself among men as a gentleman ? And Ben Jonson, in the brief character he has left us of the poet, agrees with Beeston. ' He was indeed,' says he, ' honest, and of an open and free nature.' It is but the same truth set in another light. Moreover, the evidence of the plays chimes with the evidence of the gossips. None but a gentleman could have drawn, with large and lavish hand, the women of Shakespeare. Miranda and Rosalind, Constance and Imogen, Perdita and Viola, Isabella and Cleopatra, far apart as they are one from another, could have been created only by an artist, in whom there was no touch of meanness or of guile. And that grim, strange world, inhabited by such heroes as Falstaff and Poins, as the incomparable clowns, even as the great Barnardine himself, could have been depicted by none but a gentleman. Here there is no stooping as to inferiors ; one and all of them, transcending the common measure of mankind as they do, are seen with sympathy, and fashioned without a gesture of contempt.

Again Shakespeare proves himself a gentleman in his moderation. He does not insist. He harbours no inapposite desire to make us better. Some of his critics have been saddened by the thought that his plays solve no moral problems and preach no obvious sermons—that, in fact, he is content to be a mere master of the revels, a purveyor of joy and pleasure. His refusal to preach is but another title of honour. Shakespeare was no provincial, to whom the potting-shed was an essential temple of light. He brushed aside as unimportant the tea-table squabbles of country towns. He was quite incapable of putting upon paper such a note as this of Ibsen's : ' These women of the present day, ill-used as daughters, as sisters, as wives, not educated according to their gifts, prevented from following their inclination, deprived of their inheritance, embittered in temper—it is these who furnish the mothers of the new generation. What is the result ? ' Or this other project : ' The keynote is to be. The prolific growth of our intellectual life, in literature, art, etc.—and in contrast to this : the whole of mankind gone astray.' To all such transitory subtleties as these Shakespeare was deaf and blind. He saw only the larger, plainer emotions—love, hate, jealousy, envy, ambition, cruelty—but he saw them with the clear eye of simplicity, and treated them with the knowledge and insight of one as far removed from littleness as from cynicism.

And Shakespeare, the poet of England, patriot

and Tory, has been pronounced a German by our foes ! By what right do they claim possession of a dramatist removed from them by a whole world of poetry and romance, a dramatist whose amplitude and generosity must be for ever unintelligible to them ? They claim him for theirs, I suppose, because they have heard about him in their schools and debauched him in their universities. They have made him the poor victim of their *Jahrbücher* ; they have permitted the ineffable Reinhardt to bury him, as he has buried Sophocles, beneath the weight of his hideous vulgarity. They have counted the syllables in his lines, and anatomised his words. They have gained no touch of his humanity or his good sense, and he remains, despite their anxious ministrations, the implacable foe of Teutonic pedantry and discipline.

Why, then, should the Germans have attempted to lay violent hands upon our Shakespeare ? It is but part of their general policy of pillage. Stealing comes as easy to them as it came to Bardolph and Nym, who in Calais stole a fire-shovel. Wherever they have gone they have cast a thievish eye upon what does not belong to them. They hit upon the happy plan of levying tolls upon starved Belgium. It was not enough for their greed to empty a country of food; they must extract something from its pocket, even though it be dying of hunger. We all know that the wagons which brought shells to the trenches were sent back laden with the spoils of German thievery. The strange lust which the Germans betrayed in 1870 for

clocks and watches did not leave them, and if ever
they fail to tell the hour again, it will not be for lack
of French and Belgian timepieces. Unfortunately
for them, they have not yet been able to strip England
bare of her treasures. ' Neptune's garden ' still eludes
their rifling hand. No doubt, if they came to these
shores, they would feed their fury by scattering
Shakespeare's dust to the winds of heaven. As they
are unable to sack Stratford, they do what seems to
them the next best thing : they hoist the Jolly Roger
over Shakespeare's works.

Their arrogance is busy in vain. Shakespeare shall
never be theirs. He was an English patriot, who
would always have refused to bow the knee to an
insolent alien. The vulgar brutality, which the
Germans mistake for warfare, would have been odious
to his chivalrous mind. In his own phrase, he had
no love of men who, ' having before gored the gentle
bosom of peace with pillage and robbery, make wars
their bulwark.' And the noisy apostles of *Kultur*
would find for him a second home in Leipzig !

However, it is clear that ever since Gervinus made
his fatuous discovery that Shakespeare was German,
the Germans have affected to admire our national
poet. He did not reciprocate the admiration. When
Nerissa asked Portia what she thought of the young
German, the Duke of Saxony's nephew, she got such
an answer as to-day would be regarded as *lèse-majesté*
in Germany. ' Very vilely in the morning,' said she,
' when he is sober, and most vilely in the afternoon,

when he is drunk : when he is best, he is a little worse
than a man, and when he is worst, he is little better
than a beast. An the worst fall that ever fell, I hope
I shall make shift to go without him.' Truly Portia
might have been describing the horde of Huns who
in August 1914 poured into Belgium and Northern
France.

Germany, then, would be wise if she kept her hands
off poets who do not belong to her. Even if she
could kidnap the genius of France and England, it
would not profit her. Hers is not a soil upon which
poets thrive easily. She has always looked with suspicion upon Heine, and since Heine's death she has
nothing better than grammarians to set against the
literary splendour of France and Russia and England.
Maybe, when her arrogance is abated through suffering, when she discovers that other and greater
countries live and are happy without her borders,
that her ' civilisation ' is not destined to absorb the
whole world, she may discover in humility of spirit a
literature of her own. Meantime she must know
that she cannot invade poets, as by stealthy preparation she has invaded provinces, and that Shakespeare's
priceless folio is a tabernacle, which must not be
touched by hostile undiscerning hands.

EDWARD HYDE

EARL OF CLARENDON

EDWARD HYDE, Earl of Clarendon, has always stood in especial need of defence. The Whigs, and Gardiner among them, have dealt hardly with him. They have cast upon his character the dust of misunderstanding and detraction. The consistency and loyalty which were among his virtues have seemed to them detestable. He has been belittled for the mere reason that he was a staunch upholder of the monarchy by those who forget that by his innate love of monarchy, and by nothing else, must he be tried. For a statesman of Hyde's temperament the smallest defection from kingly allegiance would have been a political crime, and his enemies have found fault even with his austere sincerity. But it is better to look at the hero as he was, than to reply to the aspersions of his opponents. And if only he be set against the proper background of his time, then all men who are not 'impartial,' with the impartiality of the Whigs, will recognise in the portrait a brave, wise, and dignified gentleman.

Born of an ancient family at Dinton, near Salisbury, in 1609, Edward Hyde grew to manhood under the

best auspices.   The sketches which he has left of both
his parents help to explain the plain, unswerving
honesty of his own career.   His father had served
Elizabeth in Parliament, and had also indulged ' his
inclination to travel beyond the seas.'   But not even
a sojourn in the Rome of Sixtus v. had made him a
wanderer, and he settled down early in life to the
simple pursuits of a scholar and a country gentleman.
' He lived,' says his son, ' with great cheerfulness and
content, . . . being a person of great knowledge and
reputation, and of so great esteem for integrity, that
most persons near him referred all matters of con-
tention and difference which did arise amongst them
to his determination ; by which that part of the
country lived in more peace and quietness than many
of their neighbours.'   Henry Hyde, then, saw most
clearly the duty which lay at his feet, and ' his wife,
who was married to him above forty years,' as her son
tells us, ' never was in London in her life ; the wisdom
and frugality of that time being such, that few gentlemen made journeys to London, or any other expen-
sive journeys, but upon important business, and their
wives never ; by which providence they enjoyed and
improved their estates in the country, and kept good
hospitality in their houses, brought up their children
well, and were beloved by their neighbours.'   The
training which he received in this home of well-ordered
simplicity had an influence upon Hyde unto the end.
What his early life lost in movement and variety it
gained in intensity, and the characteristics which

marked his maturity were already evident when he
first went to seek his fortune in London.

The first lesson which he had learned, was that
he had ' to make his fortune by his own industry ' ;
and when he had renounced an early design of taking
orders, it was natural that he should look to the law
for an avenue of preferment, so that with as much
lightness of heart as was possible to him he became
a student at the Inns of Court.   At the outset it was
life rather than law that he studied, and he threw
himself into the society of the Temple, intent upon
amusement, with considerable zest.   But he did not
wholly forget the claims of study.   ' When he did
indulge himself in the liberty,' he wrote many years
afterwards, ' it was without any signal debauchery,
and not without some hours every day, at least every
night, spent among his books.'   It was in these days
of irresponsibility that he learned to know the wits
of the town, and even sat in the ' Old Devil Tavern '
at the feet of Ben Jonson himself.   He was too young,
as yet too remote from letters, to stand high in that
great man's intimacy.   Nor was he ready to sacrifice
all to win the approval of the literary dictator.   To
know Ben Jonson was in Ben Jonson's eyes a liberal
profession.   But ' Mr. Hyde,' he tell us, ' betook
himself to business,' not being able to endorse the
poet's belief ' that business ought never to be
preferred before his company.'   However, he was
familiar enough with the ' Old Devil Tavern ' to
cherish a pious memory of its wits, and to indite

many years after a wise and flattering character of
Ben Jonson, its supreme arbiter.

Far nearer to his heart and mind was the judicious Selden, whose friendship he prized above all
things, and whose conduct he always excused, even
when he did not approve it. The passage in which
he does honour to Selden does honour to himself.
' Mr. Selden was a person,' he wrote, ' whom no
character can flatter, or transmit in any expressions
equal to his merit and virtue. He was of so stupen-
dous learning in all kinds and in all languages, that a
man would have thought he had been entirely con-
versant amongst books, and never spent an hour but
in reading and writing ; yet his humanity, courtesy,
and affability was such, that he would have been
thought to have been bred in the best courts, but
that his good nature, charity, and delight in doing
good, and in communicating all he knew, exceeded
that breeding. . . . Mr. Hyde was wont to say that he
valued himself upon nothing more than upon having
had Mr. Selden's acquaintance from the time he was
very young; and held it with great delight as long as
they were suffered to continue together in London.'
The influence of Selden's wisdom and intelligence is
seen in all that Hyde wrote and thought, and he
exaggerates not a jot the worth of the philosopher's
acquaintance.

Throughout his life Hyde was a loyal and faithful
friend. His belief in the sanctity of friendship was
whole-hearted. He knew how much might be learned

of humour and manners from the company of good and wise men. By their learning and instruction he formed his studies and mended his information. With that touch of priggishness which was not always absent from his reflections, he declared ' that he was never so proud, or thought himself so good a man, as when he was the worst man in the company.' This is a boast not always possible even for the most modest or most fortunate of men. It was not beyond the reach of the friend of Lucius Cary, Sidney Godolphin, Edmund Waller, John Earle, John Hales of Eton, and William Chillingworth. For Hyde, too, was of the privileged scholars admitted to Cary's house at Tew, whither they came ' to study in a better air, finding all the books they could desire in his library, and all the persons together, whose company they could wish, and not find in any other society.'

So it was that when Hyde threw himself into the noisy battle of politics, he was conscious of a fair equipment. He had the valuable experience which comes of converse with poets and scholars. He possessed a set of political principles which were destined to stand him in good stead, even in times of civil strife. He was a staunch upholder of King and Church, and though his eyes were never blinded to the faults of Charles I. or of Laud, he was ever ready to condone the faults of those whose sacred offices he revered. He was an aristocrat, who believed devoutly in the principle of aristocracy, and though he might deplore the injudicious counsels of his King, he could not tolerate for a moment what seemed to him the excesses of the King's adversaries. On which side he would fight there was never a doubt. Meanwhile he was a zealous member of Parliament. ' He was very much in the business of the house '—to use his own words ; ' the greatest chairman in the committees of the greatest moment ; and very diligent in attending the service both in the house and at committees.' It was at a committee appointed to examine the enclosure of certain lands that he first encountered the redoubtable Cromwell. Mandeville, the most courteous of men and rebels, was defending the enclosure, when Cromwell broke in upon the debate with great violence. ' In the end,' says Hyde, ' Cromwell's whole carriage was so tempestuous, and his behaviour so insolent, that the chairman felt himself obliged to reprehend him, . . . which he never forgave ; and took all occasions afterwards to pursue him, with the utmost malice and revenge, to his death.'

When Hyde espoused the King's cause, the only cause possible for a statesman of his strong opinions and unswerving honour, he stood at the zenith of prosperity. He was rich, fortunate, and highly esteemed. ' Under this universal acquaintance and general acceptation,' he writes with a proud candour, ' Mr. Hyde led for many years as cheerful and pleasant a life as any man did enjoy, as long as the kingdom took any pleasure in itself. His practice grew every day as much as he wished, and would have been much more, if he had wished it ; by which he not only supported his expense, greater much than men of his rank and pretences used to make, but increased his estate by some convenient pieces of land adjoining to his other.' His character had hardened with prosperity. Though in his youth he had been a complacent witness of gaming and debauchery, ' he had, by God's immediate blessing, disentangled himself from these labyrinths, . . . and was enough composed against any extravagant excursions.' With an amiable insight into his own character he confesses that he had ambition enough ' to raise his spirit to great designs of raising himself, but not to transport him to endeavour it by any crooked and indiscreet means.' It was his just boast that ' he was never suspected to flatter the greatest man, or in the least degree to dissemble his own opinions or thoughts.' Though he knew perfectly well that he was inclined to pride and passion, though his love of wrangling and disputing was troublesome enough, he was clear-sighted as to his own virtues. In a passage all the more welcome because the most of men make a practice of dissembling their good qualities, he says boldly and aloud : ' That which supported him and rendered him generally acceptable was his generosity (for he had too much a contempt for money), and the opinion men had of the goodness and justice of his nature, which was transcendent in him, in a wonderful tenderness and delight in obliging. His integrity was ever without blemish, and believed to be above temptation. He was firm and unshakable in his friendships.'

Such was the man who opposed with what energy he could the encroachments of Parliament. Openly conscious of his virtues, he could not and did not betray them. His career was one of singular evenness and uprightness. When Gardiner says that he had none of ' the larger qualities of statesmanship,' he means, no doubt, that he was not prepared to sacrifice his Tory principles upon the hastily constructed altars of new ideas. He was neither a Marten nor a Harry Vane. He believed that any attack upon the person or sovereignty of Charles I. was an unforgivable crime. But there is as much room for the exercise of the larger qualities of statesmanship in the adherence to monarchy and the monarchical principle as there is in revolution. And had Hyde been cordially supported by the King and the King's army, he might have proved himself able to stem the tide of rebellion, and to reform the Government without bloodshed : if he did not overestimate the value of that vague thing called personal liberty, he saw no sanctity in an overturned throne. Had he had his way, he would have given relief to the people and done no violence to the established order. 'This, at least, is certain,' says Sir Henry Craik, his last biographer, ' that out of the countless actors in that great drama there was not one who steered his course more straight, who was more

honest in his first choice of adherence, or maintained
more unchangeably the principles which he had set
before himself, than Edward Hyde.'

Unhappily when the crisis came in England's fate
there was no room for Hyde's dextrous moderation.
The Constitutional Monarchy which he advocated was
shaped in accord with Conservative principles, and
was unacceptable to the reckless spirit of the time.
But the war made quite clear the path which he should
follow.   With Falkland and Colepepper he gave
counsel to the King, and remained till the end his
Master's faithful servant and friend.   The King generously acknowledged his devotion.   ' I must make Ned
Hyde Secretary of State,' he wrote in a hapless letter,
which fell into the wrong hands, ' for the truth is, I
can trust no one else.'   And it was not long before
Hyde encountered a universal jealousy.   ' He had
great enviers,' he wrote, ' of many who thought he
had run too fast.'   If he ran too fast, it was in a
hopeless race.   The best advice which he or others
could give the King was powerless to save him.
Those who commanded what Hyde described as ' a
dissolute, undisciplined, wicked, beaten army, only
terrible in plunder and resolute in running away,'
were one and all unfit for their trust.   Goring did
little else than drink and play.   ' For God's sake,'
Hyde wrote to him in a memorable letter, ' let us not
fall into ill-humours which may cost us dear.   Get
good thoughts about you, and let us hear speedily
from you to a better tune.'   Goring could play no

better tune than intrigue and debauchery. Sir
Richard Grenville, on the other hand, was busy with
extortion. Few of the others thought of their
cause or their King. When the Court repaired to
Oxford, it went thither to pursue the familiar path
of luxury. The courtiers found pleasant quarters in
the ancient colleges, and counted rather for mouths
to feed than for arms to fight. Ruin and defeat were
inevitable, and they came with sure foot. Disaster
upon disaster overwhelmed the unfortunate King.
The rout of Naseby was followed by the surrender of
Bristol—a surrender all the harder to bear because
it was due to the folly and inaction of Rupert. There
seemed no hope in any quarter of the sky, and the
King did his best to save his house from extinction
by sending Prince Charles across the sea.

With the Prince went Hyde, as tutor and counsellor,
and for sixteen years he did not revisit his native
land. However much he deplored his absence from
the conduct of affairs, he turned his mind to history,
and it is perhaps to his exile that we owe an imperishable record of the Civil War. He lived in Jersey
with his friends Hopton and Capel, and was treated
by Sir George Carteret, the Deputy-Governor, with
the utmost cordiality. It was a thrifty life they led,
and if they could afford only one good meal in the
day, they had abundant consolations. Hyde enjoyed,
as he was wont to say, ' the greatest tranquillity of
mind imaginable.' When his friends were called
to serve the cause elsewhere, he took up his abode

with Sir George Carteret at Castle Elizabeth.   There
he built for himself a small lodging against the wall
of the church, on which he inscribed the motto fitted
for his quiet retreat, ' Bene vixit qui bene latuit.'
Lonely otherwise, he had the companionship of his
books and papers, and ten hours every day went to
the compiling of the first part of his great history in
its original form.   Presently his calm was disturbed
by an order to join the Prince in France, and thereafter he wandered up and down Europe, an unsuccess-
ful envoy.   Spain knew him, and Holland, until at
last he accompanied King Charles ii. on his restora-
tion to the throne.

The hopes of a happy return, which Hyde had
cherished through the long years of exile, were
speedily disappointed.   He came to an England which
he knew not, a strange, dismoded man.   He sketched
the change which had overtaken the realm in a passage
of despair. ' In a word,' said he, ' the nation was
corrupted from that integrity, good nature, and
generosity, that had been peculiar to it, and for
which it had been signal and celebrated throughout
the world ; in the room thereof the vilest craft and
dissembling had succeeded. . . . In the place of
generosity, a vile and sordid love of money was enter-
tained as the truest wisdom, and anything lawful that
would contribute to being rich.   There was a total
decay, or rather a final expiration, of all friendship ;
and to dissuade a man from anything he affected, or
to reprove him for anything he had done amiss, or to

advise him to do anything he had no mind to do, was thought an impertinence unworthy a wise man, and received with reproach and contempt.' Such, as Hyde conceived it, was the result of the Rebellion, is, indeed, ever the result of democracy, and Charles ii. did little to repair 'these dilapidations and ruins of the ancient candour and discipline.' The austere Hyde could not expect to find sympathy or support in the courtiers and mistresses of Whitehall. Nor was his position relieved of embarrassment when his daughter was secretly married to the Duke of York. His influence with the King speedily decreased. Charles ii., never eminent for gratitude, soon forgot the devotion of his ancient tutor, who had endured exile and privation in his service. He saw in Hyde a Minister inflexible alike in candour and honesty, and therefore disinclined to tolerate his extravagance or to condone his follies. At last Hyde's very presence at Court irked the King, and he bade the Duke of York ' to advise the Chancellor to be gone.' Another term of exile seemed preferable to prison or Tower Hill, and once more Clarendon, as he had now become, landed on French soil, which he was never destined to leave. For a while he sojourned at Avignon, and was driven thence ' by the multitude of dyers and silk manufacturers, and the worse smell of the Jews.' Finding Montpelier better suited to his taste, he there dwelt with dignity and in good repute. When any English came thither, none forbore to pay respect to the Chancellor. But the appreciation of Montpelier was not enough for him. He was homesick for England, and in 1671 he made a last appeal to the King, to whose service he had devoted his life. ' It is now full seven years,' he wrote to Charles, ' since I have been deprived of your Majesty's favour, with some circumstances of mortification, which have never been exercised towards any other man, and therefore I may hope from your good nature and justice, that a severity which you have never practised upon any other man for half the time, may be diminished in some degree towards me.' And he concluded his piteous appeal by praying that the King would ' at least signify his consent that he might return to beg his bread in England, and to die amongst his own children.' It is in perfect consonance with Charles ii.'s character that he left this letter without an answer. When Clarendon died three years later, it was at Rouen, which was nearer to his native land than Montpelier, and where the long-wished-for summons to return might more speedily have reached him.

Eminent as he was in council, it is as the historian of his time that Clarendon will be ever remembered. His book has its faults and limitations, no less than the masterpieces of Thucydides and Tacitus. Those who look upon history as a mere means of strengthening the Whig position will doubtless convict Clarendon of monstrous partiality, and it may be confessed that he thought it no part of his duty to look back upon events with the eyes of a Roundhead. It has been pointed out that he had little sense of natural scenery or of history's dramatic elements. He did not set the persons of his drama against any background, natural or artificial. His world has not houses, nor courts, nor fields. The personages of his drama seem to move hither and thither in vast, vacant spaces. He was interested supremely in men, not things, in the conflict of wills and the passions of the mind. Above all, he was interested in character. History for him was ' character in action,' and as he had known all the actors in the drama which unfolded itself before his eyes, and in which he had played a foremost part, he could measure their motives and discern their traits. And in this love of character he was true to the fashion of his time. Sir Thomas Overbury and John Earle, faithful disciples of Theophrastus, had not worked in vain. They had shown that it was not romantic incident alone which could move the curiosity of men. Divination of character held sway in their minds and in the minds of their readers. Clarendon did but transfer their method from the delineation of types to the delineation of individual men, and he did it with a surety unequalled save in the ancients.

So firm a foe was he to the picturesque that he is seldom familiar. He does not descend easily to those small traits which separate one man from another. He does not often describe outward appearances ; he turns his eyes aside resolutely from the details, which we should have prized, of looks and habits. He thought it no part of his business to paint costume

pieces. When he tells us that Sir Henry Vane the
younger 'had an unusual aspect, which, though it
might naturally proceed both from his father and
mother, neither of which are beautiful persons, yet
made men think there was something in him of extraordinary,' he tells it us not because he is interested
in the 'unusual aspect,' but in the 'something of
extraordinary' which it foreshadowed. He has small
traffic with wit or humour. It is with surprise that
you encounter in his pages epigram or antithesis.
Surely he was in a happy, unaccustomed mood when
he sketched the Earl of Arundel's pride: 'He resorted sometimes to the Court, because there only
was a greater man than himself; and went thither
the seldomer, because there was a greater man than
himself.' With the same happy touch he sketches
the weakness of Strafford, 'whose pride was by the
hand of Heaven strongly punished by bringing his
destruction upon him by two things that he most
despised—the People and Sir Hary Vane.' He
loved imagery as little as he loved epigram, and his
metaphors have all the more force from their rarity.
'He did swim in those troubled and boisterous
waters,' he writes of Sir Richard Weston, 'in which
the Duke of Buckingham rode as Admiral with a good
grace; when very many who were about him were
drowned or forced on shore with shrewd hurts and
bruises.' Thus his very economy of thought and
speech has its due effect upon his readers.

For him, indeed, the heroes and villains of his time

are moving bundles of moral qualities and moral
defects.   And since lists of the virtues must be tinged
always with a certain inhumanity, it is rather by their
faults that we shall recognise as real men those whom
Clarendon portrays.   His panegyric of Charles 1., for
instance, would tell us little of the King, whom he
worshipped as he worshipped none other, were it not
for the just censure, which gives it a reality.   Thus,
when we are told that Charles 1. was the worthiest
gentleman, the best master, the best husband, the
best Christian, we are convinced only of Clarendon's
admiration.   If we did not take the praise for granted,
as we should, it would not explain the King to us,
since it is not distinctive.   The mere hint that ' he
did not love strangers, nor very confident men,' helps
us to know him more intimately than would a dozen
pages of praise.   Is it not a relief to hear that ' his
kingly virtues had some mixture and alloy which
hindered him from shining in full lustre . . . that
he was not in his nature bountiful . . . and that he
paused too long in giving, which made those to
whom he gave less sensible of the benefit ' ?   The
mixture and alloy need give us no pleasure.   The
admission that the King, too, was a man with a
man's failings helps us, as mere panegyric seldom
helps us, to understand his character.

Here, too, in the phrases that follow, we catch sight
of a real King, not a merely virtuous epitome : ' He
was very fearless in his person ; but, in his riper years,
not very enterprising.   He had an excellent under-

standing, but was not confident enough of it ; which
made him oftentimes change his own opinion for a
worse, and follow the advice of men that did not judge
so well as himself. This made him more irresolute
than the conjuncture of his affairs would admit : if
he had been of a rougher and more imperious nature,
he would have found more respect and duty.' This
passage not only sets the King before us, on the
ground and not on a pedestal ; it reveals, in a flash,
the causes of his defeat and of his unhappy fate.

Indeed, while in politics Hyde naturally and
rightly took the view of an honest partisan, in the
drawing of character he was just even to his foes,
unjust, sometimes, by the desire of impartiality,
to his friends. If he could not choose but find
a few blemishes upon the silver shield of Montrose's
magnanimity, he saw the rough breastplates of the
Puritans flecked with light. He hated Oliver Cromwell, the one man of genius, in peace and war, who
emerged in the Civil Wars, with the hatred of a convinced Royalist. Yet he did not withhold from him
the tribute of his lofty praise. If Cromwell could
not but be a criminal in his eyes, he was a criminal
whose grandeur dazzled the onlooker. Here are a few
sentences, culled from Clarendon's character, which
prove his fair sense of history. Some words are
charged with malice, it is true. But the recognition
of Cromwell's greatness is unstinted. ' He was one
of those men whom his very enemies could not condemn without commending him at the same time ;

for he could never have done half that mischief without great parts of courage, industry, and judgment. . . . He achieved those things, in which none but a valiant and great man could have succeeded. . . . When he was to act the part of a great man, he did it without any indecency, notwithstanding the want of custom. . . . In all matters which did not concern the life of his jurisdiction, he seemed to have great reverence for law. . . . His greatness at home was but a shadow of the glory he had abroad. . . . He was not a man of blood, and totally declined Machiavel's method.' Here are some fragments of a tribute paid to grandeur which does as much honour to Clarendon's insight as to his good faith.

In the same spirit of impartiality he has painted for posterity the friends of Cromwell—Pym, ' the man of greatest experience in Parliament, where he had served very long, and always a man of business, being an officer in the Exchequer, and of a good reputation generally, though known to be inclined to the Puritan faction ' ; and Hampden, ' a man of much greater cunning, and, it may be, of the most discerning spirit, and of the greatest address and insinuation to bring anything to pass which he desired, of any man of that time, and who laid the design deepest.' So much is said in Hampden's favour, and then Clarendon reveals the other side : ' No man ever had a greater power over himself, or was less the man he seemed to be ; which shortly after appeared to everybody, when he cared less to keep on the masque.' Even to Sir Harry

Vane the younger—the elder he condemns utterly—
he allows 'great natural parts, a very profound dissimulation, a quick conception, a very ready, sharp,
and weighty expression.' And so it is that his
characters are neither black nor white. He paints
in streaks of light and dark colours, and he chooses his
tints with so nice a discrimination, with so fine a
taste, that you accept his portraiture as just. Falkland, his friend, is the one man in whom he sees no
spot. 'Thus fell,' he writes after the battle of New-
bury, 'that incomparable young man, in the four and
thirtieth year of his age, having so much despatched
the true business of life, that the eldest rarely attain
to that immense knowledge, and the youngest enter
not into the world with more innocency : whosoever
leads such a life, needs be the less anxious upon how
short warning it is taken from him.' And by way
of contrast look upon this other portrait, unlightened
by a single touch of hope or praise : 'Goring . . .
would, without hesitation, have broken any trust, or
done any act of treachery to have satisfied an ordinary
passion, or appetite ; and, in truth, wanted nothing
but industry (for he had wit, and courage, and understanding, and ambition, uncontrolled by any fear of
God or man) to have been as eminent and successful
in the highest attempt of wickedness, as any man in
the age he lived in, or before. Of all his qualifications
dissimulation was his masterpiece ; in which he so
much excelled, that men were not ordinarily ashamed,
or out of countenance, with being deceived but twice

by him.' Here we find a touch of irony, but even this presentment has a certain dryness, despite its invective. Clarendon is content to persuade us of Goring's wickedness. If only he had given us specimens of his evil-doing we, too, should have been content. But he disdained anecdote, and left his readers to take his judgments as they are.

In composing history, Clarendon followed the best models. He admits in a letter that Livy and Tacitus were his masters, and then adds an apology : ' I am contented you should laugh at me for a fop,' he says, ' in talking of Livy and Tacitus, when all I can hope for is to side with Hollingshead and Stowe, or (because he is a poor knight, too) Sir Richard Baker.' There was no need of an apology. Clarendon has nothing in common with such patient workmen as Hollingshead and Stowe. The only link which binds him to Sir Richard Baker, who composed his chronicles in prison, is misfortune. In aim, as in achievement, he is of the grand school. Even his faults of style came from an exuberance of mind. He uses too few words, and uses them too often. That is to say, his diction is verbose, and yet lacks variety. The compensations are obvious. As Dr. Johnson says, ' there is in his negligence a rude, inartificial majesty, which, without nicety of laboured eloquence, swells the mind by its plenitude and effusion.' On all counts his memory is entitled to our respect. He was a faithful public servant, a sound Tory, the vivid painter of a vivid age.

GILBERT BURNET

GILBERT BURNET, the son of Scottish parents, was born in 1643. On either side he was of gentle lineage, and the spirit of independence was in his blood. His father, a lawyer, 'learned in his profession, who did not rise up to the first form in practice,' was an Episcopalian of a moderate cast. His mother, in the words of her son, whose love of character-writing did not spare his own house, 'was a good, religious woman, but most violently engaged in the Presbyterian way.' With such a parentage, Gilbert Burnet could not but come to preferment, and, that his natural qualities might not rust from neglect, he submitted to a discipline as severe as that which darkened the childhood of John Stuart Mill. He went to no school, 'but was taught Latin by his father with so much success that before he was ten years old he was master of that tongue and of the classic authors.' In 1652 he entered the University of Aberdeen, studied the Aristotelian philosophy at an age when most boys are content with a primer, and took the degree of Master of Arts before he was fourteen. 'All that while,' says he, 'my father superintended my studies, making me rise at four o'clock in the morning.' With the modesty that was more often on his tongue than in his heart, he confesses also that his father increased his vanity by overloading him with learning. But his keen vitality and tireless strength enabled him to carry the burden lightly enough, and if a lack of judgment prevented him from winning a reputation for profound scholarship, it cannot be said that he made small use of his hastily acquired knowledge.

For a brief space he intended to adopt the profession of the law, for which his disputatious temper well fitted him. Had he followed his first intent, no scruple would have withheld him, even for a year, from political affairs, which were the true passion of his life, and he might have played an earlier, more dangerous, part in the history of his time. But he had not travelled far on the road of law when he changed his mind, and, to the bitter indignation of his mother, determined to become an Episcopalian minister. He precipitated himself upon theology with the same activity wherewith he had rushed upon the study of law. He read more than twenty volumes in folio of school divinity, the result of which, as he tells us ingenuously, ' was to heighten his vanity and make him despise and triumph over all who had not suffered themselves to be entangled with that cobweb stuff.'

Meantime he was taking his first steps in the world, to dominate which was always his greatest joy and pride. He possessed in liberal measure the

qualities which govern society—a handsome presence, a quick invention, indomitable courage. A
copious talker, he was never at a loss for a word
or a topic. Delighting frankly in grandeur, he was
seldom obsequious, and he was arrogantly convinced
that he carried into every company far more than he
took out of it. 'Now I began to be known to great
men '—thus he wrote with a pompous ingenuousness
of his twentieth year—' and I have ever since been
much in their company, which has brought much
envy and censure upon me from other clergymen,
who fancied that I used odd arts to compass it. But
I can give no other account of the matter than this.
I never sought the acquaintance of a great man in
my whole life, but I have often declined it. . . . I had
a facetiousness and easiness in conversation that was
entertaining; I had read a variety of things, and
could dress them in easy words, so that many liked
my company. I never imposed it on any, but I do
not deny that I had a great vanity in finding my
company so much desired.' These are the words of
truth—of truth wholly divorced from humour.
Burnet could conceal his satisfaction neither from
himself nor from others. He affected a kind of surprise at what a wiser man would take for granted.
Until the end of his life he was always a little unhappy
if he were not directing the talk in the presence of
' the great,' and his engaging simplicity dictated so
full a confession of this foible that his pride seemed
sometimes very near humility.

Nor did he always produce the effect which he hoped upon others. He is described by one who heard him discourse in 1664 in by no means sympathetic terms. 'He talked all the time,' said John Cockburn, ' and didn't suffer any of you to speak a dozen words, and he rambled from one thing to another.' Indeed he fell complacently into all the pitfalls which beset the copious and greedy talker, and forgot that he was not incapable even of boredom. Once upon a time—it was in 1683—Louis xiv. took Burnet into his coach at Versailles, and the Scot's cicerone was horrified to find that though ' he spoke the French tongue very ill, his confidence and assurance bore him fully out, and he talked for ever and as much before the King as in his own room. The courtier remonstrated, but Burnet did not amend, and the King bore all ' ! He was not the only king who was asked to bear the assured eloquence of Burnet.

And side by side with this love of the world there grew up in Burnet a subdued passion for mystic theology. He fell beneath the calm influence of Lawrence Charteris, an amiable minister, who fervently believed that ' it was a vain thing to dream of amending the world.' Burnet, who never dreamed of anything else, who was never happy unless he were attempting to do good to somebody, fondly thought that he too might find comfort in this quiet doctrine. Nothing was further remote from his hard, positive intellect. But as in later years he took refuge from the stress of affairs in algebra and chemistry, so in

his youth he boldly argued himself into the opinion
that the proper attitude of a divine was a constant
tranquillity.   He did not long preserve this attitude.
He had not been minister of Saltoun for more than
a year, when, forgetting the teaching of Charteris,
he made a bold attempt to amend the Bishops of
Scotland by a memorial.   The memorial is eminently characteristic of its author—bold and vainglorious.   A keener sense of humour than Burnet
had might have suggested that it was an impertinence in a youth of twenty-three to assault at a single
blow all the dignitaries of the Church.

But in the end his attempt was not taken amiss.
The spectacle of a David attacking not one but many
Goliaths, was at once fresh and exhilarating ; and
though Burnet's memorial drove him for a while to
retirement and asceticism, he emerged, as always,
into the world again.   In 1669 he was appointed
Professor of Theology at the University of Glasgow,
where, as always when he had a definite duty to perform, he displayed a genuine zeal and industry.
He was the most energetic professor of his time, as
he was presently the most sedulous bishop ; and
ardent though his passion for politics was becoming,
he honestly put the welfare and the training of his
pupils before the pursuits which pleased him better.

It was during his sojourn in Glasgow that he made
his first open incursion into public affairs, and it
cannot be said that he came well out of the encounter.
In 1671 the King had been married for nine years,

and the Duke of York, an avowed Roman Catholic, was heir to the throne. In the eyes of Lauderdale and Moray the State was in danger, and they gravely asked Burnet whether a childless woman might be justly divorced, or whether polygamy was in any case lawful under the Gospel. Burnet, proud to display his learning, answered 'Yes' to either question, and he must bear whatever blame attaches to the indiscretion. It is not enough to say in excuse that he was intimidated by Lauderdale. He was arrogant by disposition and an egoist by habit. He would not bend his will to another's, either from weakness or complacency. But he was a politician who in serving others hoped to serve himself. He was no mere sycophant. His character was far more complicated than mere sycophancy would imply. He did not hesitate to speak roughly, even to the highest. Nevertheless, he had a natural love of policy, and if he saw a chance of advancing himself without too great a sacrifice of pride and independence, he took it. And he took it, with disastrous effect, when he admitted to Lauderdale the equal justice of divorce or polygamy. Yet for the moment his rash opinion strengthened the bonds which bound him to the most powerful man in Scotland, and made the way easy for his reception at Court.

The first appearance of Burnet at the Court of King Charles II. was an event in both their lives, and each conducted himself on this great occasion with characteristic simplicity. 'His Majesty,' wrote

Burnet, ' ordered me to be sworn a chaplain, and admitted me to a long private audience that lasted above an hour, in which I took all the freedom with him that I thought became my profession . . . with relation to his course of life. . . . He bore it all very well and thanked me for it.' The humour of the situation is exquisite. Charles was not a man to be preached at wantonly, and Burnet, as Charles Lamb said of Coleridge, was never heard to do anything else than preach. To censure the conduct of his King at a first meeting was rash even for Gilbert Burnet, who doubtless lived to regret his temerity. But the habit was too strong for resistance. He was obliged at all costs to improve the occasion. He was a kind of Mr. Barlow, always ready with precept or anecdote to correct the morals of his auditor, and even though that auditor were a monarch of infinite humour, he did not hesitate to give his advice.

The indiscretion was as great as the courage. Burnet had lived long in the world, and had not vanity blinded his eyes he might have seen the hope-lessness of his mission. And he was conscious of nothing save an amiable reception. The King, always master of himself, sent Burnet away convinced that he had done his monarch good, and prepared still to serve him with all the eloquence at his command. Emboldened by the King's complaisance, Burnet, five years later, ventured upon another remonstrance, which was his undoing. In 1679 he addressed a letter to the King, which bears in every line the marks

of a reckless sincerity. No one who has read this
document can charge Burnet with subserviency.
It is officious and impertinent, if you will, but its
very truth is disconcerting, and Burnet, vain as he
was, proud as he was of what he believed his former
triumph, could hardly have expected Charles to make
a public repentance at the mere sight of his burning
words. That Burnet's intentions were honourable
is obvious. It is obvious also that his complete lack
of humour once more led him astray. The King
ignored the remonstrance, and ever after spoke of
Burnet with great sharpness. When Rochester
' wondered why he would use a writer of history ill,
for such people can revenge themselves,' Charles with
his own good sense replied that Burnet durst say
nothing while he was alive, and that when he was
dead he should not be the worse for what he said.
The revenge which Burnet took is known to all, and for
nothing that he said is Charles II. one whit the worse.

In truth, Burnet must have had within him the
seeds of greatness to have survived his love of intrigues
and his ill-guarded tongue. So much pleased was he
to be the repository of other men's secrets, that he
could not help betraying them. His habit of talk
fell away into reckless garrulity, and he lost friends
by the same gift whereby he won them. After his
first sight of the King, he boasted to the Duchess of
Lauderdale of the freedom he had used with him
upon his course of life. And the King was naturally
incensed when the rumour was brought to him. He

listened patiently to Burnet's defence, and then said, with an admirable appreciation of the divine's character, that ' he was afraid he had been too busy, and wished him to go home to Scotland and be more quiet.' He counselled what was impossible. Burnet was incapable of tranquillity, as none knew better than himself. Conscious of his besetting sin, he did his best to cure it, and failed utterly. ' The truth is,' he wrote in 1675, ' I had been for about a year in a perpetual agitation, and was not calm nor cool enough to reflect upon my conduct as I ought to have done. I had lost much of a spirit of devotion and recollection; and so it is no wonder if I committed great errors.' And having made full confession, he pursued his old evil course of interference. He presently estranged Sir Harbottle Grimston, a loyal friend, by revealing to the King what he had told him ; and many years later, still ardent with the spirit of reform, he allowed himself to be ' set on to speak to William III. to change his cold way.' William did not dismiss him with Charles's nonchalant wit. He called him ' een rechte Tartuffe,' and proved that he understood only one side of Burnet's duplex character.

For there was one province in which Burnet was supreme. He was the greatest preacher of an age which delighted in sermons. ' The pulpit was,' as a biographer says, ' Burnet's most appropriate sphere. An orator by temper and training, he found there ample scope for his religious fervour and his childlike love of display, his talent as an expositor, and his passion for giving advice.' The actor that was in him took full advantage of the opportunity. His gesture was as flamboyant as his style. With his unfailing naïveté he confesses that he ' took a tincture of the French way more than Scotland could well bear.' As preacher at the Rolls Chapel, he won an instant victory. He was always best when he struck off his work at a single blow ; and in the pulpit his energy of mind, his unstemmed eloquence, his quick imagination, had their fullest scope. ' I never heard a preacher equal to him,' wrote Speaker Onslow. ' There was an earnestness of heart and look and voice that is scarcely to be conceived, as it is not the fashion of the present times, and by the want of which, as much as anything, religion is every day failing with us.' And the same writer tells a story which explains Burnet's talent more clearly than pages of adulation. The orator once upon a time ' preached out the hour-glass.' Thereupon ' he held it aloft in his hand, and then turned it for another hour ; upon which the audience, a very large one for the Rolls Chapel, set up almost a shout for joy.' What preacher has ever received so lofty and sincere a compliment ?

If Burnet had a passion for intrigue, there is one subject upon which his opinion was always stoutly maintained. In hostility to what he called Popery he never wavered. He fought the battle of Protestantism with the courage that we expect of him. He was dismissed from the Rolls Chapel for preaching a bold and outspoken sermon against popish cruelty. When

James ii. came to the throne, Burnet found safety in
a wise flight. He was among the first to believe that
the hope of England lay in placing William and Mary
upon the throne; and though he did not play so
large a part in the drama as he supposed, he accompanied the Dutch prince to England, and offered
him much unacceptable counsel. He was rewarded
by the see of Salisbury, which he ruled with equal
zeal and wisdom. He preached the Coronation
sermon, in which, with memorable words, he
denounced both Tyranny and Anarchy, of which
'the one makes men beasts of prey, the other of
burden. Happy we, whose laws are neither writ on
sand—nor with blood.' To sustain the burden of
episcopal duties was perhaps the task for which he was
best fitted; and the years which he spent at Salisbury,
far removed from the turmoil of a Court which asked
not his advice, were years of dignity.

For twenty-six years he administered the affairs
of his diocese, and yet kept his hand and his eye
fixed upon the great world. He took William and
Mary under his direct patronage, and sketched, as
only he could sketch them, the relations which should
exist between them. When Peter the Great visited
these shores, Burnet, with characteristic inappro-
priateness, compared ' the great Northern Emperor '
with the Queen of Sheba, and gave him ' such infor-
mations of our religion and constitution as he was willing to receive.' In 1701 he settled with Leibnitz the
vexed question as to who should succeed to the English

throne, and was rewarded by an amiable letter from
the Electress Sophia. When William III. died, Burnet
found another deathbed suitable for his ministrations,
and presently wrote a character of his King, which
did not fail from lack of candour. He preached the
first sermon to which Queen Anne was asked to listen,
and improved the occasion by reminding ' Solomon '
that ' Saul's party was still very strong.' He died
opportunely, in 1715, just before James Edward made
a hopeless attempt to seize the crown, and was buried
to such an uproar of honour and ridicule as would
have soothed his flattered soul. The pamphleteers,
on either side, made busy with his reputation, and
the wittiest of them all, John Arbuthnot, not only
described ' the six days preceding the death of a late
Right Reverend ' prelate, but composed his epitaph
in Latin and English. Here is the English version :—

Beneath
There lies, against his own Wishes,
A man at last in PEACE.
He was Master of a Cunning, various Wit,
Agreeable to his own COUNTRY.
Great was he in Divinity, in Fable Greater,
IN POLITICS (if you 'll believe himself) greatest.
So faithful a Lover of *Truth*,
That it equally appears in his *Life*,
And *Writings*.
A violent, weighty, unwearied Preacher ;
Many have had *purer Doctrine*,

> No one stronger sides, and Lungs.
> So averse to ROME in all Points
> That he almost approached GENEVA.
> He died, to the universal grief of the
> *Dissenters* on the *Kalends of March*.

Nevertheless, it is not as a preacher, despite his oratorical gifts ; it is not as a politician, despite his faculty for intrigue, that Burnet is most happily remembered. He survives, as perhaps he expected to survive, by his writings, which gave him a place apart in our history. He was not a great man of letters. Singularly insensitive to æsthetic impressions, he wrote well rather by the stress of dramatic emotion than by a conscious effort. The best passages in his *History*, such as his account of Lord William Russell's last days and death, were composed at a time of keen excitement. He had attended him on the scaffold, and felt that he had a share in his glory, if not in his punishment. His literary masterpiece, *Some Passages of the Life and Death of the Right Honourable John Earl of Rochester*, is quick with an unforgotten experience. Within its brief compass the interlocutors, Rochester and Burnet himself, are sketched with a rare discernment. Dr. Johnson's praise is apposite and not exaggerated. With confidence he commends it to ' the critic for its elegance, the philosopher for its arguments, and the saint for its piety.' But it was written and published within a few months of Rochester's death, and was neither

spoiled by thought nor enfeebled by correction.
Moreover, it indulged Burnet's dominant passions,
always to be in at the death, and most zealously to
improve the occasion. Indeed there is no doubt
that he exaggerated Rochester's ' licentiousness ' in
order to enhance the virtue of his conversion.

As a serious historian, Burnet has a double claim
upon our regard. On the one hand, as Professor Firth
has pointed out, he was the first of the moderns
to make an adequate use of documentary evidence,
and his *History of the Reformation* is still esteemed an
authority. On the other hand, he wrote, in the
History of My Own Time, of the men whom he knew,
of the events whereof he was witness. He was at
once archivist and journalist, and by a wanton paradox it is his journalism to which he owes his immortality. The merits and faults of Burnet's most
familiar book are the merits and faults of the man
himself. It is vivid, energetic, and picturesque. It
is never dull, and it is never tired. It carries the
reader along its stream of words with as little resistance as Burnet's audience opposed to his sermons.
And the ease of its style is matched by an ease of
fancy. Burnet was a gossip in an age of gossips. He
had the same curiosity, the same love of the trivial, as
obsessed Aubrey and Anthony à Wood. He did not
disdain to record the tricks of manner and speech
which differentiate one man from another, and which
graver historians omit. For instance, he tells us that
Lauderdale's ' tongue was too big for his mouth,

which made him bedew all he talked to'; that Shaftesbury 'depended much on what a drunken physician had predicted'; that Orrery 'pretended to wit, but it was very luscious'; that Buckingham 'has no manner of literature, and all he knows is in chemistry.' So much may be set down to his credit. On the other hand, his book is, like himself, garrulous, reckless, and undisciplined. He still preaches to the personages of his *History* as he preached to them, if he might, when he and they were alive. Withal he was a finished eavesdropper, who combined the keen scent for news with the tireless indiscretion of the modern reporter; and it may be said that there is no side of his own various character that is not illustrated in the *History of My Own Time*.

His honesty and good faith have been sharply questioned. Political opponents have found in his work not a few traces of deceit and vindictiveness. But their discoveries are not justified. Burnet was an advocate who had persuaded himself that he was honest, and cared not what the others said. He did not often lie wilfully. His errors proceeded rather from want of judgment or personal vanity than from any love of falsehood. Johnson says ' he was so much prejudiced that he took no pains to find out the truth,' and compares him most wittily to ' a man who resolves to regulate his time by a certain watch, but will not inquire whether the watch is right or wrong.' That is perfectly true, but it is not the whole truth. It leaves Burnet's stupidity out of the account, and Burnet's faults sprang as much from stupidity as from prejudice. He did not see all that he thought he saw, and he understood only half that he saw. His conclusions, therefore, were often as incorrect as his impressions; and his authority, first-hand as it is, is by no means impeccable. It is difficult, for instance, to defend Burnet's character, or characters, of Charles II. The earlier draft is just and discerning. It does not hide the truth either for good or evil, and it sets the witty, pleasure-loving sovereign in not too dark a light. The later describes a monster, not a man. It introduces an infamous comparison with the Tiberius of Suetonius, for which the facts give no warrant. It brings a wicked charge against the Duchess of Orleans, for which there is not a shadow of foundation. That this change of view was not without a motive is evident, nor can we doubt that the motive was revenge. The King had not treated Burnet with the distinction which the preacher thought due to him. Burnet, in abasing himself before the King after the suicide of Essex, knew that he had been guilty of a mean action, and kept within his mind a rancour against the man who was the unwitting cause of his degradation. In any case, the offence is one which partiality cannot excuse, and which the King himself expected and discounted.

However, it is the admirable series of characters which give the greatest value to Burnet's *History*. Happily, the seventeenth century had not been taught

the heresy, that great men were powerless to direct
the course of affairs—that events were the inevitable
result of natural forces or sudden upheavals ; and
Burnet, like the best of his contemporaries, gave
generous credit to the captains and statesmen of his
time. He believed, and he believed rightly, that if
you would understand history, you must understand
the characters of those who directed the councils or
fought the battles of the State. Moreover, not
merely was character-drawing the fashion in his own
country ; it is certain that Burnet had encountered
the works of La Bruyère. And he has given us such
a gallery of portraits as you will not find outside the
pages of Clarendon. He was not so fine a painter as
his great rival, whose scrupulous tact in the selection
of virtues and vices was beyond his reach. He was
familiar, where Clarendon was austere, happily trivial
and even witty, where Clarendon was pompous or
priggish. He obtained his results not by choice and
omission, but by a careless profusion of detail, and
despite his lack of artistry, despite his prejudice, he
bears indispensable witness to one of the most
interesting periods of our history.

He has told us what he thought concerning the
greatest of his contemporaries. By way of contrast,
we will set down the opinion which two persons, who
knew him well, held of his character. His mother
declared that he ' would be a bee-headed man all his
lifetime.' The King, who, if he did not know him
as well as his mother, had the talent of swifter

judgment, thus summed up his arrogance: 'I believe he would be content to be hanged to have the
pleasure to make a speech on the scaffold; but I
would order drums to be beat, so that he should not
be heard.' Fortunately Burnet eluded the scaffold.
But had he come within the shadow of the tree he
would have been equal to the emergency. 'I would
have put my speech,' said he, 'in such hands that
the world should see it if they could not hear it';
and no doubt the last dying speech of Gilbert Burnet
would not have been without edification.

THE DUKE OF NEWCASTLE

To any politician :

Mutato nomine de te
Fabula narratur.

THOSE who believe that the world is governed
with very little wisdom can find few better
examples of incompetence in our annals than the Duke
of Newcastle. For forty-six years he interfered wantonly in the government of Great Britain ; he well-
nigh succeeded in driving his country upon the rock
of destruction; and he died still affecting, to himself
at least, the vain and pompous manners of the heaven-
sent statesman. He had made no attempt to fit
himself for the discharge of the onerous duties he
lightly assumed. Knowledge and intelligence were
completely lacking to him. The education which
Westminster School and the University of Cambridge
had offered him were thrown away upon his barren
mind. To the end of his life he kept unsullied an
inveterate ignorance. He believed that Cape Breton
was not an island, and he was once found looking for
Jamaica in a map of the Mediterranean. When, in
1755, he was asked at a meeting of the Council, what

was a squadron, he replied, ' three ships or more ! '
George II. said, with perfect truth, that Newcastle
was unfit to be the chamberlain of a petty German
prince. He could not think; he kept Stone and
Murray to do his thinking for him. Irresolute and
incapable, fussy and dishonest, he was indefatigable
in the discussion of small things. On one occasion
he argued for many hours whether the original or the
translation of a certain document should be placed
in the paper on the right or left of two parallel columns.
At the same time he so bitterly disliked the trans-
action of real business that the discipline of the army
was long suspended, because (in 1729) he would not
take the trouble to countersign the King's order for
holding courts-martial. ' Who would not laugh,'
said Horace Walpole, ' at a world where so ridiculous
a creature as the Duke of Newcastle can overturn
Ministries ? '

It seemed idle to laugh. With all his folly, Newcastle not only overturned Ministries, but made them
anew. The scorn of patriotism or the censure of
honourable men availed not to move him from his
high offices. And it must be admitted that he took
a low view of his own job. If he lacked talent himself
he did not expect it in those whom their interest or
his complaisance had advanced. ' It would be a very
bad precedent,' he said in 1737, ' to punish everybody
in office for not acting as if they had sense . . . for
everybody knew that there might be very good reasons
for giving people employment in the State besides

their having sense : they might have great titles,
great estates, great property, great zeal to serve who-
ever was in power : nay, some—I won't say all—may,
with very little sense, have great integrity and good
characters ; and such men it may be very proper for
a Government to employ in offices, where sense is
not much wanted. . . . But if such men were to see
that they were to be responsible for not acting with
all the circumspection of able men, when everybody
knows that they might as well pretend to infallibility
as ability, I think it would prevent many people from
entering into the service of the Government whom
it is very right from their property to attach to the
interest of the Government : and I think besides
that it would be as great an injustice for the House
of Lords to punish a man for being a fool as for
having the gout ; they are both infirmities, not
faults ; they are the misfortunes, not the trans-
gressions, of those who are infected with them, and
make them much more objects of compassion than
resentment.' The candour of this amazing harangue
was obviously inadvertent and unconscious. Never
once did it occur to Newcastle's cloudy mind that a
man should be chosen to do the King's business or to
serve his country merely because he was fitted by
natural gifts for those pursuits, that it would not be
prudent to enter a gouty man for a hundred yards'
race. He smiled at those who thought that the world
should be governed by a succession of talents. ' I
don't know,' said the ironic Walpole, ' whether there

are not more parts in governing without genius.' At any rate the Houses of Parliament acquiesced in their ridiculous leader, and believed, no doubt, that Pitt's gout was a worse infirmity than Newcastle's folly.

So he fumbled through life with hands ' that are always groping and sprawling, and fluttering and hurrying on the rest of his precipitate person,' *un certain tatillonnage*, a Frenchman called it; and so long as he remained in office, which he did with eminent success, he cared not what happened to his country. He had no skill in legislation. As an administrator he justly earned the contempt of all his contemporaries. He was idle, dilatory, and irresolute. He was determined that he would never do to-day what he might put off until to-morrow. Content to wait upon events, he thought there was always a chance of something favourable turning up. One desire dominated him, and one desire only : to remain in office. His ambition, restless and untiring, was satisfied with nothing less than political dominion. And for this dominion he had all the gifts that were necessary. He was intimately at home in the *coulisses*. A master of intrigue, he was at his best in the secret, corrupt management of the two Houses, in playing off one group against another, in distributing places and pensions. In a debased age, he sank triumphantly beneath the level of his kind. Not even the infamous Bubb Dodington, who knew to a penny the market value of a borough, was a match for him.

And in the purchase of votes he was never, I think,

disturbed by a false shame. He was incapable, for
instance, of the hypocrisy which persuaded Dodington
to confide to his journal in the midst of an election
that he had spent three days ' in the infamous and
disagreeable compliance with the low habits of venal
wretches.' He expected to be asked for posts and
pensions, livings and bishoprics, and if they were
handy he gave them. Were he indifferent to the fate
of England, at least he cherished a proper respect
for a man ' who could give his Majesty six members
for nothing.' Nor was there any move in the game
to which he would not willingly stoop. To counter
intrigue with intrigue, trick with trickery, was an
achievement best suited to his temper, and in this
sport, wherein alone he excelled, he spared neither
friend nor foe. How he must have laughed when
Halifax, having conspired with Dodington to contrive
a Cabinet of their own, not merely told Newcastle all
about it, but took measures with him to defeat his
and Dodington's own design ! And surely Dodington
should have known better than to be surprised at the
manœuvre, because at that very time, and ever since,
Halifax had spoken of Newcastle to him and to others
' as a knave and a fool.' There is a point at which
the ingenuousness of politicians becomes intolerable.

In war or in peace the Duke of Newcastle had but
one aim and one ambition—to purchase a general
support at the expense of the country. His power,
says Lecky, rested upon this ignoble basis—' upon
the uniform employment of all the patronage of the

Crown, and of a large proportion of the public money at his disposal, for the purpose of maintaining a parliamentary majority.' England might be beaten on land or sea—the Duke of Newcastle was indifferent to her lot. What he could not bear was that any other than he should dip his fingers in the national purse. He clung to the secret service money with the feverish despair with which a drunkard clings to the key of a wine-cellar, and in a crisis of his, and incidentally of England's fate, he deprived himself of Fox's aid, for what it was worth, because he would not surrender, and Fox, a greedier man than himself, would not forgo the control of that delectable fund. At another time, when all honest men trembled for England's safety, he would not consent to the addition of some necessary regiments to the British Army, because he could not bear to think that the Duke of Cumberland should have the privilege of appointing officers to them. Indeed, the two strongest passions of his soul were jealousy and fear. If he were unable to accomplish anything worth doing himself, he was filled with alarm at the deeds of others. Throughout a long life he pursued always the same policy of intriguing against those whom he served, or those who served him, as soon as he thought their influence too great.

He owed his first advance to Walpole, who made him Secretary of State in 1724, because he thought that the boroughs he commanded would be valuable to his interests, and because he was convinced that

Newcastle's lack of understanding would prevent him from growing into a dangerous rival. For once the astute Walpole allowed himself to be deceived. He reckoned not with Newcastle's cunning and effrontery, and before he could take steps to guard himself, he found Newcastle linking himself with anybody who would help him to stand upon his feet independently of Walpole. Thus he did his best to win Carteret to his purpose, and once when he was half-drunk— for he did not disdain the lesser vices—he waited upon Walpole with an offer of Carteret's services, and promised to go bail for Carteret's good behaviour. Walpole curtly bade him choose between him and Carteret, and presently was made the victim of Newcastle's malevolence. Lord Harvey sketched the politician's position at Walpole's fall in terms of the bitterest contempt. ' The Duke of Newcastle,' said he, ' whose envy is so strong that he is jealous of everybody, and whose understanding is so weak that nobody is jealous of him, is reciprocally made use of by these two men (Pulteney and Carteret) to promote their different ends ; and being jealous of Lord Carteret from feeling his superior interest with the King, and jealous of Mr. Pulteney from his superior interest with his brother (Mr. Pelham) in the House of Commons, is like the hungry ass in the fable between the two bundles of hay, and allured by both without knowing which to go to, tastes neither, and will starve between them.' Alas ! he did not starve. With equal greed he seized both bundles,

and was thus supported in his career of mischief.   So
in the same spirit of jealousy he quarrelled with his
brother, whose influence in the House of Commons
was too great for his endurance, and presently betrayed
Pitt to Bute in bitter envy of the victories won by
the British arms.   Bute, in whom at last he met his
match, assailed him pitilessly, expelled him from all
the offices which he held, degraded those whom he
had advanced, and left him to nurse his jealousy in
retirement.

But fear was a stronger passion of Newcastle's
mind even than jealousy.   There was nothing of
which he was not afraid.   When he was in office—
and he was always in office—he dreaded the mere
possibility of resignation.   He feared to go to war ;
he feared to remain at peace.   He was terrified by
the clamour outside the Houses of Parliament, and
had Byng shot to appease the people.   He was afraid
of the rebellious Scots, trembled before the Pretender,
and in 1745 shut himself up for days in a state of
doubting timidity.   If only he had been sure that
the Pretender would win, he would have joined him,
since Great Britain without Newcastle was a thing
he could not contemplate.   ' The other day,' wrote
Walpole, ' I concluded the Ministry knew the danger
was all over, for the Duke of Newcastle ventured to
have the Pretender's declaration burnt at the Royal
Exchange.'   Indeed this aspen of politics must have
been very sure before he dared to take so desperate
a step.   But what frightened him most of all was

the threat of a French invasion. He went about his business in a shaking tremor at the mere thought of France. And worse still, he infected his countrymen with the poison of his own cowardice. Fox declared in 1745 that ' had 5000 Frenchmen landed in any part of this island a week ago, I verily believe the entire conquest of it would not have cost them a battle.' Ten years later, Newcastle in a panic fear hurried over Hessians and Hanoverians to England rather than employ Hawke and his fleet in their proper business of defence. Well might Pitt attempt, in denouncing the cowardice of Newcastle, his ' little frivolous love of power, his ambition of being the only figure among ciphers,' to rally the English people. ' I want,' said he, ' to call this country out of that enervated state that twenty thousand Frenchmen can shake it. The maxims of our Government have degenerated, not our natives. I wish to see that breed restored, which under our old principles carried our glory so high.'

Even had Newcastle's irresolution not prevented him from making up his mind, his pusillanimity would have forced him to inaction. Horace Walpole said that he was ' always at least as much frightened at doing right as at doing wrong.' Perhaps the distinction between right and wrong was not clear in his mind. And the fear which haunted him in public pursued him to the retirement of his home. When Dr. Shaw, the King's physician, ate some mushrooms and was ill for a few hours, ' the catastrophe so much alarmed the Duke of Newcastle, that he immediately ordered all the mushroom beds to be destroyed, and even the toadstools in the park did not escape scalping in the general massacre.' So even to the hour of his death the passion of his life pursued him. He died, as he had lived, in a panic, surrounded himself with doctors, and hoped perhaps that this last lavish expenditure might save him from the grave.

There was one thing only of which he was not afraid—Parliament. The bright, well-drilled Houses presented no terror to the mind of this finished politician. The Commons and the Lords were alike his henchmen, for he had purchased most of them with public money, and the rest were looking eagerly for promotion. When Shelburne was beginning a career of politics, Henry Fox summed up in a single letter of advice the whole gospel of Newcastle. ' It is in place that I long to see you,' said he to Shelburne ; ' and it is the place-man, not the independent Lord, that can do this country good.' There in a sentence is displayed the complete ' statesman.' To be sure, there were not many independent Lords or Commoners either in the middle of the eighteenth century. Parliament itself, falling into a pit of corruption, was the slave of the Cabinet. If it had opinions, it found it profitable to suppress them, and incurred the danger of ' becoming in time rather the oppressor than the representative of the people.' As Pitt said, the House of Commons had ' degenerated into a little assembly, serving no other purpose than to register the arbitrary decrees of one too powerful subject.'

The record of Newcastle's life is the record of the
offices that he held, and the Ministries which he made
and unmade. Office was essential to him ; he could
not live without it. The service of his country would
not have interested him, even had he been capable of
it. But he delighted in comings and goings ; in
setting up A against B or C, and then betraying all
three ; in involving his nearest colleagues in intrigue,
and sacrificing them without a murmur to the popular
clamour. Nor for more than forty years was he long
deprived of the office, essential to his own poor
happiness, fatal to the poorer destiny of his country.
From the time when, in 1724, Walpole made him a
Secretary of State, unto his unlamented death in
1768, he was seldom without a seat in the Cabinet.
He served with Walpole, with Wilmington, with his
brother, Henry Pelham, with Pitt, and was disloyal
to every one of them. Upon whatever he touched
he left the mark of his incompetence. In 1743 he
made the battle of Dettingen of no effect by refusing
to assent to the Treaty of Hanau. A year earlier he
had ensured the failure of an expedition to Cartagena
by his meddling and muddling. Yet so tight was
his hold upon the public purse, so well skilled was he
in conciliating or dividing groups, that no disaster
could shake his supremacy.

At the death, in 1754, of Henry Pelham, his brother,
whom he had ever pursued with envy and malice,
he became all-powerful in England, and continued
within the space of three or four years to depress

his country to the very depths of ignominy. 'The poor Duke of Newcastle,' wrote Horace Walpole, 'conquers the torrent of his grief, and . . . rather than abandon England to its evil genius, will submit to be Lord Treasurer himself.' He was more than this : be became universal Minister, that he might mismanage all things. 'The Duke is omnipotent' —again it is Walpole who speaks—'and to show that power makes use of nothing but machines.' The failure of his plans did not disturb him. He was determined that Fox should lead the Commons and leave the control of the secret service money to him. Fox declined the dubious honour. He was determined that Pitt should resign. Pitt refused to resign. Newcastle remained 'affronted—and omnipotent.' And it was, in Dodington's phrase, 'all for Quarter Day.'

Moreover, Newcastle could do no more in an hour of stress and danger than carry the shifts and dodges of peace into a great war. He hoped that all would be well so long as Bubb Dodington and Halifax and Legge and Robinson and Fox played the old game of in and out with all the old skill, and let him draw whatever profit he could from their dissensions. What did it matter that France armed, so long as there were boroughs to be bought or given away ? When Pitt declared that ' to times of relaxation should be left that fondness for disposal of places ; wisdom should meet such rough times as these,' he was speaking a language which Newcastle could not understand,

and which, when once it had caught the popular ear, forbade the 'shifty old jobber,' for a while at least, to touch anything but the public money-bag.

The times, in 1755, were rough indeed. War with France, as any statesman would have seen plainly, was inevitable. It needed but a spark to set America in a blaze. The peace had already been broken in many a skirmish, and Newcastle refused not only to take action himself, but to see that the country was ready for action. Hungrily though he clung to power, he could not make up his mind, and let things drift as they would. In either House his majority was absolute, and he left his majority uncontrolled. Even when Braddock had been despatched on his ill-fated expedition, even when Boscawen had captured two ships of the French fleet, Newcastle persisted in the deception that we were not at war. 'There was no violence,' says Dodington, 'no oppression, no particular complaint, and yet the nation was sinking by degrees, and there was a general indisposition proceeding from the weakness and worthlessness of the Minister, who would embrace everything and was fit for nothing.'

However, in Newcastle's despite, we were soon fighting France all the world over, and the supreme Minister took no steps. As Waldegrave said, 'we first engaged in a war, and then began to prepare ourselves.' Newcastle would not prepare, even after hostilities had begun. Hawke was at Spithead with his fleet, and Newcastle was afraid to give him any definite orders. He thought it would be a good plan if ' Hawke took a turn in the Channel to exercise the fleet, without having any instructions whatever.' Thus he hoped to shift his responsibility without losing a single supporter. And when this ingenious suggestion was not approved, he proposed that ' Hawke should be ordered not to attack the enemy unless he deemed it worth while ' ; that he should not take their ships unless there were more together than ten—that he meant this only of merchantmen, for to be sure he must attack any squadrons of ships of war ; that he should take and destroy all French ships of war, but no merchantmen ; that, finally, he should be restrained from taking any ships except ships of the line. What Hawke, or any one else, made of this jumble of opposites I do not know. It is certain that Newcastle plumed himself on an ingenuity which pretended that England was simultaneously at war and at peace.

His indecision at sea was equalled by his indecision on land. While he gave contradictory orders to the Admirals, he was resolved, if he could, to make war without an army. He was quite sure that a little goodwill and hopefulness were sufficient to defeat the most desperate foe. When Pitt proposed to strengthen and to train the Militia, the House of Lords, on Newcastle's order, threw out the Bill. Compulsion and increase were alike distasteful to him. ' We have a Militia Bill,' he wrote, ' which may give us some trouble, as many of our best friends in the

House of Commons are for it, from their zeal; but
I am afraid the principles of it may prove dangerous
to this country. The expense would be certain
and immense—viz., £200,000 per annum at least.
The use very uncertain. If the scheme should succeed,
it must undoubtedly increase greatly the power of the
Crown. But that which of all things I dread, it would
breed up our people to a love of arms and military
government, and divert them from their true business
—husbandry, manufactures, etc.; and I think, upon
the whole, would tend more to make this a military
country and government than any scheme I have yet
heard of.' Zeal, indeed! What right has a self-
respecting politician to show zeal, unless it be a zeal
for the pocket? And for the rest, rather let England
perish than see the power of the Crown increased and
herself a military nation ready for defence! Thus
has the Whig spoken from the beginning, in those
far-off days when he served the Devil, the first of his
kind. Thus shall the Whig speak, until with the smug
satisfaction of a false martyrdom he beholds his land in
ruins.

The invasion, the thought of which had caused
the wretched Newcastle to tremble in his chair of
office, turned out to be a false alarm nicely contrived
to cover an attack upon Minorca. And the English
Minister did everything that was expected of him.
He made no attempt to interfere with the French
fleet, which set sail under the command of the Duc de
Richelieu from Toulon. But three days after it had

started he sent Admiral Byng, with an ill-fitted fleet, without marines, and with but a single regiment of soldiers, to defend Minorca against the superior forces of the French. So badly was Byng equipped that he thought himself obliged to linger at Gibraltar longer than was prudent, and when at last he reached Minorca, after an indecisive encounter, he decided to return to Gibraltar, and there to await reinforcements. When Byng had sailed away, the Castle of St. Philip could not hold out, and Minorca fell an easy prey to the Duc de Richelieu.

The failure of Byng was turned to excellent and instant account by the adroit Newcastle. A wave of indignation swept over the country. The Admiral was burnt in effigy from one end of England to the other. When a deputation from the City of London waited upon Newcastle to demand vengeance, the Minister showed an indecent haste in promising a scapegoat for his own incompetence. ' Oh, indeed,' he exclaimed, ' he shall be tried immediately; he shall be hanged directly,' and thenceforth the fate of Byng was sealed. He had become a pawn in the political game, and Newcastle was resolved not to lose a piece by attempting to save the life of one who might be innocent.

No sooner, then, did Byng arrive in England than he was closely imprisoned, and on December 21, 1756, began his trial before a court-martial. The sentence passed upon him was equivocal and half-hearted. He was acquitted of cowardice and disaffection, and found guilty, with many qualifications, of neglect of duty. The Court, moreover, denouncing the great severity of the 12th Article of War, earnestly recommended him to his Majesty's clemency. Argument and recommendation were alike useless. For once the King and the mobility were united to demand the punishment of Byng, and at the same time to prop up a tottering Ministry. For Newcastle, indeed, the Admiral's execution was a political necessity. Were he to escape, Lord Anson, the First Lord of the Admiralty, would be no longer secure, and the great Duke himself, the supreme bestower of patronage, would receive such a shock as had never yet fallen upon his corrupt head. So Byng's life became a mere stake in the gamble of politics. The Ministers bribed and promised, according to their wont. They saw with delight the unpopularity which Pitt and Temple incurred by protesting against what they thought a judicial murder. The blood of Byng appeared to be the best cement which could hold together the pieces of a disparted Cabinet. Newcastle, it must be admitted, left nothing undone which might strengthen him and his friends. The Duchess of Newcastle sent Lady Sophia Egerton to the Princess Amelia, begging for the death of Byng, and telling her that if Byng were spared, Lord Anson could not remain at the head of the Admiralty. 'What a complication of horrors,' exclaimed Walpole, ' women employed on a job for blood!' More than Lord Anson's position was at stake. As has been said, the great Minister himself might have been hanged if Byng had not been shot, and that in his eyes would have been the worst of national calamities.

That Byng was guilty of neglect cannot be gainsaid. As little can it be gainsaid that he ought not to have been shot. He was sent to Minorca, ill-equipped, ill-found, and with a squadron too small for the task entrusted to it. The Governor of Gibraltar refused to part with the troops which he was ordered to furnish. When Byng arrived at Minorca, the French fleet stood on the defensive. As Voltaire said, ' l'Amiral français était aussi loin de l'Amiral anglais que celui-ci l'était de l'autre.' That is incontestable, but Byng was sent to relieve St. Philip's Castle and to destroy the enemy's ships, and these objects he had failed to attain. As always happens, the sailor was punished. The politician, to whose incompetence the failure was primarily due, escaped. Long before the court-martial began, it was recognised that the sailor's escape meant the fall of the Minister. One thing is abundantly clear: if Newcastle prayed for the death of Byng, the Court was very reluctant to condemn him. It passed the sentence ' only because the law, in prescribing death, left no alternative to the discretion of the Court.'

Newcastle was not hanged. He heard with indifference the Court's recommendation to mercy ; but not even the sacrifice of Byng availed to avert his fall. For many months Pitt had attacked him without mercy and with manifest justice. Now, Pitt was not merely a greater and stronger man than any of those who bowed a willing knee to Newcastle in the two Houses of Parliament. He was made of a different clay ; he was fulfilled with a different purpose. He alone among his contemporaries had gone into the business of politics without counting what he could get out of it. He was not interested in the sale of boroughs. When he was appointed Paymaster in 1746, he had set a noble precedent by refusing to enrich himself at the expense of the nation. To his colleagues, no doubt, his conduct seemed foolish and ostentatious. They could not understand the scruple of a politician who desired simply and solely to serve his country. He appeared especially disgraceful in their eyes because, being a man of no fortune, he had refused to dip his hand in the till, and had thus set an example of political honesty which they had no intention of following. But if Pitt's sacrifice annoyed his fellows, it strengthened his hold upon the country, and gave an added weight to every blow that he struck at the quivering Newcastle. In a series of philippics, which he alone ever equalled, he prepared the way for his own advance. He knew well enough that he could not supersede the ' one too powerful subject ' until he had got him out, and that there was only one means of getting him out—by assault.

His eloquence caught the public ear, his images dazzled the people's eye. When the great conflict was engaged, his famous comparison between the Rhone and the Saone was still remembered. ' I,' he had begun with a mock modesty—' I who am at a distance from that *sanctum sanctorum* whither the priest goes for inspiration—I, who travel through a desert and am overwhelmed with mountains of obscurity, cannot easily catch a gleam to direct me to the beauties of these negotiations. But there are parts of the address which do not seem to me to come from the same quarter with the rest. I cannot unravel this mystery. Yes,' he cried, suddenly striking his forehead, ' I, too, am inspired ! Now it strikes me : I remember at Lyons to have been carried to see the conflux of the Rhone and the Saone : the one a gentle, languid, feeble stream, and, though languid, of no depth ; the other, a boisterous and impetuous torrent. But they meet at last, and long may they continue united to the comfort of each other, and to the glory, honour, and security of the nation.' The simile and its irony had an immediate and a lasting effect. The languid Newcastle and the boisterous Fox remained in men's minds, thus characterised, long after the speech had been delivered. The image of the go-cart, sketched while the fate of Byng's expedition was still in suspense, was never wholly effaced, and it completed Newcastle's discomfiture. ' If I see a child,' said Pitt, ' driving a go-cart close to the edge of a precipice with the precious freight of an old king and his family, I am bound to take the reins out of such hands.'

But before Pitt could take the reins out of the weak, crafty hands which held them, there were a hundred petty conspiracies to be set on foot and foiled. It is the curse of politics that nothing can be done simply. Even he who would save his country must first wade through the dirty water of intrigue. With the war upon us, Newcastle still deferred the day of salvation. There were secret meetings and furtive plottings. The wily old Minister thought that the game of corruption was not quite played out, and that if he yielded enough to Fox and Pitt he might still retain the pride of his place. But at last, in the stress of danger, the voice of patriotism was heard ; the thing called politics was put roughly aside ; and England, which had clamoured for a man, at last saw its call answered.

In other words, the incredible happened : Newcastle resigned. The cities of England began, with one accord, to bestow their freedom upon Pitt. As Walpole said, ' it rained gold boxes.' But the unanimous wish of the country was not enough to establish Pitt firmly in office. He could not work without the support of Parliament, and Parliament, ingeniously bought, was still in the power of Newcastle. And so, to England's shame, Newcastle had to be recalled to the Treasury, and Fox was made Paymaster of the Forces. As Pitt said himself, ' I borrowed the Duke of Newcastle's majority to carry on the business of the country.' Pitt, indeed, had stooped perforce to conquer. He had thrown to the precious pair of dogs the bone which each liked best. By an act of supreme contempt, having stripped Newcastle of power, he left him the patronage necessary to support his vanity, and to Fox he gave that opportunity of making money without which he could not live. As for Pitt, he knew that he could save England, and that no one else could; he brought her some years of shining victory; he built up empires for her in India and in Canada; he changed the very aspect of history; and he proved, incidentally, that if he had left her to be gambled for by Newcastle and the politicians, she would have come down to us stripped and pilled, the simulacrum of a second-rate Power.

'THE CROWNED PHILOSOPHER'

FREDERICK THE GREAT, as Lord Rosebery has said, is ' in a secular sense the patron saint of Germany.' It is he who has shaped his country's sinister ambition, and who held up for the emulation of future ages the supreme policy of theft. The Kaiser William, who for Frederick's motive, glory, devastated Europe, framed himself consciously and deliberately upon the model of him who delighted to call himself ' the wandering knight ' or ' the Don Quixote of the North.' Of course he fell short of his exemplar, since he was equally remote from the soldier and the pedant, who met, by a strange union, in the heart and mind of Frederick. Nevertheless, the career of Frederick is of the highest interest to us, since it helps us to understand modern Germany, and nowhere shall we find a more vivid portrait of the greatest of the Hohenzollerns than in Catt's plain and honest memoirs.

Henri de Catt was born at Morges, near Geneva, in 1728, was educated at the University of Utrecht, and was following the craft of a schoolmaster, for which nature had fitted him well enough, when—it was in 1755—he encountered Frederick the Great on

a boat at Arnheim. Three years afterwards he was
in the King of Prussia's service, allowed himself to be
absorbed heart and soul for twenty years, and then,
the victim of a sudden whim, resumed obscurity.
What he did afterwards is of no account, except that
he composed his memoirs and amply justified his
years of slavery.   Such as he was, he was born to be
the patient servitor of a tyrant. He was of those to
whom sycophancy is no dishonour. He was happy
in bending himself to another's will, in living another's
life, in thinking another's thoughts.   Though he had
something of Boswell's willingly subordinate temperament, he was not, as Boswell was, a knowing artist.
There is in his book an accidental quality, which by
no means impairs its value. He draws up the curtain
and sets Frederick the Great upon the stage, not with
the gesture of an accomplished showman, but with
the simplicity of one who has composed a drama
almost without intention. 'This is how it all
happened,' he seems to say, ' and I am as far as anybody from offering a reasonable explanation.'   In
truth, accident was the mainspring of Catt's life.
He met Frederick by accident ; by accident he entered
his service ; and in the King's service he would have
remained unto the end had it not been for some
offence given by accident and without meaning.

So faithful a character was Catt, that he is able to
boast with truth that ' the cooling off of this unique
man, so little expected, so little deserved, did not
influence his mind and heart.'   He was equally

incapable of rancour and falsehood. He tells the story of his first meeting the King with his accustomed artlessness. He chanced, as I have said, to be travelling in the same boat which was taking the King to Utrecht, and the King, disguised as the first musician of the King of Poland, invited him into his cabin. There took place the first of many hundred conversations, in which Catt played the part of listener with the greatest skill. Frederick instantly began to criticise the Dutch Government, and was told for his pains that he knew nothing about it. Then he turned lightly to religion, explained to the stern Calvinist, which was Henri de Catt, that ' creation was impossible,' got into a circle and skipped over it, ' thereupon went into such a sally upon kings, as could not in the least lead me to suppose that he was one,' shifted to literature and praised Racine enthusiastically, and when Catt launched out on Frederick's actions, interrupted him rapidly with the words : ' Nothing more of kings, monsieur ! What have we to do with them ? We will spend the rest of our voyage on more agreeable and cheering objects.' At parting the King was careful to discover Catt's name, and, remembering his patience and his tact, invited him to Breslau. Catt entered the King's service under the best auspices and with the best advice. The Marquis d'Argens, who knew ' the crowned philosopher ' as well as anybody, was ready with caution and counsel. He urged the ingenuous young scholar to keep silence, to be composed, to enter as little as possible into jests, and to show small eagerness for the confidences which would be forced upon him. 'Do not, for God's sake,' said the Marquis, ' criticise either his prose or his verse ; don't ask him for anything, no money, and see only as far as politeness permits those whom he has decided are fools, rogues, intriguers, and carpers.'.

The excellent Sir Andrew Mitchell, British envoy and Frederick's trusted adviser, showed the same understanding of the King's foible. 'Without becoming too familiar with this Prince,' said he by way of warning, ' be yet frank and open with him, and when you are together of an evening, always bring forward questions of literature, of philosophy, and especially of metaphysics, which he likes very much. Discuss the French poets with him, and if he shows you any of his verses, criticise only in so far as he requests. Allow him to speak rather than speak yourself.' Catt took all the advice proffered him with exemplary obedience. For twenty years he listened to the King's voice. He received the title of reader to his Majesty, but it was his Majesty who read. Indeed, from the moment that Catt came to Breslau, he was rather a piece of furniture than a man. Had they gone forth together, he would have played the part of walking-stick to perfection. But it was at the King's quarters that they met, and there he did his duty as a listening, sympathetic chair. At the outset, the King put Catt at his ease by assuring him that he led a dog of a life, and sketched for him the normal progress of his day. He got up at three, so he told Catt, and sometimes earlier, though he owned that it was a painful business. He did his own hair, dressed himself, took a cup of coffee, and read his despatches. While he meditated his answers to the despatches, he played for an hour or more on the flute, an instrument upon which Alcibiades said no gentleman could play, and then gave instructions to his secretaries; after which he read old books, seldom new ones, and issued the orders of the day. At noon he dined, played again on the flute or read, and was prepared, at four o'clock, to talk with Catt. It was an eager, industrious life, as he lived it, for he read and wrote with fury; and it says a vast deal for Catt's energy and persistence that for twenty years he was able to share it.

The advice which the Marquis d'Argens and Sir Andrew Mitchell gave was proved sound in the event. Despite all his professions of modesty, Frederick was one who could brook neither criticism nor contradiction. Unwilling to meet anybody on terms of equality, the victim always of a sudden caprice, he would set a slight arrogance against the fidelity of a lifetime, and dismiss the oldest of his servants for some paltry, inadequate reason. He lived and died friendless, because he did not understand that friendship meant giving as well as taking, and he was content, for the most part, to be surrounded by sycophants, whom he was free to insult either in speech or in the practical jokes of a rare brutality. His passion to be thought a poet made the task of conciliation far more difficult. He allowed himself the freedom of criticism ; he allowed it to no other, and the unfortunate Catt was compelled to hear more bad verse and to praise it than ever before had fallen to the lot of man to hear and praise. Nor was Frederick ever tired of repeating such scraps of flattery as Voltaire had thrown to him. With an ingenuous pride he declared that Voltaire had commended the doggerel in which he describes a trip to Strasburg. ' You see from this approbation,' said he, ' that I am not such a bad poet as you might believe.' One day, as a concession of kindness, he read to Catt some passages of his poem on war. ' Nothing is so difficult,' said he by way of comment, ' as to make interesting the precepts of an art, whatever it is. Voltaire assured me that I had succeeded.' And of course there was no more to be said. Nor did he understand that any higher reward could be given to those who served him than a few verses from the royal hand. These verses were to Frederick what the iron cross is to William II. They were distributed so lavishly, that they were very soon cheapened. He even paid his bets at times in the same currency. When the Empress Elizabeth was lying ill, he made a wager with Catt about her death. The winner was to pay at his discretion. ' I shall make you a present if I lose,' said the King, ' and you what you please if I win.' The Empress died, and all that the wretched Catt got for his present was an epitaph in verse ! He owned to himself

that 'this was getting off rather lightly for an
affair of this importance,' but he was too full of joy
to hint, even in jest, that the discretion was very
slight. After all, had he not shown a proper admiration of the King's poetry, his tenure of office would
have been brief indeed. And who would withhold
praise when Voltaire had given it—Voltaire who, in
the King's esteem, was a poet who never flattered, and
who was very severe in this matter ?

So Frederick, by a double error, was sure that, as
he had the poet's virtues, *teste* Voltaire, so he had
not the poet's vices. 'Do not think,' he adjured
the innocent Catt, 'that I attach any great value
to what I do! Not at all; if I have the passion
for authorship, I have assuredly not its arrogance.'
Thus he deceived himself always. If ever there was
a man who believed that he, the King, could do no
wrong, it was Frederick. He drank in praise with
all the eagerness of a thirsty soul. He knew that his
verses were masterpieces all, because he had written
them. He insisted fiercely upon having his own
opinion supported. He was, indeed, an actor, who
acted even to himself. He lived as on parade, though
none were present save Catt. The slovenliness of
his person, the squalor of his dress, were mere versions
of his pride. He was, so to say, a dandy upside down,
who knew that the Spanish snuff which besmirched
his face would call attention to him more loudly than
delicately perfumed ruffles. But his own verses apart,
he seems to have been honest in his love of letters.

Though he had but a smattering of Latin, though he made childish mistakes in spelling, though he had all the faults of the late-learner, he surrendered himself whole-heartedly to poetry and eloquence. 'With them,' he said, 'I am never bored, and I can do without anybody.' It gave him a manifest pleasure to read aloud—a pleasure which explains the necessity of the listening Catt. He adored declamation, both for its own sake and as a proper accompaniment of kingship. 'Why should I not declaim,' he asks, 'when all Nature declaims?' Thus he deceived himself, not seeing that Nature has never declaimed, except in the eighteenth century, when she was neatly clipped and barbered out of herself after the fashion of Potsdam.

Nevertheless, he carried such baggage on his campaigns as no other soldier has carried. Wherever he went, in the field or at winter quarters, a library went with him. 'Lucretius,' he boasted, 'is my breviary.' Bacon, Cæsar, Tacitus, Plutarch, Cicero—these are some of the authors who never left him, and from whom he drew the lessons of his life and trade. Overcome by grief at the death of his sister, the Margravine of Baireuth, he turned for consolation to the funeral orations of Bossuet and Fléchier, and as he was always intent to imitate what he read, to play 'the sedulous ape,' in fact, he produced himself a funeral oration upon Matthew Reinhart, master shoemaker, and presented it with pomp and circumstance to Catt. 'That, my dear sir,' said he, 'is the fruit of the readings which astonished you. Bossuet and Fléchier made funeral orations to celebrate the life and death of illustrious men. As for me, not worthy to untie the latchet of the shoes of these great preachers, I have written the funeral praise of a poor shoemaker, who by his abilities, his virtues, and his piety, was more deserving than kings and princes to pass to the most distant posterity.' There in a few phrases you have the real Frederick, a monarch histrionic and insincere, with a rare talent for the trite and a constant love for copybook headings. Fresh from the study of the masterpieces of literature, he could yet murmur in the ear of Catt such maxims as these : ' Mortals, employ your time,' or ' The fate of a king is very sad ' ; and then perplex his hearer by putting the question : ' Do you know any prince who is as much of a pedagogue as I am ? '

But he cherished one admiration always, which was sincere and complete—an admiration of Racine. The works of that great poet could never leave him, because they were stored in his brain. Not only did he know his plays by heart ; he showed at times a clear appreciation of their qualities. Indeed, it was Racine, not Lucretius, who was his true breviary. In *Athalie* or *Britannicus* or *Mithridate* he sought pleasure in his happiest, encouragement in his darkest, moments. ' To rest ourselves,' says he one day, ' let us read the tragedy of *Britannicus* ; and read it he did, with a pinch of snuff at the end of every act, until his reading was interrupted by the tears which flowed easily at the royal command. He looked even upon defeat through the words of Racine, which were for him at once a consolation and a commentary. After the disaster which befell him at Hochkirchen, Catt faced him ' in a state of extreme emotion.' He need not have yielded to his excitement. The King came up to him ' with a rather open air,' and in a quiet voice repeated these lines from *Mithridate* :

> ' Enfin. après un an, tu me revois, Arbate ;
> Non plus, comme autrefois, cet heureux Mithridate
> Qui, de *Vienne* toujours balançant le destin,
> Tenais entr'elle et moi l'univers incertain :
> Je suis vaincu. *Daunus* a saisi l'avantage
> D'une nuit qui laissait peu de place au courage.'

Did ever a beaten soldier accept disaster in so strange a spirit of literary detachment ? Frederick was, as he said, ' a poor, conquered man,' and he fell to declaiming the lines of Racine, like the consummate actor that he was. So eager was he to speak and to recite that he left the poor Catt no chance of saying a word ; and presently, in forgetfulness of literature, undid his collar, and pulled out the famous box of gold, containing eighteen opium pills, which he deemed ' sufficient to take him to that dark bourne whence we do not return.' But he was soon back at Racine, invoking God in the words of the poet :

> ' Daigne, daigne, mon Dieu, sur *Kaunitz* et sur elle
> Répandre cet esprit d'imprudence et d'erreur,
> De la chute des rois funeste avant-coureur.'

And truly it was not upon the golden box but upon the golden-tongued poet that he relied for help and succour.

But there was one poet who exerted a deeper influence upon Frederick even than Racine, and that poet was Voltaire. Voltaire, indeed, was his constant obsession. In whatever he did or wrote his first thought was : What will Voltaire think of it ? A word of praise thrown to him by the great writer was as precious to him as victory itself. He treasured piously the poor little verses of his own composing, upon which Voltaire had smiled approval. Before the great man's name he abased himself—to others. ' Voltaire has a genius for verse,' he told Catt ; ' and I haven't. I am only a poor dilettante, who has great need of indulgence.' Had another dared to hint so much, he would have chased him from his presence with insult. ' By heavens ! a letter from Voltaire,' he exclaims one day, ' what a lucky day ! ' And when he had read the letter, ' you must acknowledge, my dear sir,' he insisted to Catt, ' that this Voltaire writes like the angels.' And thereafter he expresses his gratitude, like the humblest of mortals. ' This Voltaire is admirable,' he confesses, ' to think of me, and with his letters and works to feed my mind, which has great need of good nourishment.' When he was in high spirits he would brag that he had acted the part of critic to the great man himself. ' How many times,' he recalls with rapture, ' have I not corrected Voltaire himself, yes, Voltaire.' But while he admitted Voltaire's genius, he never ceased to revile Voltaire the man. His royal vanity had been wounded too deeply for forgetfulness, though his royal taste sternly refused to be perverted. He was never tired of talking about Voltaire's 'diabolical character.' 'When you see him quiet,' says he, 'be assured that he is meditating some wickedness. His great pleasure is to set people at loggerheads, and, when he has succeeded, he roars with laughter, jumps and skips about. "The scamps," he says, with the laugh of a satyr, "the scamps; that is the way to treat them."'

At Catt's first appearance, Frederick had summed up for his profit the opinion which he held of Voltaire. 'The world has produced no finer genius than Voltaire,' he admitted; 'but I despise him supremely, because he is not upright. If he had been, what a superiority he would have had over everything that exists!' That Frederick should reproach Voltaire on a matter of conduct is supremely ridiculous, and the reproach puts in question once more the relationship which existed between the poet and the King. Truly the poet has the better of it in morals as in genius. It is Voltaire who is cast for the *beau rôle* in the tragi-comedy enacted at Potsdam and elsewhere. Manifestly superior in wit and intellect, Voltaire was superior also in the justice of his cause. The friendship which linked the two men together was a friendship of hostility. They thought that they could not live apart from one another, and they knew that they could not live together amicably. And it was Voltaire who gave far more than he received, who had every claim to regard himself as the victim of autocratic impertinence. In the poor little squabble with Maupertuis, Voltaire was in the right of it, and he covered his assailant with the ridicule which he deserved. Though Frederick desired ardently to be thought a poet, he could not enjoy the equal company of poets, because he never forgot that he was crowned. The friendship which he offered Voltaire was tainted at its source. Here is Voltaire's ' little dictionary as used by kings ' :

My *friend* means my *slave*.

My *dear friend* means *I am more than indifferent to you*.

For *I will make you happy*, read *I will endure you as long as I have use for you*.

Sup with me to-night means *I will mock at you this evening*.

It is clear, then, that Voltaire had no illusions, even though pride had blinded the eyes of Frederick. As he said himself, if he had no sceptre he had a pen, which he proceeded to use, dipped in gall. And then came the supreme insult of Frankfort, where Voltaire was arrested and imprisoned. Never did a ' crowned philosopher ' so wickedly forget his dignity as when Frederick ordered a clumsy clown called Freytag to maltreat the poet, who had been his guest. That Voltaire should never have forgiven the affront was right and proper. That he gave too violent expression to his malice is perhaps true. But for the King to shed tears over the moral delinquency of a great man, whom he thought he could use as he presently used Catt, and whom he exposed to the insolence of a petty official, was a sublime act of hypocrisy. After all, the tragi-comedy could have but one ending. There is even a kind of pathos in the King's lifelong submission to the poet, whose presence he wished for and could not endure. And Voltaire may surely be forgiven if he laughed at the memory of the poor verses and poorer philosophy, upon which he had once smiled with interested benignity.

The Frederick whom Catt sets before us, then, is Frederick the amateur, the coxcomb, the dilettante. But there is another Frederick altogether, whose policy and depredations help us to understand clearly enough the pretentious infamies of William II. It is not merely that the Kaiser took his great predecessor for his model. He shares the ambition, as he shares the blood, of the marauder. When Frederick the Great succeeded to the throne of his father, a madman who had beaten, imprisoned, and threatened to kill his son, he was known chiefly as the author of a dull refutation of the Machiavellian system. At last, thought Europe, we shall see crowned in Prussia a king who hates craft as he hates flattery, who will expect of governments the same laws of morality which he expects of private gentlemen, and will ensure the peace of the world. With characteristic effrontery Frederick disappointed Europe as soon as ever he mounted the throne. His first act was to invade Silesia, whose integrity along with the other

Austrian states his house had guaranteed, for no
better reason than that he coveted its possession.
For this act of brigandage no excuse can be found.
Frederick's motive was the motive of the burglar,
and no more. 'Ambition, interest, the desire of
making people talk about me,' said he, 'carried the day;
and I decided for war.' His crime was tenfold the
worse, because it was unexpected and unannounced.
He invaded the territory of a Queen with whom he
had no quarrel and no difference. He tore up the
scrap of paper which enjoined friendship and protection upon him with the zest which the Hohenzollerns have always shown in such enterprises, and
stealthily threw an army into undefended Silesia.
His troops were across the frontier before Maria
Theresa knew that he had made a claim upon her province. And he completed the injury with an insult-
ing message. He told the Queen that if she would
grant him Silesia he would defend the rest of her
dominions against anybody who should attack them,
and, being a Hohenzollern, he did not see that the
second promise, like the first, was worth precisely
nothing. Nor did the savagery of Frederick find its
results only in the province upon which he laid his
thievish hand. It disquieted the whole world for many
years. All the blood that was shed in Europe from
Frederick's accession until 1761 was upon his head.
As Macaulay says with justified rhetoric : ' In order
that he might rob a neighbour whom he had promised
to defend, black men fought on the coast of Coro-

mandel and red men scalped each other by the great
lakes of North America.' Who, remembering the events
which followed the outbreak of war in 1914, shall say
that history does not repeat herself ?

Unto the end of his life Frederick remained true
to his ideals of perfidy and treachery. Having promised guarantees, ' mere filigree, pretty to look at
but too brittle to bear the slightest pressure,' he
presently acted towards Poland as he had acted
towards Silesia.   Eight years after he had guaranteed
the rights and liberties of Poland he announced its
first partition, on no better plea than that the partition would contribute considerably to the prosperity
of his realm.   And if he were a true Prussian in his
policy of aggression, he was a true Prussian in his
hatred of the drudgery of war.   What he wanted
always was the palm without the dust.   He had the
love of his house for a speedy war against a defenceless
country, followed by a tyrant's peace.   But in Maria
Theresa he met his match.   That gallant Queen, if
in the end she was doomed to lose Silesia, knew how
to fight for her country and her honour.   She condemned Frederick to a life of warfare and hardship,
which he did not contemplate at the outset, and
which he endured with difficulty.   He sighed for the
peace, which did not come to him, as bitterly as the
Prussians have sighed for peace since.   Through all
his talks with Catt you may hear him bewail ' the
dog of a life ' which he led.   His enemies, he complains daily, will not give him peace.   Having stolen

what he wanted, he thought he should be allowed to go off quietly with the swag, and no questions asked. With an hypocritical effrontery, which William II. must have envied, he deplored constantly the death and misery which he brought in his train. 'You will agree that it is cruel,' said he, after he had taken Schweidnitz, 'to send so many brave and worthy people to the other world, and why ? For a few wretched roods of earth and a few huts.' With the tears rolling down his weather-beaten face, he assured his faithful henchman that 'nothing is so cruel as to be compelled to wage war unceasingly,' and he did not see that the responsibility of compulsion lies upon the man who begins it. Even the light of glory paled before his eyes when defeat and destruction threatened him. 'Ah, deuce take it !' he exclaimed ; 'a fine glory indeed of burned villages, towns in ashes, thousands of suffering men, as many massacred, horrors on all sides, and finally finishing oneself off ; speak no more of it ; my hair stands up on end.' He willed it, as his wanton successor willed it, and then let his heart bleed for the sufferings which his greed imposed upon the world, as William II. says that his heart bled for Louvain.

Thus we see in Frederick the legitimate forerunner of the Germans who have since drenched Europe in blood. He left an unexampled legacy of perfidy, rapacity, and hypocrisy. He committed the same crimes, he indulged the same sentiments, he bleated forth the same excuses as disgraced William II.

Worse than all, he formulated the pernicious doctrine that the Germans can do no wrong, that what is a vice in others is in them a manifest virtue. But in one respect he showed himself a far better man than those who have come after him. He did not always make war upon civilians ; he did not turn his arms against defenceless women and children ; he refused to count rape and pillage among the proper practices of war. ' The first man who pillages or destroys a house will be hung on the spot '—that was one of his orders. Once when a house in which he lodged had been destroyed, and a dead woman had been found in the garden, he confessed that these butcheries horrified him. He did not think that brutality was warfare. ' Princes who use such troops,' said he, ' ought to blush with shame. The blame is theirs, and they are responsible before God for all the crimes which their troops commit.' What would he say if he could witness the infamies of which Germany was guilty in Belgium and Serbia, in France and Rumania, in every country which she invaded ? Who knows ? Perhaps he would have found excuses for them as he found excuses for the Russians when they had become his allies. ' The Austrians,' said he, ' made an outcry about barbarities ; yet they had no right to complain, and they did not complain when these Cossacks burned and devastated the King's countries. Are not the horrors which march in the train of war great enough without bringing in people who make it a pleasure, a study, and a law to leave behind them the traces of destruction, murder, rape, and arson ? ' The apology is half-hearted, and leaves us doubting whether after all he would not have agreed with William II. that the German army of invasion was the poor victim of Belgian treachery.

Such was the man whom Carlyle set upon the topmost pinnacle of fame and glory, for no better reason than that he might use him for the expounding of a favourite text. In Carlyle's eyes Frederick was a strong man, and therefore justified in all that he did and said. That the panegyrist of Cromwell should make himself also the panegyrist of Frederick might seem incredible, if we did not remember that Carlyle was a slave not of facts, but of preconceptions. Having once seen Frederick in the light of a hero, he would not permit him to be besmirched even by the truth. So he preached the gospel of the Super-man many years before Nietzsche, and did his best to prepare for the doctrine of Pan-Germanism, which came near to destroying the civilisation of Europe. And Carlyle did the world a greater disservice than this. Having misunderstood Germany, he misunderstood France also. How should he understand either, when he knew no more of them than he could see from Ecclefechan and London, or gather from the books of others ? His cloudy vision would not permit him to separate the essential France—the France of Rabelais and Racine and Pascal, the France of provincial thrift and industry—from the Court of Napoleon III., with its busy pleasures and its restless frivolity. Thus it was that, when, in 1871, France was reeling beneath the weight of the blows dealt by Germany, Carlyle took up his pen to plead the cause of the conqueror. To those who asked for mercy on behalf of France he replied with all his rugged scorn. ' The question for the Germans in this crisis,' said he, ' is not one of " magnanimity," of " heroic pity and forgiveness to a fallen foe," but of solid prudence and practical consideration of what the fallen foe will in all likelihood do when once on his feet again.' It was not for the Germans to repudiate a sympathy thus eloquently expressed. The golden words of Carlyle were reproduced, by Bismarck's order, in every corner of the European press, and there can be no doubt that they brought the sunlight of satisfaction into unnumbered German homes.

To critical eyes these words of Carlyle appear dark with falsehood and prejudice. They are not the words of truth. They were inspired by lack of knowledge and by a dim perception. Carlyle's hostility to France was based upon ignorance. He believed simply and devoutly what he, the friend of Germany and the biographer of Frederick, wished to believe. In his eyes France deserved punishment, deserved even the loss of her honour, because she had been the aggressor. ' But will it save the honour of France,' he asked, ' to refuse paying for the glass she has voluntarily broken in her neighbour's window?' The attack upon the windows was her dishonour. Alas for the argument! France broke no windows.

How could she, with the watchful eye of Bismarck
upon her ?   All the breakage that was done lay solely
at Bismarck's door, and he was far too cunning to
reveal the measure of his guilt to such ardent
sympathisers as Thomas Carlyle. At last we have
discovered all the truth.   By this time the blue-
pencilling of the famous telegram is a commonplace
of history, and since we know how to apportion the
blame, we shall never again reproach France with
a catastrophe which was brought about by the
cynicism of Bismarck.

And if Carlyle, from whom the under-world of
politics was most delicately hid, misunderstood the
cause and origin of the war of 1870, he was yet more
profoundly ignorant about the characters of the combatants. Truly, as a psychologist he was sadly to
seek. Exposed to all the pitfalls of half-knowledge,
he contrasted the Germans with the French in the
easy spirit of the comic press. He vied with Momm-
sen in flattery of the Teutonic race. ' That noble,
patient, deep, and solid Germany,' he wrote, ' should
be at length welded into a nation and become Queen
of the Continent, instead of vapouring, vainglorious,
gesticulating, quarrelsome, and over-sensitive France,
seems to me the hopefullest public fact that has
occurred in my time.' How grossly the philosopher deceived himself ! The France of the Second
Empire was careless and over-sensitive, to be sure ;
she had no more talent of government than she has
to-day. But that she was supreme in intelligence

none but a philosopher whose head was packed with German metaphysics would ever have doubted. That Carlyle had an ingrained contempt for what are called *belles-lettres* is evident to a superficial reader of his works. His condemnation of the French writers of his day is none the less astonishing, as we recall it in the cool blood of a later age. ' To me at times,' wrote Carlyle, ' the mournfullest symptom in France is the figure its " men of genius," its highest literary speakers, who should be prophets and seers to it, make at present, and indeed for a generation back have been making. It is evidently their belief that new celestial wisdom is radiating out of France upon all the other overshadowed nations ; that France is the new Mount Zion of the universe ; and that all this sad, sordid, semi-delirious, and, in good part, infernal stuff which French litera- ture has been presenting to us for the last fifty years is a veritable new Gospel out of Heaven, pregnant with blessedness for all the sons of men.' And assuredly a veritable new Gospel out of Heaven was preached in France, though Carlyle heard it not, and would not have understood it had he heard it. The fifty years of which Carlyle speaks included the Romantic Movement, of all modern movements the greatest, the most keenly stimulating. If Europe had fallen in these times under the spell of France, it was because the intelligence of France exerted without effort and without question its peaceful sway. And Carlyle's error is the less easily forgiven, because had he wished he might have seen about him the noble monument which France had raised to intellect and to genius. Balzac, who with his pen had re-created his country, was still an influence. The France of 1870 was the France of Hugo and Gautier, of Renan and Taine, of Flaubert and Goncourt and Verlaine and a hundred others. What had Germany to show that might be compared for a moment with all this shining talent ? Yet Carlyle despised all that was not Teutonic, with the same dogged blindness which obscures the sight of the vain professors who boast with frenzy of German *Kultur*.

Thus are the minds of men warped by prejudice, befogged by half-knowledge, and dangerously deceived. It is not for nothing that Carlyle receives to-day the reverence of Potsdam. He deserves whatever posthumous benefits the Germany of his wilful adulation and complete misunderstanding can confer upon him. For he preached assiduously to Frederick's text that the deeds of Germans are always justified, and he must carry to the end of time his share in the burden of responsibility for the greatest war the world ever saw.

CHARLES JAMES FOX

THE outburst of enthusiasm which greeted the centenary of Charles James Fox proved that the immense superstition which he created was still alive. To read the comments of serious journals was to wonder whether there exists any standard by which the achievements of statesmen may be judged. On every hand we heard Fox described as an inspired prophet, who would have saved his country from the evils which he foresaw had he not been prevented by black-hearted opponents. One admirer was reckless enough to suggest that if Fox had been Prime Minister at the time of the French Revolution, the worst evils which overwhelmed Europe would have been avoided. In some mysterious way, we were told, Fox would have acted as a mediator between Louis xvi. and his rebellious subjects. Could any surmise be more ridiculous than this ? Is it possible that a writer lives who believes that Fox could have achieved, in a country not his own, a success which was beyond the power of Mirabeau himself, an infinitely greater man than the leader of the Whigs ? The Revolution, made by words, could be stayed only by Napoleon's sword, and Fox had nothing save words at his com-

mand. Moreover, he was distrusted in France by
either party. Louis XVI. could not be expected to
sympathise with a sentimental friend of the people,
and to the French people Fox was no better than a
faux patriote, who had grossly insulted its honour and
pretensions but a few years before the taking of the
Bastille. The truth is that Fox was no more able
to help France than to help England. His was not
the temperament of the man of action, and the suggestion I have cited is memorable only for its
absurdity. Yet it compels us to ask upon what does
the general esteem of Fox depend, and why, after a
hundred years, there are still those who would shed
upon his grave the tear of sensibility.

Concerning no politician has so much cant been
spoken and written as concerning Charles James Fox.
His name has been whispered with a reverential awe
by thousands who would have shrunk back in horror
had they discovered the truth of his career. To him
posterity has allowed a latitude which it withholds
from all others known to history. The highly sensi-
tive conscience which found Parnell's disgrace a patent
necessity does not shrink from the indiscretions of
Fox. Sir George Trevelyan celebrates in enthusiastic
terms ' the grateful veneration with which the
whole body of his Nonconformist fellow-citizens
adored him living, and mourned him dead.' Indeed,
there is an element of the grotesque in the passionate
respect in which the party of the ' conscience ' holds
this genial gamester, who loved women and the bottle

as deeply as he loved the dice-box. For his extravagances his Nonconformist friends have an ever-
ready excuse. With the bluff exclamation that 'boys
will be boys' they sun themselves in the light of his
dissipations. They take a smiling pleasure in his
vices, and describe as generosity in him what in
another they would denounce for blackguardism.
Fox might steal a horse with their gratified approval,
while Grafton, to take an obvious example, might not
look over the hedge. One of Fox's many panegyrists
finds it necessary to apologise for his conduct in 1768.
'Grafton became Prime Minister as a matter of
course,' he says, 'and Charles Fox, whom at that
age it was not easy to scandalise, readily attached himself to a leader whose bearing and address were as
full of grace as his conduct was devoid of it.' Charles
Fox, we imagine, was never easy to scandalise, but it
is certain that at no age could he have pretended,
without the grossest hypocrisy, to be shocked at
the conduct of Grafton, an eminently respectable
gentleman.

In this nonconforming admiration of Fox's light-
hearted excesses there is a plain confusion. We have
no right to say that he was a worse Minister because
he drank and gambled. We may judge his political
career without censoriously asking where he spent
his nights. At the same time, we have no right to
pretend that he was a better Minister because he
loved the bottle and the green-cloth, to look with
wonder upon his performances in the House of

Commons because he was a boon companion and a good fellow across a gaming-table. And yet this is what his foolish admirers ask us to do. They describe him travelling all night from Newmarket to address the House, or speaking with eloquence after sitting twenty-four hours at quinze, and declare that it is genius. Genius it may be—the genius of endurance—but it is not political genius. And we shall not understand the career of Charles James Fox unless we keep his two *rôles* rigorously apart, and judge him separately as politician and man of pleasure.

As a man of pleasure he was supereminent. In an age of hard drinking and reckless gambling, Charles Fox had no equal. His education encouraged a natural talent. Lord Holland, grown rich upon the spoils of office, brought up his son upon a generous method of his own. He denied him nothing; he encouraged him in all his whims and all his extravagances. With the best will in the world, he deprived him of his childhood and its simple joys. When Charles was barely three years old, he dined *tête-à-tête* with him, and delighted in his already mature conversation. Once the child announced his intention of destroying a watch. 'Well,' said Lord Holland, 'if you must, I suppose you must.' When Charles was no more than fourteen, Lord Holland took him to the Continent on a tour of dissipation. At Spa he taught him the rudiments of gambling, and sent him ' every night to the gaming-

table with a pocketful of gold.' Not content with
this first lesson in life, ' the parent took not a little
pains to contrive that the boy should leave France
a finished rake,' and it is not surprising that on his
return to Eton, Charles, with his knowledge of Spa
and Paris, and his diverting tales of gambling-hells
and their frequenters, should have done much to
destroy the discipline of the school.

A few years at Oxford did not change the habits of
Charles Fox, though it vastly increased his learning,
and when he came to London he was ready to take
his place with the most daring of the rakes. At sixteen he was a member of Brooks's, and from that day
it may be said that he never looked back. For many
years the chief occupation of his life was gambling.
He played cards, he backed horses, he made bets.
There was no accident of life or politics which he did
not think worth a wager. At whist, quinze, and
piquet his skill was unrivalled. He had so profound
a knowledge of Newmarket that he seldom left the
Heath with an empty pocket, and the betting-book
at Brooks's is clear evidence of his sound judgment
in affairs. His tireless and energetic temperament
was the best that could support a gambler. He would
sit at the table all night and yet pursue his business
the next day. A bold player and a cheerful loser, he
was familiar with all the hells of Europe ; and had he
never sat in the House of Commons, he would still
have been notorious. Casanova, generally a truthful
witness, encountered him at Lausanne, won all his

money at Geneva, and once lent him £50, which were repaid three years afterwards.

But his real battlefield was St. James's Street. At Brooks's there was no one who played so fantastic a part as 'Charles.' A macaroni, with dirty hands and soiled clothes, he moved in the most exclusive set, and exacted respect from all those who won his money. And truly for many years his losses were prodigious. Again and again Lord Holland settled his affairs. Again and again he plunged deeper into the quagmire of debt. At his father's death he is said to have owed £140,000, and it is not strange that his estate in Thanet, and all that he inherited, fell, with his furniture and his books, into the hands of the Jews. Yet he bore no malice. Like Charles Surface, for whom he might have sat, he softened even the Hebrew hearts of the moneylenders, and forgot all his displeasure when he had called the waiting-room of his house his Jerusalem Chamber. In truth, he was one to whom money could never have been of the slightest service. When he won it, he was restless until he had lost it. His pocket was an unplumbed pit of thriftlessness, and an entry in the betting-book of his club proves how just an estimate one of his most familiar friends had formed of him. 'Lord Clermont,' thus runs the entry, 'has given Mr. Crawford 10 guineas, upon the condition of receiving £500 from him, whenever Mr. Charles Fox shall be worth £100,000 clear of debts.'

Now the character of the gamester is not unamiable.

We may even cherish an admiration for the man who, regarding money as dross, flings it carelessly away to purchase a few hours' excitement. But we cannot extend the sympathy we feel for the punter to him who holds the bank. To sit at the receipt of custom is neither noble nor glorious. The bank has a cold advantage which cannot appeal to our sense of romance; and assuredly the worst blot upon the private character of Fox is that in 1781, having been long a pigeon, he determined to play the part of a rook. He set up a bank at Brooks's, with Hare and Fitzpatrick as partners, appointed Lord Robert Spencer dealer at the handsome figure of five guineas an hour, and prepared to win the money of the town. The four associates were able to relieve one another at their pleasant toil, and for a year or two the play was continuous. It would be difficult to match the cynical effrontery wherewith they advertised their proceedings. Their clients gave them cards bearing the legend, ' Received from Messrs. Fox and Co.' in acknowledgment of money paid. No one could walk down St. James's Street without discovering their enterprise. ' This Pharo bank,' we are told, ' is held in a manner which, being so exposed to public view, bids defiance to all decency and police. The whole town as it passes views the dealer and the punters by means of the candles, and the windows being levelled with the ground. The Opposition, which has Charles for its ablest advocate, is quite ashamed of the proceeding, and hates to hear it mentioned.'

No wonder the Opposition hated to hear it mentioned, for the episode was discreditable to all who had a hand in it. To encourage speculation, Fox or Fitzpatrick would at their own bank lose £1000 in one deal and win it back in the next. The case against them was put with perfect force by Selwyn. 'Hare opened the Pharo bank in the great room,' wrote he in November 1780, ' but had so few and poor punters that Charles and Richard were obliged to sit down from time to time as decoy ducks. . . . I do not think that the people who frequent Brooks's will suffer this pillage another campaign.' But while the game lasted, Charles and Richard were in high cash. Their winnings were fabulous. ' I have not been at Brooks's for I do not know when,' wrote Selwyn in 1782 ; ' that *maudite banque* of Charles's *aspirera avec le tems tout l'argent de Londres, au moins de notre quartier.*' Upon Fox the success had an immediate effect. ' I saw Charles to-day,' says Selwyn, ' in a new hat, frock, waistcoat, shirt, and stockings ; he was as clean and smug as a gentleman, and upon perceiving my surprise, he told me it was from the Pharo bank. He then talked of the thousands it had lost, which I told him only proved its substance and the advantage of its trade. He smiled, and seemed perfectly satisfied with that which he had taken up ; he was in such a sort of humour that I should like to have dined with him. His old clothes have been burned like the paupers' at Salt Hill.'

Nor was it only his wardrobe that profited by the

winnings of his bank. While Fox and Fitzpatrick
were emptying the pockets of the town, the bailiffs
were ransacking Fox's house to satisfy a debt of Fitzpatrick's making. And Fox did not let the opportunity slip. His old and broken furniture having
been seized, he determined to replace it with the
magnificence which became the master of a thriving
business. 'His house,' said Selwyn, 'I mean the
place of execution, where he is to go soon, is the
sprucest to look at from the street I ever saw. I
never saw such a transition from distress to opulency,
or from dirt to cleanliness.' And then, as Cincinnatus
was called from the plough, so Fox was summoned
from the Pharo bank to take part in the counsels of
his country. He did not forget his accomplices at
the gaming-table. Hare became his private secretary,
and Fitzpatrick was sent as Chief Secretary to Ireland.
Nothing was omitted to enhance the absurd contrast.
The new Minister was interrupted at Brooks's so
often that he could neither punt nor deal for a quarter
of an hour without giving audience to one or other
of his colleagues. Was not the scene, in Selwyn's
words, *la plus parfaitement comique que l'on puisse
imaginer* ? And is it not eminently characteristic of
Fox that it appeared to nobody more truly risible
than to himself ?

The bank at Brooks's, which would have added no
distinction to a simple man about town, throws a
curious sidelight upon Fox's failure as a politician.
A statesman who took so trivial a view of his own

responsibilities could hardly hope to be a leader of
men. And the truth is that politics were for Charles
Fox but another field for the exercise of his fierce
activity. He went into them without principles,
and, though with the passing years he adopted a
party, without principles he remained to the end.
His eminent qualities of courage and address never
found him a large following in his own day. He
passed the greater part of his career in the discomfort
of Opposition. His amazing eloquence, his genius
for debate, stood him in small stead. His power of
rhetoric was even a hindrance to him, for within a week
he would cover the same man with equal floods of
flattery and vituperation, and his hearers, admiring
both, knew that neither was sincere. And so he
lost the faith of the vast majority. The king most
properly distrusted the politician who had approved
and abetted the disloyalty and dissipation of his son.
And the people, though it made far less of gossip
and rumour than to-day seems possible, could not
close its eyes to the street-ballads nor its ears to the
common talk. In spite of an inclination to admire
one who had cut a figure in many worlds, it could not
always condone Fox's flippancy or overlook his vain
inconsistency.

That he changed the lightly held opinions of his
youth is in no way discreditable to him. A boy may
turn from gospel to heresy without suspicion or reproach, and there was no blot on Fox's political honour
until in 1783 he made a coalition with North, whom

he had attacked for years with a perfect fury of indignation. That, indeed, was the wreckage of his fame. Nobody could believe him honest, when he allied himself with one who, he had prayed, should hear of his misdeeds at the tribunal of justice, and expiate them on the public scaffold. But we shall not understand Fox if we do not remember that he was a partisan. He aimed always at the triumph of himself and his friends, and he cared not if in that triumph England were broken in pieces. ' As a party man,' he said once, ' I think it a good thing for my party to come into office, were it only for a month.' And that is not the worst. Fox went far beyond a mere hunger for office. Whenever the opposite party was in power, he ranged himself openly and fiercely with the enemies of his country.

He put no bounds upon his hatred of England, and he thought it not shameful to intrigue with foreigners against the safety and credit of the land to which he belonged. Wherever there was a foe to England, there was a friend of Fox. America, Ireland, France, each in turn inspired his enthusiasm. When Howe was victorious at Brooklyn, he publicly deplored ' the terrible news.' After Valmy he did not hesitate to express his joy. ' No public event,' he wrote, ' not excepting Yorktown and Saratoga, ever happened that gave me so much delight. I could not allow myself to believe it for some days for fear of disappointment.' More bitter, if possible, was his venom in 1801. ' To tell the truth,' he said, ' I am gone something further in hate to the English Government than perhaps you and the rest of my friends are, and certainly further than can with prudence be avowed. The trumph of the French Government over the English does, in fact, afford me a degree of pleasure which it is very difficult to disguise.'

The open treacheries of Fox are by this familiar. But his policy cannot be considered without a repetition of them. By his own confession he was a constant contemner of his country, and his career cannot but suggest the question : How far is patriotism necessary to the equipment of a statesman ? Now patriotism, out of fashion though it be to-day, should be the first and plainest of the virtues. It is but an extension of the feeling for family, which is the foundation of all society. A man who insults his father and despises his mother is a bad son. He is a bad citizen, who despises and insults his country. And a bad citizen, though he has every right to exist, is not likely to prove the wisest ruler. No one need love his country—that the experience of England has fully demonstrated. It is the privilege of all, we suppose, to defame the land of their birth, and a vast number has always claimed the privilege. But it may be said, perhaps without exaggeration or malice, that he who loathes his country is not best fitted by nature to govern it. And why should he wish to govern it ? Had Fox been logical, he would have shaken the dust of England from his feet, and given what aid his rhetoric might afford to England's foes. But he would not do that. He stayed at home to rejoice if he might in the defeat of his compatriots, and to sing the praises of foreign tyrants in the name of freedom.

It is not a pleasant career to contemplate, for, if politics be not an idle game or a momentary excitement, then an honourable patriotism should be esteemed at more than a feather's weight. There is no compulsion put upon any man to be a politician, but if of his own will he becomes one, it is his business to protect his country against insult and attack. It is, then, in no spirit of partisanship that Fox is condemned. He who gives comfort to the king's enemies should have no place in either party. And Fox was not content to comfort with words. On one conspicuous occasion he was engaged actively against the interest of England. When Robert Adair went on a mission to St. Petersburg, it was Fox who procured him letters of introduction, and who said, as he bade the informal emissary good-bye: 'Well, if you are determined to go, send us all the news.' Moreover, that no detail might escape him, he urged Adair to use Burgoyne's cipher; and ' to puzzle them the more,' said he, ' you may put some of your figures in red ink.' Adair, with great indignation, denied many years after that Fox had anything to do with his celebrated journey. But as Fox furnished him with letters, demanded news, and suggested a cipher, Adair's denial seems a mere quibble.

And since Adair's day much light has been thrown on the intrigue by the publication of the *Dropmore Papers*. From them it is clear that Adair made his journey with the utmost expedition, seeing no one on the way save the Russian Ambassador at Vienna; that he lived much with M. Woronzow and the Imperial Minister; that he was received with every mark of respect by the Empress, who treated the accredited English representative with contempt; that he held 'language dictated by the most virulent opposition to his Majesty's Administration, and calculated to counteract the effect of a negotiation.' Lord Grenville was convinced that it was Woronzow who had suggested the idea of employing Mr. Adair as envoy from Mr. Fox to the Empress, and the one bright spot in an unpleasant business was its complete failure. 'It is, I confess, no small satisfaction to me,' wrote Whitworth, ' to witness the disappointment of Mr. Adair: the language he has held has been calculated to produce a far different effect, and his expectations were considerably raised. His journey has, however, been ineffectual, and he will, I flatter myself, have but a bad report to make to his principals.' There can be no doubt, indeed, that Adair's journey to St. Petersburg was carefully arranged, and it matters not a jot whether Fox initiated it or merely acquiesced in it. It was taken on behalf of Fox's party, and it was Fox who would have profited had it been carried to a successful conclusion.

So throughout the war with Napoleon, Fox did his best to aid the enemy and to thwart his own countrymen. He supported the treasonable clubs and associations which were formed all over England in pious imitation of Paris. He defended the rebels, wherever they were found, and he opposed with all his energy any attempt to put down sedition. When in 1792 it was proposed to strengthen the hands of the Government by a coalition with the Whigs, Fox alone declined to coalesce. And he declined in 'anger and rudeness,' because he was an ardent Jacobin. Gilbert Elliot, himself a staunch Whig, thought that Fox's conduct 'went to overthrow the country, and that it was essential for their honour and the sake of the country to separate from him.' And, as his party diminished, Fox's acrimony increased, his determination to embarrass his country grew stronger. At a moment when there was war abroad and rebellion at home, when it needed all the courage and skill of Pitt to save the country, Fox, with his customary levity, decided that it was the duty of the House at that moment to cherish the spirit of freedom in the people.

Such was the pose that Fox preserved unto the end, a pose of embarrassment and hostility to the imperious interests of England. Yet, while he was passionately admired by a mere handful during his lifetime, his reputation has been constantly enhanced since his death. Upon what, then, in addition to the constant adulation of Holland House, does the superstition depend ? Largely, we think, upon the legend of his affability. He was one whose misdeeds were always excused by his friends. When, by refusing to pay Lord Carlisle what he owed him, he kept that hapless peer a prisoner at his country seat, Carlisle neither felt nor expressed resentment. When Foley, in a vain attempt to plead Carlisle's cause, confronted the magician, he retired hopelessly worsted. With the conference at its acutest Fox burst into tears. ' However,' said Foley with a pardonable pride, ' I carried two points out of four, but I was obliged to leave him, not being able to resist the force of sensibility.'

And in being unable to resist Fox, Foley was not singular. Nobody who knew him could resist him, and the town was forced to set up a new standard of morality for his benefit. That which would have covered any other man with eternal ridicule provoked no more than a kindly smile if it happened to Charles. When a monstrous impostor, who called herself the Hon. Mrs. Grieve, involved him for her own purposes in a wild scheme of marriage, a poor copy of verses celebrated the event, and on the morrow it was forgotten. And it must be admitted, too, that the romantic contrasts of his career have helped to keep his memory green. The light hand and the easy manner, which permitted him to turn without absurdity from the Pharo bank to the Treasury bench, deserve some recognition. But these qualities have no touch with politics, and Fox's political reputation is still unexplained. That he was never a statesman is obvious. The opportunity of statesmanship did not come to him, and in opposition he behaved with the dignity and discretion of a vestryman. Why, then, should he appear as a guide to the footsteps of our modern Radicals ? His hatred of England, of course, entitles him to some respect in their eyes ; but it is not enough of itself to justify the adulation that is still showered upon his name.

The real cause of his glory is his unfailing sentimentality. He is the hero of men who love copybook headings, and who would compensate for evil deeds with good phrases. The tinkling of empty words such as ' freedom ' and ' the people ' was always heard when he rose to address the House. He did not want to give the people freedom, and he could not have given it if he would. But the words had a solemn sound, and he knew that his friends would respond to them instantly. And, apart from his skill in words and phrases, he was one of the ablest debaters that ever addressed an assembly. He possessed all the arts of rhetoric and eloquence which are a danger to the community. He could persuade his audience for the moment that the worse was the better cause with an ease which not even Burke could rival. And yet, though we understand how it was that his speeches appeal to a rhetoric-loving age, we cannot read them to-day without perceiving the poverty of their thought, the inadequacy of their argument. In brief, Fox's political record is as barren as Sheridan's. He added nothing to the dignity or the amenity of public life. When Sir George Trevelyan tells us that Fox 'of all men did most to reform the corruption of politics,' I am unable to understand him. If to put party in front of the State, if to increase acrimony in a moment of national peril, be a means of reform, then Fox was a reformer. But it is difficult to discover in a long life one signal service that he rendered to England. Statesmanship was as far beyond his reach as patriotism; and the best that can be said of him is that he engrossed the vices of the professional politician.

By a strange irony, then, Providence, who withheld from Fox so many precious gifts, endowed him with a charm of speech which seems to have rendered the meaning of what he said immaterial. His bitterest opponents listened to him with complaisance, if without approval. 'I can hear him,' said Selwyn, 'which is a singular thing, with the same pleasure as if I gave ample credit to what he said. . . . It is as impossible not to love him as it is to love his adversary (Lord North). . . . Charles aims sometimes at humour—he has not an atom of it; or rather it is wit, which is better; but that is not his talent neither. . . . Charles's poignancy and misapplication of truth, making the most known falsehoods serve his purpose better—in all that, he is admirable. His quotations are natural and pleasing and à propos, and if he had any judgment, or conduct, or character, he would and ought to be the first man in the country. But that place, I am assured now, is destined for another.'

Happily for England it was destined for another. But Selwyn's character is as just a character of Fox as can be drawn. There was no place he might not have filled had he had judgment and conduct and character. As it was, he had to be content with winning a hostile audience by his affable speech, and with amazing his hearers by his apposite quotations. And this brings us to another of Fox's perplexing and contradictory qualities. He found time, amid the distraction of gambling and politics, to make himself a good scholar and a sound critic. His taste equalled his erudition. He knew the classics as well as any man of his time, and he read and re-read them with never-failing devotion. History shows us few pleasanter pictures than Fox amid his books and his friends in the retirement of St. Anne's. But it is a Fox who has forgotten the ferocity of political contests and the rattle of the dice-box. And it is a Fox far nearer to reality than the foolish bogey invented by the Nonconformist Conscience. However, as you look back upon a career which might have caused the destruction of England, you can afford to smile at the hypocrisy which has converted Charles James Fox into a saviour of his country. His own contemporaries, who loved him in spite of his politics, knew him far too well to accept his opinions. The Radicals of to-day, with an imperfect knowledge of his qualities, worship him as one who hated England.

How he would have laughed at the absurdity of this, his own image ! And how unfortunate is the party which, in spite of its active ' conscience' and high professions, can find no better saints to reverence than John Wilkes and Charles James Fox !

A FAMOUS TSAR

SOME men there are whom destiny casts for a romantic part upon the grand stage of life, whether they will it or not. Though all the impulses of their hearts drive them to retired thought and tranquil speculation, they are forced not only into great situations but into conflict with great men. Alexander Paulovitch, for instance, known to history as Alexander i. of Russia, was well fitted by temperament and character to be a political philosopher or an amiable philanthropist ; it was his fate to dominate for a while the councils of Europe, to confront and ultimately to foil Napoleon himself, and rising to the height of his opportunity with a strength which not even his friends suspected in him, to break the last desperate attempt that was made before the adventure of William ii. at universal sovereignty.

The grandson and favourite of the great Catherine, he was but a boy when the savagery of the French Revolution burst upon Europe. By a natural reaction he eagerly caught up the opinions of the foolish enthusiasts, who made the streets of Paris run with blood. He became curious concerning the sins of monarchs and the rights of men. A mild liberalism

filled his heart and brain. He was seized with a
grave desire to do good, a desire which would have
found little sympathy at Court, had he dared to reveal
there his hopes and purposes. The only begetter
of these vague aspirations, of these brave, unpractical
ideals, was M. de la Harpe, whom the Empress
Catherine, persuaded by her love of intelligence and
her interest in the Encyclopædists, had procured him
for tutor. Now M. de la Harpe, who had been a
member of the *directoire helvétique*, was one of the
many prigs who had fed their fancies upon the
illusions of the dying eighteenth century, who devoutly believed that the crooked world might be
set straight by phrases, and who saw in their own
doctrine a new philosopher's stone, a universal remedy
which should explain all and cure all. He was not
the best kind of instructor that could be found for
a young prince, and it was consonant with Catherine's
intellectual cynicism that she should have chosen him.
Doubtless she thought that no man of her house,
least of all her loved and elect successor, could possibly
take any harm from the teaching of a philosopher.
She did not understand the quick receptivity of
Alexander's mind ; she did not appreciate the con-
stancy of his temper, which bade him never withhold a friendship he once had given.

For some years Alexander kept his hopes and fears
locked within his own breast. It was not until he
encountered Prince Adam Czartoryski that he discovered a companion to whom he might intrust his

secret thoughts. Nor could he have found a wiser, better counsellor, whose loyalty equalled his candour, whose allegiance never weakened, despite the sufferings of Poland, and who loved Alexander too well ever to deceive him. The decisive conversation took place at the Palace of the Tauris in 1796. The Polish Prince regretted always that he could not remember the exact date of an interview which profoundly influenced his own life and the destinies of his country. What he did remember was the precise terms of the confidence which was made to him in Alexander's English garden. The Grand Duke freely confessed that he did not share the ideas or the doctrines of the Cabinet and the Court, that he was far from approving either the policy or the conduct of his grandmother, that all his wishes were for Poland and her glorious struggle, that he deplored her fall, that Kosciuszko was a great man in his eyes both for his virtues and for the cause which he defended—the cause of humanity and justice.

It is easy to imagine the enthusiasm which these warm words excited in the patriotic breast of Czartoryski, who believed that Russia and the rest of Europe existed for no other purpose than to right the wrongs of Poland. And Alexander was as yet but on the threshold of confession. He admitted that he hated despotism wherever it was found and in whatever manner it was practised, that he loved liberty, the equal rights of all men, that he took the liveliest interest in the French Revolution, though

he did not approve its enormities, and that he wished
the happiest success to the French Republic. These
were pretty views for an autocrat to hold! And
Alexander held them, as views merely, until the end
of his life. We may imagine that he did not hold them
very strongly or obstinately. The gift of persistence,
save in friendship, was never his. His liberalism was
a wayward, moving influence, like many other of his
dreams and fancies. Moreover, it was necessarily
superficial. It was not held deep in his soul by knowledge or experience. Adam Czartoryski admits that
his friend, in spite of his political zeal, had never read
a serious book unto the end. Nevertheless he was
a willing pupil of the French Revolutionaries; he
echoed with at least a passing sincerity the solemn
words of the amiable M. de la Harpe.

Czartoryski, young and enthusiastic as his master,
marvelled greatly at what he heard. That these
words should be spoken by a prince of Russia, the
successor of Catherine, the well-loved grandson and
pupil, whom, discarding her own son, she wished to
reign after her, was a wonder indeed! And though
the talk in the garden, though the many walks to the
villages about Tsarkoé-Sélo, had no direct result,
though Alexander fortunately did not on account of
de la Harpe's benighted reasoning give Russia a
constitution or demolish his own throne, he won for
himself a lifelong friend, whom no disappointment
could estrange, and no political difference could turn
from the habit of plain speaking.

Meanwhile, though in one part of his brain Alexander kept neatly docketed a fine set of liberal opinions and a sympathetic interest in revolution, in another he cherished the proper pomposity of princes.   He was greatly subject to what Czartoryski calls ' paradomania.' He delighted in reviews and official spectacles, in the details of uniforms, in all the manifold trappings of a soldier's profession.   So busily indeed was he engaged with his duties in the army that he had no leisure for study, and he cultivated politics only in talk with half a dozen intimates, who remained with him as an inner and informal council, even after he had ascended the throne, and the foremost of whom was always Czartoryski.   The death of Catherine and the accession of his father, Paul, left him still free to pursue that liberal policy, which in other countries besides Russia has seemed the privilege of an heir to the throne.   And then suddenly there came upon him the tragedy of death, with which his house was already familiar, and which compelled him to lay aside the vague hopes of boyhood, to face with what courage he might the crisis of his fate.

In 1801 the Emperor Paul was brutally murdered by a mob of conspirators, who went insolently beyond their instructions.   That the safety of Russia demanded the abdication of Paul was evident.   Catherine, in her foresight, had wished the immediate succession of Alexander, who himself had approved and shared the plan to remove the Emperor Paul from the throne.   But Alexander had not envisaged for

a moment the possibility of murder. He had devised
for his father, in his own mind, a retirement of splendour and luxury. And when Nicholas Zubov found
him expecting, in disquietude and doubt, the news
of an abdication, and announced in his raucous
voice that ' all was over,' Alexander fell into the very
depth of sorrow and despair. Like a Hamlet, dimly
conscious that he was not guiltless of his father's
blood, he was paralysed to inaction. He knew not
how to discover the actual murderers, or how to deal
with them if he found them. He let ' I dare not wait
upon I would,' and like all vacillators incurred the
blame of both sides. These reproached him for disloyalty to the men who had placed him on the throne,
Those charged him with a cynical inactivity of
revenge. The truth is, he followed the right, and
middle course. On the one hand, he could not make
a scandal and punish the offenders by the public processes of the law ; on the other he could not tolerate
near the throne the murderers of his father. So,
holding in horror all those whose persuasion had
made him a party even to the plot of abdication, he
sent them off to the Caucasus or some other outpost
of the Empire, where they died of the bleak climate
or of disappointed ambition.

Never was there a more melancholy coronation
than Alexander's. Shaken by remorse, he passed
through the ceremonies of Moscow like one in a tor-
tured dream. He spent hours in silence, with fixed
and haggard eyes. His friends feared for his reason,

and had Czartoryski not been there to recall him to
the proper discharge of his duties, he might have sunk
into a state of leaden despair. Nor even did the
conflict of Napoleon, and the great drama in which
he played an eminent part, wholly save him from
self-chastisement. He relapsed when the strain was
relaxed into the moody mysticism, the disgust of life,
which confused and darkened his last years.

It may be doubted whether he would ever have
put into practice the liberal ideas of his youth had
leisure and peace been given to him. The common
experience of history proves that a philosophic heir
to the throne accepts lightly enough the burden of
autocracy. At any rate, the times in which Alexander lived were not favourable to speculation or
reform. Destiny forced upon him the duty, for
which his wayward temper, shot with manifold
changes of mood and fancy, did not wholly fit him,
of facing an implacable invader. When it would have
pleased him to devise a new constitution or to establish Poland as a free and independent kingdom, he was
asked to liberate his country from the dominion of
Napoleon. And if the task was not congenial to him,
he possessed one gift which made it easy for him to
attach the willing service of others—the gift of com-
pelling worship. The ' paradomania ' of his youth
had developed in him a fine sense of spectacle. Wherever he went he was followed by the eager glances of
his countrymen, not because he was their Emperor
—emperors were not sacred to those who had strangled

his father—but because he was Alexander himself,
gravely smiling in the exercise of his authority. In
Moscow he was spoken of as the Angel Incarnate,
and miraculous influences were ascribed to him. The
atmosphere of tragedy in which he seemed to move
intensified men's respect and admiration. There
was something sacred in the moral sufferings which
his subjects knew had been his.

Tolstoi in his *Peace and War* has ascribed to Rostov
the devotion which was felt by the whole nation. The
scene is familiar to all. The Tsar appears unex-
pectedly to the young soldier, who recognises in a
half surprise his lamented, his idolised sovereign.
' " But it can't be he, alone in the middle of this
empty field," thought Rostov. At that moment
Alexander turned his head, and Rostov saw the
beloved features, vividly imprinted on his memory.
The Tsar was pale, his cheeks looked sunken, and his
eyes hollow, but the charm, the mildness of his face
struck his worshipper the more poignantly. Rostov
felt happy in the certainty that the report of the
Emperor's wound was false. He was happy that he
was seeing him. He knew that he might, that he
ought, indeed, to go straight to him and to give him
the message he had been commanded to give by
Dolgosukov.' Yet, timid as a youth in love, Rostov,
now that the long-desired moment had come, fears
to approach his sovereign, and Tolstoi in the devout
hesitation of one soldier makes his readers realise and
understand something of the mystic influence which

Alexander exerted almost unconsciously upon his compatriots. Even if he were infirm of purpose, if, as Adam Czartoryski declared, he was dilatory in the performance of his political duties, he was still to the Army and to his simple people a miraculous apparition, a phantom Emperor whom all were content to live and to die for and to wonder at.

Such was the Tsar of Russia, who, still gracious after defeat, met Napoleon at Tilsit in the unequal combat of wits. The two men presented all the glaring contrast which drama demands of life. ' Napoléon,' says M. Vandal, ' c'est action ; Alexandre, c'est le rêve.' The differences between the two could not be more concisely or more clearly stated. They opposed one to the other not only their own temperaments, but the temperaments of their countries. Napoleon was a man with no rough edges. His outlines are still plainly defined against the sky of the past. He knew precisely what he wanted, and by what means he could attain it. Even the rapidity of his imagination, the sureness of his fancy, never ran in opposition to the laws of logic. He had defeated Alexander in fair fight, and he meant to get all the advantage he could out of the victory. The necessary result of his amazing triumph at Friedland was peace. Harbouring no resentment against his beaten foe, he was resolved to turn the new friendship to the best account. In 1807 he had but one end and one aim, to achieve a general peace by the conquest of England. He might for the moment

be engaged with other countries, but every march
he made, every battle he fought were but steps upon
the same road.   England was the enemy, and must
be destroyed !   And he was sure that Russia might
serve better than any other to help him in the grati-
fying of his supreme ambition.

So he came into the conference—a man of action,
armed for the discussion at all points.   And opposite
him sat Alexander, a child of romance, a dreamer of
the Steppes, mysterious and deceptive, like his
northern atmosphere, knowing not what he sought
nor what he hoped of the future.   *Ondoyant et divers,*
to use the words of Montaigne, he varied in mood
and policy from day to day, completely unconscious
that his very variableness would prove in the end the
best of weapons wherewith to oppose Napoleon.   In
subtlety and cunning he was no match for his adversary, who was his superior also in years and in experience.   A master of all the arts of flattery and
cajolery, Napoleon had no difficulty at the first onset
in outwitting Alexander.   He spoke to him with a
cunning sympathy of his liberal ideas and of the
happy dreams of his youth.   Like the great captain
that he was, he told him tales of victories won in the
field, of the vast ambitions which he cherished of
universal dominion.   In brief, he drew the feather of
hope and wild surmise across the eyes of Alexander,
who saw himself for the moment a proud sharer with
Napoleon in the sovereignty of the world.

The setting of the stage was worthy the impassioned

drama itself.   Upon a raft in the Niemen the quick
hands of the French had fashioned *une maisonnette
très-joliment meublée,* as a Russian Minister described
it.   Garlands of flowers hid the bareness of the walls,
and everywhere the monograms of Napoleon and
Alexander were seen interlaced.   In this pavilion
Napoleon received his august visitor, whom he saw
now for the first time, and if he made a speedy conquest of Alexander, Alexander's pleasant gift of intimacy set him instantly at his ease.   For the first
time in his life he was received by an autocrat,
whom yesterday he was fighting, without disdain and
without rancour.   With a single phrase the Tsar
laid what seemed a solid foundation to their friendship.   ' I hate the English as much as you do.'
' Then,' answered Napoleon, ' peace is made.'

Thereafter followed military reviews and brilliant
spectacles.   In amœbean strains the two Emperors
strove to show which could pay the other the better
compliment.   When they discussed which Ministers
of State should represent them, ' I will be your
secretary,' said Napoleon, ' and you shall be mine.'
Truly, had it not been for the King of Prussia, whom
Napoleon rightly detested, and who, lodging in a mill
hard by, was admitted now and then, like a poor
relation, into the imperial presence, the many conferences would have passed without a word of dispute.
Unfortunately for himself, Alexander would not surrender the fettered Prussian to his fate.   Better had it
been for his country and for Europe if he had allowed

the supine Frederick William to lie where he had fallen. But he did his best to save an unworthy friend, and the world has suffered ever since for his ill-judged complaisance.

However, Napoleon's tact brushed the Prussian bogey aside, and when they came to the making of terms Alexander accepted willingly the map of Europe as France had re-drawn it, and made no objection to any of her conquests. He even undertook the thankless task of mediating between England and France, promising to exact that she should grant that freedom of which we have heard so much ever since, and recognise that ' the flags of all the Powers should enjoy an equal and perfect independence upon the seas.' In brief, it was Alexander's hopeless task to persuade England to renounce all the advantages of her insularity and to present her throat to the knife of the first sovereign who resented her power and her ambition. Alexander failed in this project, as all others have failed who have striven to enchain the liberty of England ; and though the cant phrase, ' the liberty of the seas,' will, we hope, never be spoken with approval by an English tongue, Napoleon and Alexander must have been strangely sanguine if they thought that by the mere promise of an insecure peace they could deceive the generation still proud of Aboukir Bay and Trafalgar.

The brilliant spectacle of Tilsit faded away, leaving behind it nothing more solid than a vague friendship and a dream of Eastern conquest. England brusquely declined the mediation of Russia, because the secret clauses in the agreement of Tilsit were concealed from her, and, much to the chagrin of Napoleon, presently made it clear, through the mouths of her Ministers, that she would fight the pretension of the French to the dominion of Europe to her last man and her last bullet. But it was not England and her invincible fleet that touched the imagination of the Tsar. He was under the spell of a fairy story. When Napoleon spoke to him of the East and the triumphs which together they would achieve there, he became as a child, listening for the first time to the Arabian Nights. It was indeed the East which carried Napoleon on the strongest wing of eloquence. He painted in the liveliest colours how great would be his victory over England, if only with Russian aid he could pierce the Balkans and make himself master of Constantinople. It was his hope to use Turkey as a point of departure for an attack upon India. It was easier, thought he, to conquer the East than to cross the narrow, baffling Straits of Dover. All should conspire to the ruin of England. The Mediterranean should become a French lake, and an attack upon Egypt would not only shake to its foundations England's Asiatic Empire, and threaten her routes to India both by sea and by land, but it would utterly destroy her prestige, so that she would be ready to accept any terms that Napoleon might fling to her, as a bone to a dog.

That Napoleon had touched Alexander's imagina-

tion there is no doubt. That he had entirely overcome his distrust is less certain. Like all those
cynics, who break their pledged words and tear up
pieces of paper, Napoleon was pursued in all that he
said and did by a just suspicion. And if Alexander
was for the moment beguiled, his people was resolute
in opposition. Count Tolstoi, indeed, when he went
to represent his sovereign in Paris, never succeeded
in hiding a just distrust of Napoleon and his marshals,
and once upon a time, returning from a review, almost
came to fisticuffs with Ney. Nor in the tedious
negotiations which followed the sentimentality of
Tilsit could either side be brought to a decision. To
Alexander the dominion of the East seemed a many-
coloured dream, until he saw in his imagination
Napoleon supreme at Constantinople and master of
the Straits. And Napoleon, though he offered grimly
to distribute the countries of other people, did not
intend that Alexander should ever profit by a one-
sided bargain. He had but one object—to throw
dust in his friend's eyes and thus to deceive him into
a political slavery. In his eager egoism he thought
that he could make use of Alexander ; he was resolved
that Alexander should not make use of him. Bernadotte, speaking with the knowledge of later years,
declared that Napoleon meditated war against Alexander at the very moment that he signed the Treaty
of Tilsit, and Bernadotte no doubt was in the right
of it. Moreover, Napoleon was not at the pains to
understand Alexander's complex character ; he did not

perceive that Alexander's irresolution was of itself
an accident of strength. At any rate, Alexander
was incapable of adopting suddenly and irrevocably
a policy disastrous for himself.

So Erfurt followed Tilsit, but the glorious rapture
of the first meeting on the banks of the Niemen was
never recaptured. What Napoleon in his amiable
flattery called *le style de Tilsit* was dead and done with.
Though in his patronage of Wieland and Goethe
Napoleon proved himself once more the forerunner
of romance in modern Europe, and once more did
his best to dazzle the Tsar, the ancient charm had
ceased to work. And there was Talleyrand, schem-
ing for France against her Emperor, ready to pour the
poison of dissension into Alexander's ear. ' Sire,'
said he, ' what do you come here to do ? It is for you
to save Europe, and you can succeed in that enterprise only by holding your own against Napoleon.
The French people is civilised ; its sovereign is not.
The sovereign of Russia is civilised ; his people is
not : it is, then, the duty of the sovereign of Russia
to become the ally of the French people.'

Such subtle counsel as this could not but have
effect upon the mind of Alexander, whose youthful
liberalism, combined with the influence of Speranski,
the son of a pope and a violent reformer, suddenly
appointed privy counsellor, convinced him that his
duty was owed not to the French Emperor but to the
Russian people. It was still Alexander's ambition to
link Russia to the chain of Western civilisation—to

create a nation, in fact, higher in its moral and intellectual level than that which the great Catherine had bequeathed to him. He saw at last that he could succeed in this purpose only by serving his own people and by putting away from his eyes the glamour of Napoleon. There remained his foolish attachment for the cause of the Prussians—' poor miserable creatures,' Napoleon called them ; and the loyal sympathy, which he preserved for the abject Frederick William, made still wider the breach which began to yawn between the sworn brothers of Tilsit.

Meanwhile Napoleon was seduced by another adventure from what he deemed the main purpose of his life. In Spain and Portugal he had turned a deaf ear for a time to the imperative call of the East. Far from him then was the dream of 1807. Nor did the Tsar's refusal of his sister's hand and his own marriage with Marie Louise help to strengthen the weakening ties. Another cause of dissension was a friendship formed in Napoleon's despite between Bernadotte, now Crown Prince of Sweden, and the Tsar of Russia. Bernadotte, chosen heir to the throne, if not with Napoleon's approval, at least without his dissent, discovered rightly enough that he owed allegiance not to his late master but to his adopting country, and saw profit for Sweden in a close friendship with Russia. Napoleon's exasperation knew no bounds at what he thought the defection of a servant. He crossed the Niemen with an army, and sent away the Tsar's envoy of peace with scorn and contumely. In Tolstoi's *Peace and War*, a master-piece of fiction based upon accurate documents, Napoleon's fury against Balashov, Alexander's emis-sary, is described in the terms of truth. ' As for the Swedes,' said he, ' it 's their destiny to be governed by mad kings. Their king was mad. They changed him for another, Bernadotte, who promptly went mad ; for no one not a madman could, being a Swede, ally himself with Russia. . . . . Yes, I 'll thrust you beyond the Dwina, beyond the Dnieper, and I 'll restore the frontier that Europe was criminal and blind to let you overstep. Yes, that 's in store for you, that 's what you will gain by alienating me. And yet what a fine reign your master might have had.'

The ' fine reign ' of Balashov's master was indeed but just beginning. As it was Napoleon's flattery which had once dazzled his fancy, so it was Napoleon's rancour which enabled him at last to see things as they were. For once this dreamer put away his dreams ; for once this waverer formed a resolution, which nothing save death and destruction could break or bend. In the letters which passed between Alex-ander and Bernadotte in the year of destiny, 1812, you may see how strong was the Tsar's determination, supported by Bernadotte's wise counsel, to make an end for ever of Napoleon's aggression. No longer did he use the suave style of Tilsit. He was ready to accept a peace if Napoleon would grant what he asked, and if as a preliminary every French soldier was withdrawn from Russian soil. He admitted

the force of Bernadotte's warning that it was still
Napoleon's object to divide the great states one against
the other, and thus to facilitate the old project of the
European hegemony. ' I am making a war of delays,'
wrote Alexander, ' and since a superior force is march-
ing upon us, I am retiring to a fortified position,
which I have prepared to that end. . . . Meanwhile
you may be sure that, when once the war is begun,
it is my firm resolve to make it last for years if
necessary.'

With this end in view the Tsar avoided general
engagements, and betook himself to the heart of his
empire that he might inspire his people with the
hope of conquest, and persuade it to make fresh
sacrifices, to form new armies of reserve. His policy
won the whole-hearted approval of Bernadotte,
who never wavered in his belief, even when the
armies of Napoleon were overrunning Russia, that
the ultimate victory must be Alexander's. ' He
may gain the first, the second, even the third battle,'
he wrote ; ' the fourth will be undecided, and if your
Majesty perseveres you will certainly gain the fifth.'

Then suddenly there comes news of disaster.
Kutusof has not profited by his victory ; the road
to Moscow lies open to the enemy ; the capital has
fallen into the hands of the French, who find there
none to welcome them but the porters of the houses.
Yet Alexander's resolution was still adamant. ' It
is a cruel loss, I admit, but of moral and political
rather than military import. At any rate it will give

me the chance of proving to the whole of Europe that
I mean to sustain this struggle against the oppressor
with all possible perseverance, for after this wound
everything else will seem but a scratch.' Thus the
famous retreat of the Russians was victoriously
achieved, and the urgent overtures of Napoleon contemptuously dismissed. What was his letter of peace
but a mass of *fanfaronnades* ? Thus the burning of
Moscow was endured by a brave people with a shrug.
And then, in October, came the crowning reward of
the Tsar's persistence and resolution.

' Monsieur mon Frère et Cousin,' wrote Alexander
to Bernadotte, ' I have with the utmost fidelity kept
your Royal Highness exactly informed of my re-
verses ; it is but just that I relate to you the successes
which the Russian armies have lately won.' And so
he goes on to describe, without exaltation or boast-
fulness, the marvellous victories which his brave
generals had wrested from the French. Here the
Bavarians were beaten, and lost in their defeat eight
guns and twenty-two flags. There the King of
Naples was put to flight, leaving upon the field a
standard and thirty pieces of artillery. The Polish
general, Tischekwistschk, of whose prowess Napoleon
had proudly boasted, had surrendered with 2000
men. The Emperor Napoleon had gone hot-foot
to Smolensk, telling his army to follow by the same
route. All the roads of Russia leading west were
strewn with dead horses and abandoned munitions of
war. Never were good tidings more plainly told or

more joyously received. A few weeks later there
was still better news to tell. Ney's lot was the most
deplorable. His retreat being completely cut off,
he lost in two days 117 pieces and 20,000 men, with
four generals. Thus victory followed upon victory,
triumph upon triumph. There was but one disappointment—that Napoleon himself escaped from
Russia with the few poor remnants of his army. But
it mattered not. As the retreat from Moscow was the
end of Napoleon's hopes of conquest, so it was the
beginning of Europe's liberation. Once more the
plain truth was established that Russia was uncon-
querable, that it is at his peril that the bravest invader dared to cross the river which divides East and
West.

The campaign of Moscow was an interlude in
Alexander's life of dreams. Not long before
Napoleon's disastrous invasion he had been on the
verge of accepting Speranski's project of a Constitution. The sudden impulse of action destroyed
the project and sent Speranski into banishment.
But the lessons of La Harpe and Czartoryski were
not obliterated from Alexander's brain ; they were
merely blurred ; and they might have taken a practical
shape, had not Waterloo and Mme. de Krüdener
intervened. The defeat of Napoleon, who for
twenty years had ravaged Europe, drove all liberal
ideas from the minds of men. And Alexander was
strengthened in a contempt for the past—even for
his own past—by the pious ministrations of Mme. de

Krüdener. This female prophet, who had exchanged the sentimentalities of *Valérie* for a love of prayer meetings, gained a complete ascendancy over the Tsar, whose mysticism persuaded him that the burning of Moscow had illuminated his soul, that henceforth he was, by the grace of God, the arbiter of the world, the sanction of the unbroken right of Russia. Thus with the aid of Mme. de Krüdener he sketched the scheme of the Holy Alliance. For twenty years the world had been torn in pieces by Jacobins. Henceforth it was to be made ' safe for ' autocracy. The lessons which Europe had learned from Napoleon and his lawless combating, were not to be thrown away. Any attempt at revolution, wherever and by whomsoever it was made, should promptly be suppressed by the armed forces of the Alliance. The aspirations of the Tsar were Christian and monarchical and reactionary, and, encouraged by Mme. de Krüdener, he believed them irresistible. With him it was a pious doctrine that for the rest of time princes should look upon one another as brothers, should treat their peoples as their children, and establish their actions upon the firm and sacred principles of the gospel of Christ.

Alexander himself forgot in his new worship all the old hopes and dreams of reform. He fondly believed for the moment that he was giving ' a lofty satisfaction to divine Providence.' Metternich denounced the Alliance as ' a loud-sounding nothing,' and presently interpreted it, according to his will, as a guarantee

of legitimate sovereignty. For Castlereagh it was
'a sublime piece of mysticism and nonsense,' and
though he, too, prayed that Europe in the future
should be protected against revolution, he saw no
safety in Alexander's phantasies. Meanwhile, he
received the project with an ironical politeness.
'The benign principles of the Alliance of the 26th of
September 1815,' he wrote, 'may be considered as
constituting the European system in the matter of
political conscience. It would, however, be dero-
gatory to the solemn act of the sovereigns to mix its
discussion with the ordinary diplomatic obligations,
which bind state to state, and which are to be looked
for alone in the treaties which have been concluded
in the accustomed form.' A civil, ingenious method,
truly, of shelving an awkward question.

And presently England, with the joint aid of
Castlereagh and Canning, took the decisive step in
the dissolution of the Holy Alliance. The mystical
doctrine of Alexander, translated into a practical
policy by Metternich, threatened to involve Europe
in perpetual wars. When once an international
police force has been established, there will always be
found work for it to do. And Castlereagh and Canning
formulated their sane and sound policy of intervention in the nick of time. If the nations are not
to live in chains, then each one of them must be free
to choose the form of government which suits it,
whether it be autocracy, or oligarchy, or democracy.
No one ever devised a scheme of greater futility than

that all men should measure their corn by his bushel. For acquiescence can be achieved only by force of arms, and the fiercest pedant upon earth will hardly contemplate with cheerfulness a perpetual state of war. Nor shall we best ensure the growth of liberty, if we cut off in his prime every obstinate citizen who refuses to be free.

So Alexander's attempt to stop the clock of time, to check the growth and change of the world at an arbitrarily chosen hour failed, as all such attempts must fail. And he, poor man, fell to dreaming again of liberty and free constitutions, until the excesses of Arakcheieff doubled his suspicions, and yet more darkly clouded his morose, unhappy mind. He died, as he had lived, a sphinx, who put to his people such riddles as it could never guess ; a vague Hamlet, whose conscience was seared by the memory of his father's death, a prince disillusioned by an implacable fate, and disappointed of the coloured dreams of youth.

TALLEYRAND

NO man of his time has been so bitterly attacked and so lamely defended as Charles Maurice Talleyrand de Périgord. He was said by his enemies to engross the vices of the old and new *régimes*. Napoleon led the chorus of abuse. 'Talleyrand,' said he, 'is a scoundrel, like Marmont: he has betrayed religion, Louis XVI., the Constituent Assembly, the Directorate. Why did I not have him shot ? ' And a thousand others have followed Napoleon's lead. A stranger to honour and virtue, declared one, he sacrificed his country to an insensate love of money. A monster of disloyalty, murmured another, he witnessed the ruin of his benefactors with a complacent smile, and cheerfully profited by the disasters of his friends. Even his statecraft has been decried as cunning, and his diplomacy as a mere trick of dissembling. Nor did Talleyrand often condescend to defend himself against his contemporaries. He countered insult with a smile, and, when charged with lack of principle, was content to observe that the only sound principle was to have none. His unpopularity, then, is easily intelligible. Nothing alienates people more thoroughly than indifference, unless it be a rasping wit; and when Talleyrand spoke at all, he would always rather lose a friend than a jest.

Moreover, he was for many years a fearless king-maker. He dispensed crowns as monarchs distribute portfolios. Dynasties were his playthings. He set up thrones and overturned them; and at each revolution he created for himself a new mob of enemies. He was, in truth, a finished specimen of the *homme politique*. He aspired to govern not empires, but rulers; and such being his profession, it is not strange that vices and even crimes were imputed to him by those who lacked his knowledge and humour. But if he disdained to answer his accusers, he never ceased to believe in the loftiness of his patriotism and the grandeur of his policy. 'Animated by the most devoted love of France,' thus he wrote at the end of his career, ' I have always served her conscientiously, and sought for her honestly that which I honestly believed to be most advantageous for her.'

Born in 1754 to a noble family, he was passed over by his parents in favour of a younger brother, and sent into the Church, because a limping leg rendered him unfit for the profession of arms. Neglect did but sharpen his wit and increase the quiet severity of his temper. Moreover, he looked upon the Church, for which he had no exalted regard, as a convenient method of preferment; and being appointed Bishop of Autun in 1789, he was able to play a distinguished part in the Revolution. With a prudent regret he foresaw the triumph of the popular cause, and, as it was always his habit to hail a rising star, he dedicated his energy and courage to the service of the people. But he did not share the illusions of his sentimental contemporaries. ' A democracy,' he asked in derision, ' what is it but an aristocracy of blackguards ? ' Meanwhile no hostile critic saw the weakness of France more clearly than he. ' The Nation,' said he to Gouverneur Morris, ' is a parvenu, and, like all parvenus, is insolent.' Moreover, he preserved a sturdy contempt for the heroes of humble birth who were his colleagues in rebellion, and who, in his own phrase, ' had never walked on the *parquet*.' As for himself, ' he dressed like a coxcomb, thought like a deist, and preached like a saint.'

And he understood life as he understood politics. He was a man of the world as well as a master of finance ; and since he was troubled neither by prejudices nor passions, he instantly assumed a leadership among the rabble. So he was a member of the Constituent Assembly, and, in spite of his bishopric, he urged the Government to lay hands upon the landed estate of the Church. Like Wolsey—a still greater Churchman—he thought it no dishonour to tax his own house ; and with a better excuse, since, in his eyes, the Church was no more than a means of advancement. A student of Montesquieu, and a patient admirer of the English Constitution, he affected to prefer a limited monarchy to other forms of government, and so long as safety permitted he was the zealous champion of Louis XVI. That he would have bowed to the storm is not improbable. Happily for him, he was in exile during the Terror, and he was not asked to soil his hands with blood. When, therefore, he returned from America, fortified by the lessons taught him by Alexander Hamilton, he could take up his broken career under the most favourable auspices, and unstained by the foolish crime of regicide.

Determined to rule through the established government, he was confronted by a desperate task. The Directory was neither sympathetic nor amenable. Its members regarded Talleyrand with suspicion, and even with hatred. In their eyes he was an aristocrat, an *emigré*, a friend of Mirabeau, who was waiting his chance to bring back the Royal House of France. Rewbell could find no words too brutal for what he thought the Bishop of Autun's treachery. ' He is the powdered lackey of the ancient *régime*,' said he ; ' at most he could be used as a servant for purposes of parade, were he only provided with a decent pair of legs, but he has no more legs than heart.' Talleyrand marked the hostility, and, after his habit of discretion, resented nothing openly. He shrugged his shoulders, and ' set the women going.' He plainly told Madame de Staël that if she did not find him a place he must blow his brains out, and Madame de Staël willingly used her influence to prevent so grave a tragedy. She assailed Barras with a passionate eloquence ; she sang the praises of her hero, who

wished nothing else than ' the honour of serving the
Republic and of showing his love of liberty ' ; and
Talleyrand, having proclaimed his unfailing devotion
to the Directory, was appointed Minister of Foreign
Affairs by Rewbell and Barras, the very men who had
most bitterly distrusted and assailed him. Admirably did he play his part in the comedy until the end
of the act. He employed all his marvellous gifts of
diplomacy to cajole the Directors, and he resigned
his office as soon as he knew that Napoleon's ascendancy was inevitable. While he had served France
with all his energy and prudence, he cherished a profound contempt for those who gave him his opportunity. ' These were the men,' said he in his
Mémoires, after describing a disgraceful quarrel
between Carnot and Barras, ' who held the reins of
government, and with whom, perforce, I attempted
to restore France into the society of Europe.'

The Directory, however, did Talleyrand an
eminent service : it first brought him face to face
with Napoleon. When the young general returned
from his glorious campaign in Italy, Talleyrand was
selected to pronounce his panegyric, and he instantly
fell under the triumphant spell. ' The winning of
twenty battles,' said he, ' accords admirably with
his youth, his good looks, his pallor, and a suspicion
of fatigue.' And it was not merely the picturesque
aspect of Napoleon which captivated him. He saw
in the victorious soldier the one man capable of re-
generating France, and at the outset supported his

schemes with unwavering devotion. If he could, he would have made Napoleon king, and thus put into practice his favourite theory of government. But kingship being impossible, he took care that Napoleon's power should be unhampered. The conspiracy of the 18th Brumaire could not have been made without the help of Talleyrand ; he approved the consulate ; and he delighted in the empire. The pomp and ceremony which the Emperor restored to France were in perfect harmony with the temper of one who throughout the fury of revolution never forgot that he was an aristocrat.

Thus during the first years of Napoleon's sovereignty Talleyrand exercised a wide and deep influence. As Madame de Rémusat says, he ruled France through his master. But two men so far different in temperament and ambition could not for ever follow the same path. Talleyrand always subordinated military glory to the security of France. Napoleon hesitated to leave the field, on which he believed himself invincible. While the soldier aimed at universal dominion, the statesman would have preferred a stable balance of power, and at last a separation became inevitable. ' I do not wish to be the executioner of Europe,' said Talleyrand in opposition to Napoleon's schemes of aggrandisement ; and so strongly did he disapprove of the policy pursued in Spain, that he was dismissed from the Ministry of Foreign Affairs. Henceforth he remained in Paris, watched and watchful. He played an energetic part in the downfall of the Emperor, and he has ever since been charged with treachery and ingratitude.

As has been said, Napoleon regretted that he had not shot Talleyrand, and from Napoleon's point of view the regret was perhaps justified. But it cannot be argued with justice that the Emperor had an honourable grievance against his Minister. There was no treachery, because Talleyrand served France, not Napoleon. There was no ingratitude, because Talleyrand owed no more to Napoleon than Napoleon owed to Talleyrand. Napoleon, said his Minister, was raised to the supreme power that he might oppose the forces of anarchy. Duped by his imagination, he determined to surround France 'with a rampart of thrones held by members of his own family.' And in this enterprise Talleyrand saw the ruin of his country. In 1807 Napoleon, by restoring peace to Europe, might have given to France a lasting supremacy. He preferred to seek adventures in Spain and Russia, and, by what seemed a reckless disregard of his country's interests, made Talleyrand's defection and his own downfall inevitable. Indignantly did Talleyrand deny that he had conspired against the Emperor. 'I have never conspired in my life,' said he, 'except when I had the majority of France for my accomplice.' Such are the ostensible differences which separated Napoleon and Talleyrand. But beneath them, and greater than they, was the struggle of temperaments, the struggle between genius and talent, between glory and tact, between imagination and subtlety, between dreams and practice. And it is not surprising, in the conditions of modern life, that talent won the ultimate victory.

'Napoleon,' said Talleyrand, 'had remade the bed of the Bourbons,' and the adroit Minister had no other choice than to smooth the pillows. In another sense he had performed the same office for Barras years before, and the Director had proved more grateful than the King. After Talleyrand had played a conspicuous part at Vienna, and realised at last the dream of his life—a constitutional monarchy, he found his occupation gone. Louis XVIII. would have none of him, despite the pressure of Wellington and the advice of Guizot. For once Talleyrand's tact deserted him. He did not gauge the obstinacy of the King, and thought that he might rule by force, where hitherto he had found cunning all-sufficient. And so King and Minister exchanged sarcasms and parted.

When Louis XVIII. asked him how he had contrived to wreck so many dynasties, 'there is something about me,' he replied, 'which brings ill-luck on Governments that neglect me.' The King did not entirely neglect him, since he gave him a sinecure worth 100,000 francs a year, and the throne withstood all his attempts to overturn it. So for fifteen years he remained a simple courtier, quietly organising an opposition, and waiting for better times. His last chance came when in 1830 he placed Louis Philippe upon the throne of France, and chose as his reward the post of Ambassador at St. James's. In London he proved that his talent for affairs was unimpaired, and he succeeded in strengthening the ties of friendship which bound England and France. Greville pictures him as a favourer ' of moderate and healing counsels,' as ' a statesman like Burleigh or Clarendon for prudence, temperance, and discretion.' The transformation of the volatile Abbé, of the unscrupulous Bishop, was indeed complete, and yet he was distinguished by that unity of character which may always be detected in the great.

He had controlled as many dynasties as Louis XVIII. declared that he had wrecked. He had encouraged the first signs of revolution ; he had governed France through the Directory ; his had been the unseen hand behind the Imperial throne ; he had established a limited monarchy. As it was never his ambition to stand first, so he cared not who had the semblance of power so long as he had the reality. And in all that he had accomplished, he might well boast that in serving himself he had also served France. But though his motives were as simple as his ambition, he appeared to his contemporaries little short of a criminal. Even Gouverneur Morris, a most judicious observer of men and events, has nothing better to say of him than that he ' would rather do right than wrong,' as became a man who was ' indifferent between virtue and vice.' The misconception was partly due to Talleyrand himself ; partly, and in a higher degree, to the age in which he happened to play his part. Cynical in all things, he studiously rid himself

of the qualities which were not either pleasant or useful, and he did not acclaim as virtuous that which
he knew to be expedient. He himself rebutted the
common charge with an insouciance that did but
increase the rancour of his enemies. ' Did you ever
know crime of use to a sensible man ? ' he asked
Lamartine. ' It is the resource of political fools, and
is like the breaker which returns and overwhelms you.
I had my failings, some say vices—*mais des crimes, fi
donc !* '

To the age of revolution, ebullient with ideas, this
political wisdom seemed a clear proof of villainy.
The heroes of the Terror, their hands red with blood,
believed that they might rule the world with pious
maxims. ' Be virtuous and you will be happy,' they
murmured, as the tumbril carried its innocent load
to the guillotine. But Talleyrand knew that these
amiable platitudes were not the most useful instruments of policy. He would sacrifice nothing to ideas
—' not even if they were his own.' He would not
have murdered his bitterest foe for the sake of a moral
saying. In other words, he was sternly practical.
He would be turned aside neither by love nor hate,
neither by virtue nor vice, from the business of government. And this persistence best illustrates the unity,
the oneness of his character—selfish in the cause of
France, with which he identified himself ; pitiless and
inexorable to those who checked her advance and his.
The task which he had set himself compelled him to
worship success. ' The courtier of destiny,' said

Lamartine with perfect truth, ' he served the strong, he despised the maladroit, he abandoned the unfortunate.' Such qualities, used in the commerce of daily life, would make a bad friend and a worse enemy. In times of stress they may be the necessary weapons of a statesman, and those who condemn the means which Talleyrand employed lack either the will or the intelligence to understand the end and aim of his ambition.

To achieve his purpose he spent his whole life, as it were, on guard. He divested himself of passion and sentiment. He remained silent in company, lest he should betray his thought. With so stern a hand did he govern his impulses that he was never known to lose his temper. In all the relations of life he let wit and sarcasm perform the work of anger. If there was that in his mind which must be spoken, he made a speech ; otherwise he held his tongue, and he astonished the Foreign Ministers whom he met in conference by an obstinate reticence. Indifferent to the opinions of others, he read himself to sleep with pamphlets written to insult him. Yet if he were cold in his manner, he was never rough or brusque. With him discretion did not degenerate into insolence, and he was not a slave even to his discretion.

When he came to London as Ambassador, he surprised our statesmen with the openness of his speech and demeanour, which was perfectly adapted to the occasion. But in eulogising Reinhard, who had served him for many years, he sketched the qualities

which are necessary to a Minister of Foreign Affairs
with an authority which is indisputable, with a candour which plainly reveals his own method, and which
is the most eloquent answer to his detractors. ' A
Minister of Foreign Affairs,' he said, ' must be endowed with a kind of instinct, which should save
him, by a prompt warning, from ever compromising
himself. He must possess the faculty of seeming
open, while remaining impenetrable ; he must cover
his reserve with a mask of frankness ; he must be
adroit even in the choice of his distractions ; his
conversation should be simple, various, unexpected,
always natural, and sometimes ingenuous. In a word,
he must never cease for one moment in the twenty-
four hours to be a Minister of Foreign Affairs.'

To this arduous ideal Talleyrand showed a constant
loyalty. He was a Minister of Foreign Affairs always,
and in all circumstances ; he was no amateur,
who dabbled in politics when sport or bric-à-brac
failed him ; he thought no labour excessive which
should further the interests of France and of the prevailing dynasty. But, he proceeds in his panegyric
of Reinhard, ' the rarest qualities are of no avail in
diplomacy if they do not find their guarantee in good
faith.' Thus he rebuts, in Reinhard's name, the
charge that was so often brought against himself,
and for once in a long career stooped to answer his
opponents. Thus with the full emphasis of his
authority he attempts to destroy a general prejudice.
' No,' says he, ' diplomacy is not a science of craft

and duplicity. If good faith is necessary anywhere, it is necesssary in political transactions, for it alone can render them solid and durable. The world has been pleased to confuse reserve with cunning. Good faith never authorises cunning, though it admits reserve ; and reserve has this characteristic—it increases confidence.' Thus spoke Talleyrand in what may be called his *apologia*, and it can be said that never in his dealings with foreign States was he guilty of bad faith. He did not always treat his own compatriots with the same magnanimity. At the outset of his career, when he was attempting to force the door of politics which he feared was closed against him, he employed with excellent effect all the arts of cunning. He flattered and cajoled the men whom in his heart he despised, and whom he was resolved to oust from power. But he was playing a purposed part, and when once he was master of himself and his position he proved that wisdom and silence, not cunning and chicane, are the true instruments of statesmanship.

If he thought as a diplomatist, it was as an aristocrat that he always presented himself to the world. He preserved through all vicissitudes the dandyism of the ancient *régime*. Though his policy forced him into strange companionships, he never forgot that by birth and habit he was a gentleman, and his wit, which was a survival of another age, protected him against the assaults of insolence and familiarity. His retorts, courteous even in their bitterness, long ago became the commonplaces of polite conversation, and have been so recklessly perverted that their author, could he hear, would not recognise them. Of his faults, the worst in private was his ingratitude to women—he dismissed Mme. de Staël, his benefactress, with the curt refusal of an invitation ; the worst in public was his insatiable greed. So sharply had he felt the pinch of poverty, that he used the opportunities of power without scruple to fill his pocket. When Napoleon wondered at his wealth, 'I did but buy *rentes* on the 18th Brumaire,' said he, ' and sell them on the 19th.' The compliment, adroit as it was, concealed the truth ; and Talleyrand, no doubt, vied with his colleagues in seeking and accepting bribes. Nor can any better excuse be found for him than that he followed the fashion of dangerous times, and took a necessary precaution against the future.

And, thus fortified against discomfort, he faced the approach of age—it was very old age—with a dignity and nonchalance which well became him. ' Je suis un vieux homme,' he wrote to Lady Jersey in 1834, ' mais je ne veux pas que d'autres soient dans le cas de le trouver,' echoing unconsciously a phrase of Lord Chesterfield's, a man of kindred temper and talent. Four years later he died, reconciled with the Church. ' He was always a man of pacification,' said Roger Collard at this final act of diplomacy, and these words might well serve for his epitaph.

METTERNICH

WHEN Metternich first saw the monarch whom he was destined to rule for so many years, he was but a boy of seventeen. Fortunate in birth as in opportunity, he was appointed in 1790 Master of the Ceremonies which embellished the coronation of Leopold II. at Frankfort. The high office flattered his love of pomp and pageantry; and his meeting with Francis, then an Archduke, pointed the way to a career of diplomacy. In his allegiance to this prince, who two years later succeeded to the throne of Leopold, he never wavered. Even at the time when he knew himself to be an autocrat, he cherished the fiction of devotion and obedience. With a simple reverence for kingship, he gladly yielded the glory of his own exploits to his master, and declared, in writing his own autobiography, that his sole desire was to paint his monarch such as he was. He was never tired of celebrating the calm which the Emperor displayed in the greatest crises, and ' the force of soul and the firmness of character, which are the appanage of princes born to rule '; he sang pæans to the Emperor's virtues, both public and domestic, with an enthusiasm which history has not justified; and he found an ample reward when the dying Francis called him ' his best friend.' But the deeds of Francis were in truth the deeds of Metternich, and to the Minister, who for nearly half a century directed the counsels of Austria, must be given the praise and the blame which follow achievement or disaster.

Metternich's education was, so to say, guided by the hand of fate. He entered the University of Strasburg as Napoleon quitted it. He sat in the same class-rooms, he received instruction from the same masters as his great adversary, and if he never heard the hero's name mentioned, he, too, listened with an eager interest to the first news of the Revolution. His preceptor was a Jacobin, who did his utmost to inspire his distinguished pupil with the ominous doctrines of liberty, equality, and fraternity —and in vain. Metternich was naturally inaccessible to new ideas. He was born and grew up with a lofty respect for law and order, and the aberrations of others did but confirm him in an austere habit of thought. And if at Strasburg he had an opportunity of observing what were cynically called ' the rights of n. in,' at Mayence, whither he went to study law, he was confronted with the emigrants, ' those Jacobins of Coblentz,' as M. de Bouille called them, whose levity persuaded them that in a few weeks they would be restored to Paris in triumph. At the siege of Valenciennes he learned his first lesson in the art of war, and in 1794 he witnessed the departure of Admiral Howe's fleet from Portsmouth—the fleet which won the glorious victory of the 1st of June. At the age of twenty-one, therefore, he had a clear and practical knowledge of the problems which perplexed Europe; he had seen something of the means by which they would be solved; and he was ready to take his part in the greatest game that ever it was the lot of a statesman to play.

Yet he would have us believe that he had no natural love of diplomacy, that the fires of ambition never burned within his breast. He declares that public affairs never attracted him, and that, had he been permitted to choose his own career, he would have devoted his days and nights to the study of science. When in 1801 the Emperor called him to his service, he obeyed the summons with a show of reluctance. 'Your Majesty,' said he, ' wishes me to throw myself into a profession which I do not think is mine.' Thus pleasantly he deceived himself. Politics were the first necessity of his being. As Napoleon was born to be a military despot, so Metternich was born to be a calm, cold, calculating diplomatist, and neither the one nor the other could avoid his destiny. Meanwhile, Metternich had already frequented the society of such astute Ministers as Pozzo di Borgo. He had already made an appearance at the Congress of Rastadt. Above all, he proved that he understood the conditions of his craft by his choice of a mission. Dresden and Copenhagen being offered to him, he selected Dresden, which was a stage on the road from St. Petersburg to Berlin, and which was thus an

excellent post of observation.   To what good purpose
he put the watch-tower of his choice the years proved :
he detected the weakness of others without revealing
his own strength ; and when he stood face to face
with the forces of disorder, he was prepared by knowledge and experience for the encounter.

From the moment that he entered the service of
the Emperor Francis he understood his appointed
task.   The enemy which he fought with a simple
courage and a tireless energy was the French Revolution and the opinions which it enforced.   Determined to save his own country from terror and sub-
version, determined to preserve the balance of power
in Europe, he set his face sternly against the excesses of
thought and action which had filled the gutters of
Paris with blood.   Like the trained soldier that he
was, he had studied his enemies' positions, and had
armed himself efficiently for the fray.   His passionless
intellect permitted him to form a clear judgment of all
parties.   He esteemed the Emigrants as lightly as
the Sansculottes.   He knew all the men of the Revo-
lutionary Government, and he saw as clearly as their
master that they were good workmen, who fondly
believed themselves architects.   It was his foible to
believe that he alone in Europe understood the true
meaning of the French Revolution ; he held that a
military despotism was the only logical result of the
Terror ; and the triumph of Napoleon was the best
justification of his arrogance.

After Austerlitz Metternich was appointed Am-

bassador at Paris, and then it was that the determined
duel commenced, to which history can hardly find a
parallel. On either side the battle was fought with
perfect consciousness and without rancour. Napoleon
found the society of Metternich so agreeable that he
demanded his presence in Paris, while Metternich
never concealed his lofty appreciation of the man
whose schemes it was his duty to oppose. If the
Ambassador was shocked now and again at the harsh
manners of the Emperor, whom his aristocratic soul
regarded as an upstart, if he was sometimes appalled
at Napoleon's insufficient culture, he never made the
mistake of underrating his adversary. With an infinite patience and an imperturbable temper he set
himself to study the Emperor's character and ambitions. To Napoleon's strength he opposed a quietly
assured cunning. He listened obediently to the
characteristic garrulity of the Corsican, and, while
he silently criticised all that he heard, he never committed himself or his Government by an indiscreet
reply. The contest was unequal from the first. It
was again, as with Talleyrand, talent against genius,
realism against romance, and if for the sake of diversion you regret the issue, you cannot but admire
the calmness, the deliberation, and the address
of the Ambassador who won the last triumphant
round.

Metternich possessed one conspicuous advantage
over all his colleagues—he was never afraid of
Napoleon. His well-bred serenity was impervious

to assault, and, doubtless, the Emperor liked him all the better when he discovered the hopelessness of attempting to browbeat him. And, when Metternich looked back upon the glories of his career, it was the audience of August 15, 1808, that most generously flattered his pride. Napoleon was highly incensed at the news which he had received of Austria's warlike preparations, and he determined, in revenge, to make a public example of Metternich. Approaching him, with menace in his mien, before all the diplomatists, he addressed him at the top of his voice. 'Well, Mr. Ambassador,' said he, 'what is it your master, the Emperor, wants? Does he think he will drag me back to Vienna?' No shade of embarrassment passed over Metternich's face. He opposed a perfect calm to the Emperor's anger. If he raised his tone and his voice to his opponent's level, it was to prove that he was still master of himself. And so the two great adversaries shouted louder and louder. Diplomatic irony was more than a match for imperial pride, and at last Napoleon, having vainly striven to involve Count Tolstoi in the argument, turned on his heel and left the room. But no spark of malice burned in his mind. He hastened to assure Metternich that his words were inspired by no personal animosity— that he had no other aim than to understand the situation; and Metternich, strong in the pride of having taught the Emperor a lesson, might have received the apology with a better grace. 'Europe,' said he with an ungenerous pomp, 'will decide on

which side are reason and justice.' And there the
matter ended.

Whatever advantage Metternich's serenity had
gained in Paris was lost at Vienna in less than a year.
After spending some months as Napoleon's prisoner
at Schönbrunn, the Ambassador was appointed
Minister of Foreign Affairs in time to give a forced
approval to the disastrous Treaty of Vienna, which,
as he truly said, ' enclosed the Empire in a circle of
iron.' The humiliation of Austria was complete ; for
her resistance was impossible ; and the Emperor
Francis accepted the pitiless terms of Napoleon with
what spirit he could. But even in the moment of
disaster Metternich was subtly preparing his revenge.
His emissaries had already instilled into the mind of
Napoleon the poisonous hint of an ambitious marriage.
Though in his *Memoirs*, as in his life, Metternich
affected to believe that the proposal for the hand of
Marie-Louise came from Napoleon, there is no doubt
that the cunning mind of the diplomatist suggested
the alliance. It was well for the dignity of the
Austrian Court to confer with the Archduchess. It
was well for the sake of traditional morality to prate
of sacrifices made in the cause of duty and of peace.
But Metternich, with his unfailing prudence, had
foreseen the consequences of Napoleon's false step.
Austria pacified and Russia alienated—were these
objects not worth striving for ? Napoleon discovered his error too late. ' J'ai fait une bien grande
sottise,' he confessed, in 1813, ' en épousant une

Archiduchesse d'Autriche.' Metternich recognised the folly when he accompanied Marie-Louise to France, and found no difficulty in acquiescence.

The Imperial marriage was, indeed, a masterpiece of nicely calculated diplomacy. Yet Metternich, like the polished actor that he was, assumed an air of innocent surprise. He declared that he could not understand Napoleon's motive in espousing Marie-Louise. For six months he pretended to seek the light in a dark situation, and to seek it in vain. He told Napoleon that he wanted to find a line of conduct which he might follow in the far-distant future. ' Stay a few weeks longer,' replied the Emperor, ' and you will have satisfaction.' And all the while he held the balance of events in his own hand. The marriage, which ensured a peace to Austria, presently involved France and Russia in war. Metternich, by proclaiming an armed neutrality, stood well with either side. Though 30,000 Austrian troops went to the aid of France, the Tsar was assured that the aid was not seriously given, and he still regarded the Emperor Francis as his ally. Metternich, with a rare modesty, declared that history could not show a situation so strangely eccentric as this. If it were eccentric, it was also of infinite advantage. The issue of the struggle was immaterial. Whichever won, Austria's hands were free for a settlement, and, if Napoleon hoped that a sentiment for the husband of Marie-Louise would intervene, he was doomed to disappointment.

After Moscow, Metternich, conscious that he

dominated the situation, wisely declared that Austria's attitude was that of a *puissance médiatrice armée*, and set about the making of a durable peace with perfect sincerity. He knew that he had won the victory against the forces of revolution, but he wished to use his victory with moderation, and it was vastly honourable to him that he showed no anger against Napoleon. Indeed, had the great Emperor been willing to make terms at Prague, he would have saved his throne and his dynasty. France, Italy, Belgium, and Holland would still have lain at his feet, while Prussia would have found her boundary at the Elbe. But Napoleon must have the world or nothing, and he angrily rejected the terms that were offered him. 'You want war,' said he to Metternich. 'Very well, then, you shall have it.' And Metternich, who looked upon himself as 'the representative of the whole of European society,' reluctantly took up the challenge. Even after Leipzig, Metternich would have secured Napoleon upon the throne of France. He wished for Austria no aggrandisement nor extension. If only he might ensure the balance of power, he would have been content, but he knew how desperate was the hope that Napoleon would be persuaded to moderation by defeat. 'The Emperor Napoleon will not make peace,' said he; 'that is my profession of faith, and nothing will give me greater happiness than to be wrong.' He was not wrong. Napoleon still believed himself superior to circumstances, and Elba and Waterloo were the result.

During the troubled years, 1813-14, Metternich showed astounding skill in the management of affairs. He had studied the character of Napoleon with so eager a precision, that his policy was nearer to science than to art. If the ultimate downfall of Napoleon was assured by the energy and statecraft of Pitt, it was the diplomacy of Metternich which hastened the *coup de grâce*. Had Metternich gone into retirement after Waterloo, he would have bequeathed to posterity an unbroken reputation. He had achieved his purpose with singular success. The Revolution, which he had set himself to destroy, was crumbled in pieces. The man of genius who had turned the forces of disorder to his own use was a lonely, hopeless exile. Metternich's work was done, his wages ta'en. But he lacked the imagination to understand his own achievement. Though anarchy was dead for the moment, he was still eager to fight it. He persisted in his policy of counter-revolution, long after the necessity had passed away. The fall of Napoleon gave him no sense of security, and with the aid of the Holy Alliance, which was established upon a patriarchal basis to secure the interest of all thrones, he determined to govern Europe with an iron hand. For the Napoleonic system he substituted a system of his own. He announced himself the friend of all absolute monarchs, and he declared that no country had any other hope of salvation than in a benevolent despotism. His aim and purpose was to check the growth of representative government wherever it threatened an appearance. Europe was at peace, and he still shaped his policy as though Napoleon were leading to victory an army of Jacobins. Not content to govern Austria, he wished to exert his influence in every capital. At Teplitz he set forth his views to the King of Prussia in a few words. 'The whole question is reduced to this,' said he, 'if your majesty has made up his mind not to introduce national representation into his kingdom, the evil may be exorcised. Otherwise there is no safety.'

And thus it was that Metternich, by ignoring the changed circumstances of Europe, made the reaction against his policy inevitable. He became the slave of his own consistency, and thought that the only cure for discontent was suppression. Had he had a vast army at his back, with a general of genius to lead it, he might have realised his ambition, and seen the Continent one vast autocracy. But the Holy Alliance put its trust not in arms but in conferences, and Metternich could not persuade a world devastated by war to resume the field for the sake of a system. It was in Naples that the voice of protest was first heard, and presently Spain echoed the complaint. The question of Greece set Metternich in opposition not merely to Russia but to England. And Metternich held to his course with admirable tenacity. No reverse dismayed him, and it is the best proof of his strength that he survived the prophecy of his downfall many years.

In 1835 died the Emperor Francis, whom he had

served faithfully and ruled with a firm hand, and Palmerston believed and hoped that the appointment of a family council was the prelude to Metternich's decline. The wish was father to the thought. Metternich remained inflexible for ten years, and bowed at last to the storm which his policy had raised in Hungary. Resolved to suppress the Hungarian language, and at the same time to levy heavier taxes and to demand more recruits, he aroused the opposition of Kossuth, and in 1848 found himself once more face to face with revolution. Deserted by the Emperor, and alone in council, he resigned, not to save his life, but in obedience to the Imperial will. Had he lived in an earlier century, he would have laid his head upon the block. Being a modern, he went away quietly by train. The mob which he had restrained, as he believed, for its own good, took a characteristic revenge by burning his villa. For himself he feared nothing, he regretted nothing, he would have changed nothing. ' If I had to begin my career again,' said he, with superb arrogance, ' I would follow the course I have taken, and would not deviate from it for an instant.' But the truth is, he had outlived his age. He was already an anachronism in 1848. Unwillingly he witnessed the reversal of his cherished policy. He saw Napoleon III. mount the throne of France, and his deathbed may have been disturbed by the echo of the shouts which greeted the victory of Magenta.

Metternich was a diplomatist of the old school,

polished, suave, impenetrable. Nothing ever persuaded him to betray an emotion. When in 1813 he left Napoleon after his last audience, the generals gathered round him to see what impression the interview had made upon his face. ' I don't think I satisfied their curiosity,' said he, with a characteristic pride in his grave and cunning demeanour. At the same time he looked with a jealous eye upon his craft. He hated what he called ' the policy of egoism, the policy of good pleasure.' In his view the rival States were all members of human society, of which reciprocal forbearance was the first duty. ' Do not unto others,' said he, ' that which you would not have others do to you.' An inflexible bureaucrat, he preserved his principles inviolate, and thus he was able to look back upon a singularly uniform career. He adopted for his device *la force dans le droit*, and he was certain that the right was always on his side. He resented nothing so much as the accusation that he had attempted to impose a system upon Europe. ' That which is called the system of Metternich,' said he, ' was not a system, but the application of the laws which govern the world. Revolutions rest upon systems ; the eternal laws are outside and above that which has no other value than that of a system.'

To speak of ' eternal laws ' is to beg the question, but Metternich's meaning is plain. He was a statesman of practice, not of theory. ' I have been of the number of men of action,' said he, ' and I have proved it during my long years of service in peace and in war.' He dealt quite rightly in prose, not in poetry. ' My temperament,' said he, ' is a historical temperament, antipathetic to all that is romantic ' ; which explains his constant opposition to Napoleon. At the same time, he was not without illusions concerning his own character. He declared in his political testament that he had always regarded despotism as a sign of weakness, and yet a despotism was the starting-point of his policy. Still more rashly, he thought that he had come into the world too late or too soon. Had he lived earlier, he would have had his share in the prosperity of the epoch. Had he lived later, he would have played his part in the reconstruction of things. ' I should have been born in 1900,' said he, ' and have had the twentieth century before me.' How men deceive themselves ! One thing is very sure, that in the twentieth century there is no place for Metternichs.

An accomplished courtier, a great gentleman, Metternich loved all the ornaments of life. Never for one moment had he known the hazard of the adventurer, as Talleyrand knew it. Rich and well-born, he was early inured to splendour, and he cherished a very proper respect for stars, orders, protocols, and the other appurtenances of his craft. Something of a dandy himself, he could not endure the prevailing fashion, and he looked with contempt upon the false elegance of upstarts like Robespierre. All his life he held bad company in horror, and he was shocked at the detestable circles to which some of the princes

of his time condescended. A cold, marmoreal nature
saved him from frivolity, and rendered him incapable of condoning frivolity in others. But it was
an invincible pride, of triple brass, which most
efficiently protected him against the assaults of
fortune. When he fell, it was Europe, not Metternich, which suffered humiliation. 'I draw a line
between that which was and that which is,' said he
with composure. 'The demarcation begins at the
eleventh hour of the night between the 13th and 14th
of March 1848.' That is to say, in his own eyes
Metternich's resignation changed the whole spirit of
the universe. Though he lived to see the work of his
hands undone, a sublime self-esteem softened his
regret. 'I am the man of that which was,' said he,
and was content.

NAPOLEON VITUPERATOR

THE cult of Napoleon, pursued for many years
with fanatical ardour, has resulted in a sad
misunderstanding of the great man. None of that
familiarity which breeds contempt has been spared
his memory. He has been presented to the world in
an attitude of mild flirtation; he has been pictured
at the pompous dining-table of Fontainebleau, or set
down, in his own despite, to an amiable game of back-
gammon. Certain sisters of the Church which he
treated with so lofty a disdain are still found teaching
that, by his own confession, he was never so happy
as when he was admitted to his first Communion.
Worse than this, a foolish drama once made him the
hero of a washtub, and ascribed a hundred trivial
pleasantries to this iron-handed soldier. Even at his
stateliest, he scowls upon a litter of Empire furniture,
with arms imperturbably folded, or fitfully meets
the reproachful gaze of Madame Mère. His official
editors have aided and abetted the general mystifica-
tion, by excluding from his correspondence those
letters, which cast the clearest light upon his
mind and character. But the documents which
Napoleon III. placed upon the index, were gathered
together some twenty years ago, and they effectually

destroy the legend of sentimentality. In truth, no man ever harboured so sincere a contempt for anecdotal obsequiousness and vapid admiration. Once upon a time he condemned a journalist to prison who sought to win him glory by the invention of unperformed generosities; and could he revisit the world of to-day, the dungeons of France would speedily be filled with indiscreet flatterers and too faithful partisans.

The Napoleon who lays bare his naked soul in his *Lettres Inédites* is not a hero for the schoolroom or the pulpit. He is no warrior in kid gloves, anxious to do good and obey the rules of morality. He is, on the contrary, an egoist, magnificent and profound, who knows no other law than tyranny and triumph. Though France and her glory are ever on his tongue, it is Napoleon alone that governs his heart; and on every page he betrays his hatred and contempt for everything and everybody that opposes his progress towards the headship of the civilised world. He is Machiavelli in action, Machiavelli strengthened by the belief that his theory of cunning may instantly be put into practice. Not only had he the hand to strike; he had the brain which knew where to direct the blow, and knew, moreover, precisely what would be the effect of his castigation. His, indeed, was that swift intellect, that complete clairvoyance, which penetrated in a flash the inevitable stupidity of mankind. 'I judge by my judgment and my reason,' he wrote proudly,

'and not by the opinions of others.' And assuredly
he never stooped to take counsel of any man. His
policy was to keep his intimates in ignorance, that
they might not mar the performance of his designs
by a scanty half-knowledge of their own. 'Ney knows
less of my affairs,' he asserted, 'than the youngest
drummer-boy in my army'; and when you remember
how vast were his schemes, you may estimate the
burden which his necessary independence laid upon
him.

'In Spain,' said he, 'I shall find the Pillars of Her-
cules, but not the limits of my power'; and this
power none might wield, none might even understand,
except the tireless hero who knew not how to delegate
it. When his affairs were discussed in Paris he was
furious. 'They would do better,' he growled, 'to
go to the Opera, to *fêtes*, and to the Bois de Boulogne.
. . . Paris wants wit.' And he told the land he
governed no more than he chose, and tightened so
firm a grasp on the Press that no man dared report
the truth without his special sanction. But while
he would keep others in darkness, he would master
everything himself. No detail was too insignificant
for his interest; he knew more of finance than his
Chancellor of the Exchequer, more of crime than
Fouché himself; and the astutest of his Ambassadors
received his instructions in a proper spirit of humility.
An expert in corn and cotton, a better theologian
(so he says) than the whole College of Cardinals, a
constant critic of the Opera, he still found time to

dictate articles for the journals, and to sketch caricatures in ridicule of his enemies. Nothing was
hidden from this active soldier, whose education began
and ended in Plutarch and Livy—excellent masters
both ; and it is the omniscient statesman rather than
the peerless general that he displayed, when he took
his pen in his hand.

He knew all things, and scarce a letter passed
through the post without his cognisance. If General
Clement receives improper guests at his dinner-table,
he does not escape the Consul's notice. When
Rochebrune, a disreputable printer of Marseilles,
visits Paris, Napoleon is ready with a warning. If
une nommée D. receives letters from Prince Eugène,
the secret is instantly revealed to him, and he is quick
with a denunciation of ' this mud of Paris.' He has
eyes and ears in every capital of Europe, and the
tributary kings can neither lift their finger nor open
their mouths without word and action being reported
to the Emperor. His curiosity is keen on the march
as at Paris, and the hardships of a campaign are no
drag on his agile spirit of discovery. Nor was it
politics alone that engrossed his attention ; a common
case of poisoning is sufficient to arouse his energy.
' The man Pascal,' he informs Fouché in 1807, ' certainly poisoned his wife on the 2nd of Floréal in the
Year XIII., at four o'clock in the morning. If the magis-
trate cares to interrogate the women about Madame
Pascal and the brother-in-law of Monsieur Pascal, and
to have the dog opened who was poisoned, they will

find sufficient evidence for the arrest of this scoundrel, who seems to be so perverted a criminal that there is a danger of his going to further excesses.' All the details were familiar to him, down to the poisoned dog and the very moment of the crime. Abroad also he was on sure ground, and could discuss the varying policy pursued by the *Times* and the *Morning Chronicle*; and while in one letter he prescribes the policy to be pursued by the School of Medicine, in another he ordains what his soldiers shall eat and drink, and even lays the table for his officers. But with all his lust of knowledge, he knew the value of deception, and maybe he really believed that the ' affair of Vittoria ' was a triumph for the arms of France. And so little was he a pedant that he could even sing the praises of ignorance. ' The art of the police,' he wrote to his Minister, ' is not to see that which it is useless for it to see.'

His omniscience never tempered his ferocity. Cruel, relentless, unscrupulous, he fought the world of Pitt and Burke, of Wordsworth and Chateaubriand, with the weapons of the Middle Ages. He treated the august States of Europe with as slight a courtesy as he would have treated a rival village in Corsica had he never found a larger theatre for his enterprise. In his native land the inhabitant of the next valley was his natural foe; and had this foe sounded the horn upon the mountain as he passed by, he would have slain him for his insolence. So in Europe, no man might blow the trumpet of revolt; and, since he cared nothing for justice, since he exacted both eyes and a dozen teeth for the smallest infraction, his vengeance was always swift, ample, and unquestioned. ' Arrest this man,' he writes to Fouché, ' and imprison him for three months ' ; and never once does he hint at the pedantic necessity of trial or inquiry. He condemned and sentenced whomever he chose, and thus facilitated the work of government. The Revolution is always imagined by enthusiasts as a belated revenge for the majesty of Louis xiv. ; yet the Great King himself never for one instant knew the omnipotent tyranny enjoyed by Napoleon, the elect of the people. For a parallel you must return to Louis xi., and you will find this ancient King a miracle of mildness compared with the Consul. As early as the month of Pluviôse in the Year xii. he ordered Fouché to put to the torture a sailor caught in communication with the English, and his treatment of criminals never ceased to be mediæval in its cruelty. He would lay traps for the unwary with an adroitness which puts the modern practice of *la cuisine* to the blush. He explicitly orders Talleyrand to entangle a Spanish Prince in a love affair. ' Invite Madame Talleyrand with four or five women to meet him,' he recommends : ' if the Prince of the Asturias attaches himself to a pretty woman, and you are sure of her, that would be no harm, since you would have an extra chance of watching him.'

' Shoot the burgomaster,' that is the naked eloquence of a letter to General Clarke. Once upon a time he hears that an actor is a dangerous intriguer. 'If this refers to politics,' says he to Fouché, 'arrest him and have him whipped, as all this riff-raff deserves when it meddles with serious things.' So his ferocity increases, and he bids his Minister 'shut up Doctor Mayer *au cachot et au secret*, to teach him to preach sentiments against honour.' When the appearance of some actors in French uniform inspired a Konigsberg audience to hiss, Napoleon demanded exemplary justice for the insult. 'I refuse to evacuate the place,' he wrote, 'until the two principal offenders are shot, and if the King of Prussia permits me to be thus outraged, he need not come to Berlin, for he would not stay there long.' Not even then was he satisfied : he insisted that the Prussian Envoys should be recalled from Paris, and concluded with the threat that if 'these rascals, as cowardly on the battlefield as they are arrogant in the wings of a theatre, continue to behave in this manner, the Prussian monarchy won't last long.'

So Hersfeld was pillaged from floor to ceiling for the insult which 'she has offered to sixty of my troops.' Padua fared still worse. 'As for Padua,' he protested, 'if there is any great family there that has conducted itself badly, I wish it to be destroyed from top to bottom, that it may serve for an example in the annals of Padua.' Mercy was completely foreign to his nature. When a charge was brought against General Duhesme, a valiant officer, he had him summoned instantly to Paris. 'If he is innocent,' he exclaimed, 'let him be purged at once; if he be guilty, let him lose his head on the scaffold.' His common policy with offenders was short and sharp. He suppressed the trial, and merely announced that the first time they came within forty leagues of Paris they would be arrested and banished. But he reached a climax in the punishment of two Italians. 'I have received the sentence upon Cifenti and Sassi della Tosa,' he wrote to the Governor of the Castle of Vincennes. 'You will execute the first, who is a miserable spy. As for Sassi della Tosa, I grant him a respite from execution; but you will have him led to the place of punishment, and after the execution of Cifenti, at the moment when Sassi della Tosa should mount the scaffold, you will bid a page appear with the order of release; but I desire that Sassi should have under his eyes the whole example of the punishment for his crime.' It would be difficult to match that in the annals of mediæval France or of modern Russia.

It was in the spirit of the Middle Ages, too, that he interpreted the law of nations. He meant to govern Europe for himself and by himself; and, though he yielded to none in his admiration of useful pomp and proper ceremony, he would tread all the *convenances* underfoot if he deemed it profitable. Other monarchs should display 'the grand manner'—upon that he always insisted. In their dealings with him they should respect the most delicate rules of conduct.

But his own manner was grander still, and he felt it his own peculiar privilege to despise all the ordinances which hitherto had controlled the intercourse of foreign Powers. In his treatment of the Church he went far beyond the licence of that most Christian King, Louis XI., for Louis did no more than hang up a Cardinal in a cage, and Napoleon not only kept a vast colony of imprisoned prelates, but he even dared to kidnap a Pope. Ambassadors fared as ill at his hands as Cardinals. 'My police,' he exclaims in a passage of real magnificence, 'knows not an Ambassador. I am master in my own house.' Nor would he suffer the slightest interference even at the hands of a friendly State. 'I am well enough with Russia,' he acknowledges in a moment of coquetry; 'but I will not accept counsel from her nor from anybody.' Yet, though he would be tyrannical and independent as a Khan of Tartary, he pretended to cherish enlightened views of government. Had he completely subjugated the world, he might even have become a benevolent despot; and it may have been the consciousness that he was fighting against overwhelming odds which bade him persevere in the path of tyranny. 'It is with reason and policy that States are governed,' said he with a touch of scorn, 'not with a bitter and vitiated lymph'; and he hoped, did this imperious overlord, that the publication of the Code Napoleon would mean the end of feudalism. And so it might, had not the door of 'progress' been barred by a sterner monarch than ever feudalism imagined.   His theory of government, if brusque, was efficient : his orders should be obeyed, though obedience meant the ruin of the world.   ' I did not undertake the government of Holland,' he confessed, ' to consult the populace of Amsterdam ' ; and Amsterdam, he thought, should have been content, since it is better to be bullied by the tyranny of genius than disgraced by the prudent futility of the People's elect.

Nowhere may Napoleon's style be better studied than in his prescribed letters.   His style was essentially a style of command, and found a fitting occasion in the arrogant denunciation of his foes. Now, Napoleon was not merely the greatest general of his time; he was master of an eloquence which was the more impressive for its severity.   Before all other men, he had the gift of direct utterance ; he never wasted a word or slurred a thought.   He cut away from his plain, eager statement every ornament that might embellish or confuse, and he conveyed a truth or passed a sentence in naked, irresistible periods.   As you read him, you are caught up in a very whirlwind of command; face to face with this terrific intelligence, which expressed itself with perfect clarity because it never knew doubt, you suffer the fatigue of exhausted wonder ; you shudder at the passionate intensity thrown into half a dozen words.   Blow after blow hits its mark with the surety of a hammer on its anvil.   In a letter addressed to M. de Champagny he comes near to formulating a theory of style. ' Tell the man Lefebvre,' says he, ' that the tone of his despatch is not what it should be to his Minister ; he should try to seize his Minister's intention, and not to make epigrams. Let him follow the direction given, not give a direction of his own. Inform him that after reading the despatch I asked his age, and that it seemed to me to be written by a man of twenty.' In truth it was no part of Napoleon's business to make epigrams : with him eloquence was not a separate art ; it was his policy put into words ; and it received its force from the fact that it was backed by an all-powerful will, which knew neither pity nor hesitation. Yet, personal though it was, it had its origin in the study of the ancients. Its classic severity proceeds directly from Cæsar, from Plutarch, from Livy ; nor can there be any doubt that Napoleon's policy was immensely strengthened by this talent of militant concision.

' Arrest him,' ' shoot him,' ' tell him,' it is in such phrases as these that his commands are expressed. ' I disapprove of your conduct,' he writes to one of his brothers, where another might have expostulated ; and again, he says to Joseph, ' don't answer this letter until Scylla and Reggio are yours.' Above all he excelled in vituperation. No monarch ever addressed his Ministers in so forcible a tone of familiarity. If he distrusts a man, that man instantly becomes a ' coquin ' or a ' polisson.' To-day the Pope is a ' violent madman ' ; to-morrow he has the air of

Sainte-Nitouche; but in all circumstances the priests
of Italy are 'vermin,' and the monks of Spain
mere 'butcher boys.' Fouché has a 'spoiled head'
and Benjamin Constant is a 'cad.' 'Why did you
send General Morio to me?' he asks in a fury;
'he is a kind of ass whom I despise.' Once he
credited Lucien Bonaparte with sense; he revises his
opinion, and pronounces him 'nothing but a fool.'
Blame, blame, blame you find on every page of the
book, and the monotony of sentiment heightens the
effect of persistent authority. In vain you look for
humour or the discussion of common topics. For
Napoleon the external world did not exist, save as the
undiscerned theatre of enterprise. 'It is splendid
weather,' he writes in December from Madrid, 'it is
absolutely the month of May,' and that is his sole
descent from the lofty platform of scornful eloquence
or impassioned command.

Stendhal has said that Napoleon never hated anybody except a Jacobin; and the Emperor's banished
letters abundantly refute this over-amiable judgment.
It would be nearer the truth to declare that he
loathed all men. His correspondence contains a very
gospel of hate. In the first place, he hated stupidity,
and, alas! he encountered it in all those to whom he
entrusted the performance of his designs. Then he
hated opposition by whomsoever offered; and, remembering the superiority of his intelligence, you are not
surprised that his hate expressed itself in a general
irritation. But he reserved for three objects a pecu-

liarly active detestation, and there is hardly a page
in which Madame de Staël, England, and the Pope
do not receive a share of abuse. The Emperor's
furious indignation against the author of *Corinne* is
not easily intelligible, and it certainly gave its victim
an undeserved repute. Had she been left alone to
her little *salon* in the Rue du Bac, she never could
have posed for a shaker of dynasties ; and, if once
the discomfort of exile be set aside, she certainly
gained far more than she lost by Napoleon's perse-
cution. However, this lady, ambitious as she was
to ' collect ' great men, never succeeded in winning
their regard. Byron flouted her, and the Prince de
Ligne, for all her editorial service, could not endure
her presence. But it was her greatest glory to have
aroused the loathing of the great Napoleon, who
pursued her with a tireless zeal.

The attack was begun as early as 1800. ' M. de
Staël,' he writes to the Citizen Joseph, ' is in the
deepest poverty, while his wife gives dinners and
balls. If you continue to see her, could you not
compel this woman to grant her husband an allowance of one or two thousand francs a month ? '
He would have her judged as a man, and pertinently
asks what the world would have thought had the
positions been reversed, and the husband had
left the wife to starve. As yet there is no talk
of exile, though by 1805 she is banished from the
capital as an element of discord. ' She pretends,'
he tells Fouché, ' that I have allowed her to come to

Paris, and she wants to stay there. Let her be off
to Coppet : you know that I am not imbecile enough
to wish her within twenty leagues of Paris.' A
year later he is convinced that this ' coquine ' is
not far off, and again he orders her not to approach
his capital. But her persistence is almost as great as
his own, and in a few months another order is necessary to remove the mischievous intriguer forty leagues
from Paris. In 1807 he despatches another furious
letter. ' Among the thousand and one things which
fall into my hands from Madame de Staël ' (Fouché
is again the recipient), ' this letter will show you what
a good Frenchwoman we have in her. If it were
Prince Louis, our frantic enemy, who compassed the
loss of his monarchy, she would have done her best
to see him. My intention is that she will never leave
Geneva. Let her go, if she likes, with the friends of
Prince Louis. To-day she toadies the great ; to-
morrow she is a patriot and democrat ; and in truth
you cannot curb your indignation when you see all
the forms assumed by this —— ' ; even the French
editor suppresses the word ; and presently the
Emperor consigns her for ever to her Coppet, to her
Genevese, and her Maison Necker.

Nor would he leave her in peace even in that distant
seclusion. He keeps a record of her visitors, and is
ready to treat the slightest friendship with her as a
crime. He falls in an access of rage upon Prince
Augustus of Prussia, whose ill-conduct at Berlin is
reported to him. ' I am not surprised,' he admits to

Marshal Victor, ' for he has no sense. He has passed his time in paying court to Madame de Staël at Coppet, where he could not pick up any but bad principles. . . . Tell him that at the very first word you will have him arrested and shut up in a castle, and that you will send Madame de Staël to console him. *Il n'y a rien de plat comme tous ces Princes de Prusse!* ' You would think that the limit of detestation and contempt was reached, but presently Napoleon devises a more stringent method of suppression. At last he finds the lady in correspondence with one Gentz, who belongs to a gang of shufflers in London. Henceforth banishment is insufficient for her crime. ' I desire that she should be watched at Coppet,' says he to Fouché, ' and you will give the necessary orders to the Prefect of Geneva. A *liaison* with this individual can only be for the detriment of France. You will inform her that hitherto she has only been regarded as mad, but that to-day she enters into a plot against the public tranquillity. I have also ordered my Minister of Foreign Affairs to instruct my agents in foreign Courts, and to have her watched wherever she goes.' But he struck his heaviest blow when she published her book on Germany, the fruit of long exile and deep research. First he demanded whether she had a right to the dignity of Baroness, which was flourished on the title-page, and then he suppressed so many passages that the book did not appear in its proper shape for many years. Such is his campaign against this persistent blue-stocking, and whether she was worth his ceaseless vigilance and his fierce resentment or not, at least he succeeded in the suppression of what he said was a danger to the State.

His hatred of England is more easily intelligible, and far worthier his Imperial majesty. For England was his one serious antagonist, and, despite his loudly expressed contempt, he was unable to conceal from himself her dangerous rivalry. In his eyes she was the general enemy, and nothing but her complete humiliation was necessary to the peace and prosperity of Europe. Wherefore it was his dream to send her to a kind of political Coventry, to exclude her ships from every foreign port, and to make any intercourse with an Englishman a capital offence. With what energy and success he pursued this policy of exclusion is made abundantly clear. A general who dared to receive an Englishman at dinner was in immediate disgrace. The King of Holland was always the enemy of France because he was unable to exclude the ships of Great Britain from his ports. In 1807 the Emperor contemplated a descent upon the recalcitrant island. His fleet, said he, was ready, and a vast army was stationed at Boulogne. Meanwhile he gave orders that all the English diplomatists should be driven from the Courts of Europe, and that the whole Continent should be 'purged' of the enemy's presence.

There was no city, from the Channel to Siberia, where letters were admitted which bore the mark of London. 'Seize them all,' he cried, 'and throw them in the fire.' When Sir Arthur Wellesley began his victorious campaign in the Peninsula, the Emperor denounced the 'impudence' of the English, who should dare to undertake a war on land, and it was long before he would believe in the possibility of defeat. 'The English,' he wrote, 'are in flight, and have sent for ten thousand horses that they may get away the more speedily.' And with his inexhaustible fertility he insisted that this cowardice should be celebrated in caricatures and comic songs, and that the songs should be translated into German and Italian and thrown broadcast over Europe. He goes even further : he suggests articles which should appear in the journals to England's discredit, and even sketches the line that the leader-writer should adopt. Moreover, there was none of English birth in the whole Continent of Europe whom he did not watch with sleepless ferocity. He had as keen a scent for English blood as a hound for a fox. The humblest menial did not escape him. 'There is no reason,' he told the police, 'why M. de Chevreuse should not have a governess for his children, but there is every reason why that governess should not be an Englishwoman.' And straightway she was deported or imprisoned. The policy was spirited, and it failed because it could not be carried out by one man. The world has known but one Napoleon, and it needed a battalion to follow his designs to a successful conclusion.

His hatred of the Church was yet more bitter and

contemptuous. The Pope must recognise his supremacy, and give an implicit belief to his Divine headship of the world, or the Pope was meaner than the
meanest huckster.   Napoleon was as little hampered
by an old-fashioned respect as by an old-fashioned
morality ; and it is noteworthy that he reserved his
choicest scorn for the Church to which his subjects
bowed the willing, reverential knee.   And here he
showed his greatest courage, his loudest arrogance.
Whatever was the creed, religion, or superstition, he
put his iron Imperial heel upon it when it threatened
to thwart the smallest of his schemes.   His feud with
the Pope began early, and ended only when the Pope
and all his Cardinals submitted to defeat.   The first
blow was struck in the Year x., when his Holiness
declined to secularise Citizen Talleyrand.   The
Consul insisted.   He pronounced it a measure
agreeable to the Government of France and to the
dignity of the Church, and he fortified his opinion
with an array of precedents, from the fifteenth, the
sixteenth, and the seventeenth centuries, which must
have astounded the Holy Father.

When his troops entered Rome he beat opposition
aside with a scornful admirable cynicism. ' My troops
have entered Rome,' he wrote ; ' it is useless to speak
of it, but if any one mentioned it to you, say that, the
Pope being the head of my country's religion, it is
proper that I should assure myself of the direction
du spirituel ; it is not an extension of territory, it is
prudence.'   As for the sanctity of priests and Car-

dinals, he knew not what it meant. 'If they behave badly,' he wrote to Cardinal Fesch, 'I shall punish them far more rigorously than ordinary citizens, since they are better educated, and their character is more holy. As for the rest of your letter, I see in it nothing more than the effect of a delirious imagination, and I advise you and all others who create such monsters, as only exist in their own imaginations, to take cold baths.' The Cardinals moderating their zeal in cold baths! Was ever the Church so roughly entreated?

But this was only the beginning of the campaign. When the Pope excommunicated him, he turned the tables with a laugh of scorn. 'The excommunication,' said he, with a magnificent disregard, 'is aimed at himself. No more parleyings; he is a furious madman who must be shut up.' Nor would he yield to the Pope in a knowledge of divinity. 'I am a better theologian than the lot of them,' he boasted. 'I shall not cross the line; but I shall take good care that no one else crosses it either.' A few years later he summed up in a phrase the whole drift of his teaching. 'Was it to curse sovereigns,' he asks, 'that Jesus Christ was crucified?' And not even the Pope could find in his heart an answer to that sally. Thus all the clergy fared badly at his hands. 'Inform the Bishop of Gand,' he writes to his *Ministre des Cultes*, 'that I am displeased with the manner in which he governs his diocese, with his weakness, and with the small attachment that he manifests for my person.' Cardinals and priests he arrested by the hundred, and the prisons of Italy were filled with them. At one moment five hundred were shut up in Parma, and with a grim humour he ordered their distribution. ' Send two hundred to Bologna,' he suggested ; ' they will be very well there.' And all the while he regarded himself as the head of the Church, as of the world ; and when he carried the Pope to Fontainebleau, his excuse was cynically worthy the occasion. ' It is right that he should be at the head of Christianity,' he told Fouché; ' the first few months it will be a novelty, but that will soon finish.' Yet, although the Pope was at the head of Christianity, he was still a prisoner, kept under the strictest surveillance ; his letters were read and opened as though he were an Englishman, and his faithful Cardinals were secretly arrested by dead of night, and carried to a discreet distance beyond the borders of Paris.

Nowhere, in fact, did Napoleon show his disregard of history and tradition so candidly as in this firm treatment of the Church. He had more monks, priests, cardinals, and bishops under lock and key than he could count. He had set himself to achieve the mastery of the world, and nothing was allowed to impede his march. His daring outstripped the bravest conceptions of Cæsar or of Alexander. He invented a new world for himself, like Shakespeare, and, like Shakespeare, tore it to pieces that he might have no worthy followers. England, the Pope, Madame de Staël—how he hated them all ! And if

only he had trampled England into the same mire
wherein he flung the Church, he never would have
seen the coastline of St. Helena. A man has only
one brain and two hands, and not even Napoleon
could do the work of a thousand. His brothers could
not help him, and herein lay his deepest tragedy.
He loved Louis and he loved Joseph, and he believed
that the blood which flowed in their veins was the
blood that flowed in his. But what had he, the
greatest monster of the modern world, to do with
brothers or cousins or uncles ? He stood by himself,
and lived his own life, and grumbled ever at the inevitable failure of others. The letters addressed to the
King of Holland are pathetic in their misery. 'Are
you the ally of England or of France ? ' he asked
piteously; 'I do not know.' Louis has not 'the
grand manner.' How should he, poor devil ? 'The
future grandeur of your people is in your hands,' he
wrote another time. 'If you govern by jeremiads,
you will furnish me with nothing more than the
miserable 6000 men that are in Hanover, and you will
be more useless than the Duke of Baden.' Louis
was helpless even after such a letter. The final
appeal, *de l'énergie, de l'énergie*, fell upon an ear
deafened by his people's indifference, and he could
but listen despairingly to the monumental postscript :
'It is only by braving the opinion of the weak and
ignorant that you can assure the good of your people.'

But it was Jérome who received the stateliest reproof, and who was honoured by the letters of most

eloquent reproach. ' In war,' wrote Napoleon from
Schönbrunn, ' there is neither the brother of the
Emperor, nor the King of Westphalia, but a general
who commands his corps.' And on the same day he
sends another letter : ' You are King and brother
to an Emperor, qualities ridiculous in war. You must
be *soldat, et puis soldat, et encore soldat.* You need
neither Minister, nor diplomatists, nor pomp ; you
must bivouac with your advance-guard, you must
be day and night in the saddle, you must march with
your advance-guard to get news ; or else you must
stay with your seraglio. You make war like a satrap.'
Does not that reproof come like a thunder-clap ?
And the contrast between himself and his brother is
still more eloquent. ' The trade of soldier and the
trade of courtier are far apart. I was scarcely your
age when I had conquered the whole of Italy and
had beaten Austrian armies three times as numerous
as my own. But I had neither flatterers nor diplomatists in my suite. I made war like a soldier ;
there is no other way of making it. I did not pretend
to be brother to an emperor or king ; I did all that I
must to beat the enemy.' Thus it was to his brothers
that he sent his austerest passages of prose. And
Jérome he signalled out for favour above the rest.
' My friend, I love you,' he set in his own handwriting
at the end of a stern reproach ; ' but you are *furieuse-
ment jeune.* Keep Siméon and Beugnot without oath
at least another year. *Alors comme alors !* '

Alors comme alors ! And when failure and defeat

overwhelmed him, it was still of his brothers that he thought. In a tragic letter addressed to Madame Mère he insists that Louis should stand by the throne, already in peril, as a French prince ; and with Europe invaded he makes the same demand of Joseph. History cannot show more deeply impassioned, more closely reasoned appeals than these, made to the loyalty of brothers on the eve of his ruin. And his grasp of details weakened no more than his dignity. To the very end he would control the world, and show himself the supreme hero that he was. 'To-day, as at Austerlitz,' he wrote to Joseph from Reims, 'I am master.' His will was not equal to circumstances, and having sent back the Pope, and having recommended economy to every one, he was forced to retire to Elba. During the Hundred Days he pursued the countless occupations which, perhaps, had diverted his genius ; once more he picked up the myriad threads of government. With his brain distracted by the appointment of prefects and the control of the police, how should he design his last campaign ? Yet even after Waterloo he was not hopeless. 'All is not lost,' he assured Joseph. Within three days he believed he could put himself at the head of 50,000 men. Above all, he exclaimed, *du courage et de la fermeté*. It was too late for firmness or courage. Napoleon had fallen, and with his fall there died that renowned style, which found its sanction in limitless power, and which for brutality and persuasiveness cannot be matched in the literature of the world.

LORD MELBOURNE

A LEISURED study of letters and documents cannot but revise many of the world's judgments. Political opinions are based of necessity upon an imperfect foundation. We believe that we know what this man thought from the words he spoke—often a baseless assumption. We know from the records what that man did. The motives which induced the thought or the action, too often evade us. We are wont to mistake the compulsion of circumstances for malice. We arrive at a half-truth, which is far more misleading than a whole lie. And then the revelation of documents flashes upon us. The dark places are illumined. The lamp of justice shines with equal brilliance on the overpraised and the misunderstood. And only the honourable man, only the upright Minister, fears not the discovering hand of time.

Of all those who during the first twenty-five years of the Queen's reign were called to advise her, none survives the ordeal of knowledge so triumphantly as Lord Melbourne. Research does but embellish his character. His dignity, his intelligence, his perfect fairness of mind, are made, by the passage of time, increasingly evident. And it was not the least of the

Queen's good fortune to ascend the throne under
the auspices of so brave and faithful a Minister.   For
Melbourne had none of the vices of the politician.
He had measured more accurately than any of his
contemporaries the strength and weakness of all
governments.   He knew with the certainty of intelligence that the pulse of the country beat with a better
strength outside than inside the House of Commons.
He recognised the plain truth that no policy, not even
if it were a policy of revolution, had one-tenth of the
influence which its eager, narrow-minded advocates
ascribed to it.   If he adopted the profession of
statesmanship, it was because that profession was, in
the early nineteenth century, best adapted to his
position and his talent.   The son of a rich man and a
peer, he seemed destined to the profession of affairs.
Brought up in a house which regarded Charles James
Fox as nothing less than divine, he naturally espoused
the cause of the Whigs.   That his own sympathy was
opposed to this course mattered nothing to him.   He
devoutly believed that an English gentleman owed
his first duty to the tradition of his house.   He might
have gone over to the other side, with which he was
in closest accord, had he not been restrained by the
habit and loyalty of years.   Yet, with one interval,
in which he served under the banner of Canning, he
fought the battle of the Whigs with all his force and
with what sincerity he might.

Acutely conscious of his inconsistency, he justified
his action with an honest cynicism.   ' In politics,'

he wrote once, ' you may serve the cause of wisdom
and justice better by remaining with those to whom
you have attached yourself, even after you disapprove of much of their conduct and prefer that of
their adversaries, than by leaving them.' It is not a
counsel of perfection ; but Melbourne knew that
perfection was inaccessible to modern statesmanship.
It is not the gospel of idealism, but Melbourne never
concealed from himself the plain truth that idealists
might be a danger to the State. It is even a hazard-
ous doctrine, which has been used by the dishonest
to cover up many disreputable acts and shameful com-
promises. But it is not without a certain common
sense, which more than once has saved England from
revolution, and enabled a prudent driver to put the
drag upon the coach wheel when he approached a
sudden and precipitous declivity.

For though Melbourne called himself a Whig, he
did not share the vices of his class. He did not exult
in the misfortunes of England when he had outgrown
his callow youth. The hatred which Fox and Lord
Holland professed for their own country was repugnant
to his sense of honour. He did not detect in Napoleon
the saviour of the human race merely because his
armies threatened the existence of Great Britain.
He agreed with Pitt that, even if reform had been
good in itself, it was monstrous to propose it in a
time of war, and in a most luminous passage he protested against inapposite legislation.

' One great difference,' he wrote, ' between the

conduct of the reformers of the present day and those
of the days of Charles 1. is that the latter chose a
period of perfect tranquillity and security from external enemies—a period when almost all foreign
nations were by their own distractions disabled from
interfering with England—for putting into execution
their schemes of amelioration. The former exclaimed against grievances, and pressed the most vital
measures at a moment when the power and inveteracy
of France threatened our existence as an independent
nation.'

The wisdom of these words is strongly at variance
with the faith and practice of the Whigs. It was at
the very moment of threatened disaster that Fox
acclaimed the majesty of the people. It was when
Napoleon was universally triumphant that the
Jacobins of England demanded annual parliaments
and manhood suffrage. Instead of standing in solid
order against the foe, the Friends of the People
thought it becoming to embarrass the hands of those
who were protecting them against invasion by making
insolent demands and clamouring for a false thing
called Freedom. But Melbourne would not for an
instant tolerate such treason as this. Though his
party was pledged to conciliate the democracy, reform
was always repugnant to him, and it was the supreme
irony of his career that he was in office in 1832. His
conservative instincts rebelled fiercely against the
policy of Lord Grey. He ' really believed that there
was no strong feeling in the country for the measure '

of reform. He objected strongly to the abolition of
the rotten boroughs, which he regarded as a bulwark
against the encroaching mob. He would not, if he
could help it, have enfranchised the big boroughs
such as Manchester. Yet he bowed before the storm
of popular opinion, and aided the passage of a measure
of which he gravely disapproved.

The motive of his action was generally misunderstood. His contemporaries seem to have believed
that he yielded to his colleagues ' because it suited
his ease and convenience to do so, and because he was
actuated by no strong political principles or opinions.'
This is not true. It was not ease and convenience
which persuaded him to take an uncongenial path.
As has been said, he did not like to depart from his
allegiance. In a letter to the Queen, he once quoted,
with manifest approval, Napoleon's saying, *un gentil-
homme ne change jamais la religion*, and he applied this
principle, less worthily, to statesmanship. He knew
that his party was following an evil path, and he
would not desert it. He thought, with his customary
cynicism, that ' it was more necessary to stand by his
friends when they were in the wrong than when they
were in the right,' and he did his utmost to get the
unwelcome question answered and set aside.

And he stood by them after his own characteristic
fashion. While his colleagues in and out the House
let off the glittering fireworks of their eloquence,
prating of Freedom and the Rights of Man, he remained sternly in the Home Office, and took care

that those whom he was helping to make free and independent electors should not too clamorously assert their privileges. He rigorously suppressed the first signs of sedition, and would not permit those about to become citizens to anticipate the sweets of liberty. And when the Bill was passed he was still uneasy. ' I do not myself much like the complexion of the public meetings of constituents,' he wrote to his brother in 1833, ' of which I read in the newspapers. They seem to me to be very violent, and to be demanding pledges in a very positive manner, which are given rather too readily and to a too great extent.' He recognised that the harm was done, and he resolved that he would take no other hand in the game of revolution. ' There is no knowing to what one may be led by circumstances,' said he ; ' but at present I am determined to make my stand here, and not to advance any further '—a vain boast, for no man can, when he will, put a spoke in the wheel of what is called progress.

The truth is, that Melbourne rejected in a block all the doctrines of the Radical. He had a natural and a wholesome dislike of change. When Lord John Russell desired to express his restlessness in some tinkering of the constitution, Melbourne was content to ask : ' Why not leave it alone ? ' He saw in the ballot nothing but an opportunity of chicane and intrigue. He urged those who would have made experiments in education to ' moderate their zeal,' pointing out to them, with perfect wisdom, ' examples of men who, without education, had made good their advancement in life.' In other words, he looked upon facts with an honest eye. He did not pretend even to himself that an Act of Parliament could atone for the sloth and carelessness of the individual. He knew by experience that a lofty position could be held only by right of conquest, and that they did a disservice to others who made the road of advance too easy. In brief, he shrank from sentimentality wherever he found it. He abhorred high-sounding talk and insincere professions. 'Nobody ever did anything very foolish except from some strong principle,' said he, thus anticipating the supreme folly of the generation which succeeded his own. Similarly he mistrusted doctrinaires in politics or religion. 'I do not like the Dissenters,' he once wrote. 'They are more zealous, and consequently more intolerant, than the Established Church. Their only object is power.'

How abundantly has our subsequent experience justified this sound opinion! On the other hand, his assumed indifference was never caused by a lack of zeal for England. He was a staunch patriot, to whom the treasonable practices of his friends were always distasteful. Much as he hesitated to reveal his emotions, he took alarm openly if war or disaster threatened. In 1840 he was so anxiously disturbed by the state of affairs in Europe that he could not eat nor drink nor sleep. In a moment the idleness which he assumed was laid aside, and he was ready to sacrifice his ease, his life even, for the sake of his country. And this is the paradox of his career. He was a patriot who saw the danger of change. He acknowledged that reform was unattended with any of the benefits expected from it ; that the appetite of revolt grew in eating ; and that in the end the constitution would be threatened. And he supported reform because he was called a Whig, and because his party demanded his aid.

The paradox is not so great as it appears at first sight. Melbourne's career was made possible only by his temperament. He possessed that acute intelligence which sees the good and bad on either side, and which naturally inclines to moderation. The great master of men, the leader of forlorn hopes, cannot succeed without a grain of stupidity. He cannot reach the pinnacle of courage or conviction if he understands the reason of his adversary's action as well as of his own. Melbourne's strength was his weakness also. He knew so much that he was too often reduced to a condition of stable equilibrium. Above all, his knowledge and interest were not limited by politics. There was no province of human skill or intelligence which he did not regard with an eager curiosity. He was deeply read in many literatures. He had studied the poets and historians of Greece and Rome with an acute understanding. He could illustrate the events of his own day by the experience of Thucydides. He scorned translations, and read Herodotus, for example, in the original, with great profit to himself. And he could discourse with a ready eloquence of what he knew.

None of those who frequented Holland House shone in conversation with a radiance equal to Melbourne's. He was neither pedantic, like Allen, nor greedy, like Macaulay. Greville is an eager witness of his prowess. ' Melbourne's excellent scholarship and universal information,' he writes, ' remarkably display themselves in society, and he delivers himself with an energy which shows how deeply his mind is impressed with literary subjects.' His judgment kept pace with his energy. It is impossible to read his comments upon literature without a profound respect for his taste and enterprise. Nor did the stress of office interfere with his devotion to humane letters. In the very crisis of 1832 he solaced his leisure by studying the tracts of Gosson, Stubbes, and Heywood concerning the abuses of the theatre. With the same intelligence he gave himself to theology, in which he was profoundly versed, and he was thus able to discourse of religion, which he loved to do, with authority and moderation. But, in truth, nothing came amiss to him, and he remained a student unto the end of his life. He knew the danger of thus ' pursuing ' knowledge, and with his usual candour made ample confession of it. ' I have read too much, and too little,' he said. ' So much that it has extinguished all the original fire of my genius, and yet not enough to furnish me with the power of writing books of mature thinking and solid instruction.' He need have harboured no regret. He read not for others, but for himself and for reading's sake, and he was thus able to look upon politics with the broad and tolerant eye which few politicians may boast.

It may be said that in many pursuits he dissipated his energies. That is true enough. In fact, he might be described as what was known to the eighteenth century as a lounger. He passed easily from one age, from one book, to another. He changed his diligence with his humour. But he was a lounger of activity. He was diligent always, and, as he said himself, he looked back with remorse only to those hours which he had spent in sleep and sauntering. And with his lounging habit was associated in men's minds a kind of nonchalance which he affected. Greville declared that he was ' habitually careless and *insouciant* ' ; and he hated squabbles and contests so bitterly that he would avoid them sometimes at a loss of dignity or decision. Talleyrand interpreted this temper with a gentle irony. Melbourne, he said, is ' *trop camarade* for a Prime Minister.' Wellington's testimony, though not so briefly expressed, is to the same purpose. Melbourne, he said, ' was a man apt to treat matters too lightly, or *poco curante*, but in the main an honest and an honourable man.' That seems rather to underrate the Minister's excellent qualities. At the same time, it may be admitted that Melbourne encouraged a general opinion of indifference.

His contempt of fuss persuaded him to wear a cloak

oι carelessness. He refused to detect a gravity in
trivial things. He persistently esteemed politics at
their proper value. It was not his habit to pretend
that an Act of Parliament would bring into being a
new heaven and a new earth. This habit irritated
his more pompous colleagues, and being known to the
world brought him into an unmerited discredit.
Men lacking in humour were busy with reproach
against a philosophic temper which they could not
understand. Once upon a time—it was in 1841—
Lord John Russell proposed to substitute a fixed
duty of 8s. on wheat for a graduated duty. To the
proposer this measure appeared to be of the highest
import, and he expected it to be received with
becoming solemnity. And then Melbourne poured
upon Lord John's enthusiasm the cold water of his
wit. ' By the bye,' said he on leaving the room,
' there is one thing we haven't agreed upon, which
is, what we are to say. Is it to make our corn dearer
or cheaper, or to make the price steady ? I don't
care which, but we had better all be in the same
story.' And this is not Melbourne's highest achievement in *insouciance*. It is reported, on sound
authority, that once, when he was Prime Minister, he
fell asleep at a Cabinet meeting. This feat is probably unrivalled.

In private as in public Melbourne had rid himself
of the common superstitions. If he had ever felt
the impulses of jealousy or malice, he did not for an
instant betray their influence. He was a practical

philosopher, who took all things for granted. He
had learned the lesson which few are able to learn,
that nothing external to himself debased or im-
poverished his soul. And he was able to endure the
blows of fortune with a light heart. For instance,
he regarded the eccentricities of his wife with a noble
detachment. He judged her faithlessness—if so
harsh a word as ' judgment ' may be used—with the
amiable indulgence which might be expected of a
wholly disinterested adviser. He overlooked the
scandal of Lord Byron and *Glenarvon*, silently and
without reproach. And when Lady Caroline's extravagant humours made life under the same roof with
her intolerable, he left her with a genuine regret.
Her last hours were solaced by his presence, and her
brother paid the highest tribute to his magnanimity.
' William Lamb,' said he, ' behaved throughout as I
always knew he would.' But this magnanimity did
not proceed from a lack of dignity or a too easy-
going good humour. It was the result of a very
candid and evenly balanced mind. Melbourne saw
both faces of life, as he saw both faces of politics, and
being (as has been said) a practical philosopher, he
recognised that there was not a vast difference
between this face and that. At any rate, it was not
for him to pass sentence, and since the subtlety of
his brain eluded his contemporaries, it is not surprising that his actions were ascribed to a culpable
apathy.

His practical philosophy naturally encouraged a

love of paradox. The polite society of Holland House, used as it was to the bigotry of Allen, was surprised at times, or even shocked, at the unexpected flashes of Melbourne's wit. And as he dealt in irony [1] as well as in paradox, it is not strange that he was commonly misunderstood. His sayings were quoted as though it were his sole object to frighten the Philistines. When Prince Albert insisted that ' a closer line should be drawn ' in the matter of appointments, Melbourne complained that ' that damned morality would undo us all.' His meaning is clear enough, but the words, used, contrary to his intention, in their literal significance, might easily be turned to his discredit. The truth is, he hated humbug and hypocrisy wherever he found them, and his sense of picturesqueness persuaded him very often to overstate his case. But this over-statement was but another expression of his virtue and honesty ; and though England has known some greater Ministers than Melbourne, she has put her trust in few innately wiser or more simply devoted to her interests.

---

[1] Of his paradoxes only the merest echo is heard. An example of his irony is quoted from a commonplace book in Mr. Lloyd Sanders's excellent edition of his *Papers*. ' Give every subject and every expression, if you can, an indecent turn,' he wrote, remembering Swift ; ' that makes a witty man. Impute to every action a base or wicked motive ; that makes a profound and sagacious man. Act without regard to times and circumstances in a manner which is best calculated to defeat your own objects ; that makes an incorrupt and honest man.'

By temperament and training, then, Melbourne was perfectly fitted to guide the footsteps of a young Queen. He was in the highest sense a man of the world, without prejudice or disguise, and he gladly accepted the charge which fortune had put into his hands. Nor has history revealed to us a wiser education of a monarch than this. The first volume of the Queen's *Letters* is not unlike a modern *Cyropædeia*. Melbourne forgot nothing which should improve the natural talent of Queen Victoria. He was ready with advice on all subjects, and on all occasions. Not merely did he teach her the first lessons of statecraft ; he gave her his opinions freely concerning literature, theology, and history. Now he tells her what he thinks of Adolphus's *History*, and recommends Horace Walpole's *Letters* by way of illustration. Now he declares that ' Hallam is right about Ireland,' and that ' her advocates are very loud in their outcry, but she has not really very much to complain of '—two simple truths which were abundantly confirmed in the course of the Queen's reign. In one letter he comments with severity and good sense upon Macaulay's *Essay on Madame d'Arblay* ; in another he discourses pleasantly and plainly upon *As You Like It*, and recalls the excellence of Mrs. Jordan in the part of Rosalind.

Thus he brought into the palace a breath of his own humanity and humour. His letters are not mere formal state papers. They are alive and alert with the writer's sound sense, and not unillumined

by the writer's flippancy. Above all, he did his best
to instruct the Queen in the mysteries of character,
and to inspire her with something of his own
moderation. When, in 1839, she was loud in her
reprobation of Peel, Melbourne counselled a better
opinion. 'Lord Melbourne earnestly entreats your
Majesty,' he wrote, 'not to suffer yourself to be
affected by any faultiness of manner which you may
observe. Depend upon it, there is no personal
hostility to Lord Melbourne, nor any bitter feeling
against him. Sir Robert is the most cautious and
reserved of mankind. Nobody seems to Lord Melbourne to know him, but he is not therefore deceitful
or dishonest. Many a very false man has a very open,
sincere manner, and *vice versâ.*' The moderation of
this advice matches its loyalty, and no better words
could be spoken in the ear of one whose business it
was to mitigate the stress of party politics.

Between the Queen and her favourite Minister
the sympathy and understanding were complete.
From the first she recognised in the Minister 'a
straightforward, honest, and good man.' She confessed that he was 'to her quite a parent.' Again
and again she expresses her high appreciation of his
service and talents. 'The more I see him,' she
wrote, 'the more confidence I have in him. . . . He
is of the greatest use to me both politically and
privately.' And the Queen's affection and regard
were faithfully reciprocated. Greville says that Melbourne looked upon the Queen as he might have looked

upon a daughter if he had had one. He felt the inevitable separation most acutely. In 1845, we are told, he could not mention the Queen's name without tears coming into his eyes. Nor did the Queen yield to him in sorrow. Melbourne's resignation was the first blow which she was asked to bear. And she did not minimise its weight. 'The Queen thinks Ld. Melbourne may possibly wish to know how she is this morning'—thus she wrote in 1839. 'The Queen is somewhat calmer : she was in a wretched state till nine o'clock last night, when she tried to occupy herself and to think less gloomily of this dreadful change, and she succeeded in calming herself till she went to bed at twelve, and she slept well ; but on waking this morning all—all that had happened in one short uneventful day, came most forcibly to her mind, and brought back her grief.' And when Peel succeeded Melbourne in office, the Queen insisted that she should still be permitted to exchange letters with her old adviser—a privilege which, despite the suspicious voice of rumour, neither Queen nor Minister misused.

Thus till Melbourne's death the unequal friendship was zealously maintained. The statesman's visits to Windsor were always recorded by the Queen with a kind of joyousness. 'Good Lord Melbourne was here from Saturday till this morning,' we read in a letter dated 1843, 'looking very well. I almost fancied happy old times were returned ; but alas ! the dream is passed'—as none knew better than Melbourne, who confessed that he ' continually missed and regretted the time when he had daily confidential communications with your Majesty.' His loneliness, indeed, was unrelieved, and the repeal of the Corn Laws made it increasingly difficult for the old confidence to be renewed. Like the stern Conservative that he was, Melbourne wished to leave things as they were. He feared the violent change of policy, of which not even its enthusiastic supporters could see the end. Above all, he thought that Peel had betrayed his party. Greville sketches a curious scene at Windsor, and there is no reason to doubt its verisimilitude. ' It was at dinner,' says he, ' when Lord Melbourne was sitting next to the Queen. Some allusion was made to passing events and to the expected measure, when Melbourne suddenly broke out, " Ma'am, it is a damned dishonest act." The Queen laughed, and tried to quiet him, but he repeated, " I say it is a very dishonest act " ; and then he continued a tirade against the abolition of the Corn Laws, the people not knowing how to look, and the Queen only laughing.' Though the difference of opinion did not impair the Queen's regard for Melbourne, it made his presence at Windsor an embarrassment ; and he was driven back more and more to the books which he loved well, and knew well how to read.

The last years of Melbourne's life were years of gathering gloom. He did not easily endure the change from strength to weakness. Greville said that he seemed ' to bear on his face a perpetual consciousness of glory obscured.' A spark of irony flashes now and again in his letters, as when he assures the Queen that he has been reading ' Cicero on Old Age—a very pretty treatise, but he does not find much consolation after it.' He was tired, he was out of the world, which he had dominated by his wisdom and his wit, and the seclusion of age irked him. Yet he might have found some comfort in the thought that his work was done, and that, though the Queen listened to other counsellors, he had taught her such lessons of life and politics as the years even of her long reign would not wholly efface.

SIR JAMES GRAHAM

THE fact that Sir James Graham has already passed
from the memory of man is an eloquent comment upon the insecurity of political fame. For thirty
years he assisted at the councils of the nation. He
held high office in many administrations. He was
warmly praised by men of all parties, to most of which
he had belonged in the course of a long career. He
was at once the friend of Croker and of Lord John
Russell. For many years he was the chief support
of Sir Robert Peel. After Peel's death Disraeli invited him to take command of the reunited Conservatives and Peelites. In 1852 Roebuck ' looked to
him to be the leader of the Liberal party.' Mr. Gladstone often told Sir Algernon West that ' he considered Sir James the greatest administrator of his
time, and the only statesman whose merits never
received due recognition from the Press.' On four
occasions Sir James declined the Governorship-
General of India. ' The more I study that generation,' says Mr. Morley, ' the more do I incline to put
Sir James Graham in the very front for sagacity, pure
sense of public duty, and for moral depth of character,
all in combination.' This chorus of praise might be

infinitely swelled. Yet this enthusiasm has met with no popular response. *Laudatur et alget*—he is acclaimed, and grows cold with the coldness of oblivion. And his career, as set forth in Mr. Parker's well-edited and impartial biography, puts, if it does not answer, the question : Why is the glory of statesmen as short-lived as the glory of actors or of bishops ?

Oblivion overtakes them because, in the first place, they are not of so vast an importance as they appear to their colleagues and to their generation. Countries are governed by accident or by one man. Secretaries of State and First Lords play their part in the public pageant ; they hold too large a space in the general esteem while they are alive ; and posterity takes its customary revenge, and forgets them when they are gone. Nor is posterity wholly unfair in taking this revenge. The compensation is accurately esteemed, and in the end a rough justice is done. But there is a second reason why the world should have a short memory for such public servants as Sir James Graham. Fame is a sort of scandal, which does not attach itself to the merely virtuous, uninventive man. He who would catch the public eye must be consciously or unconsciously something of a histrion. The easiest method by which a politician may acquire immortality is to create a legend of himself. When once this is done the rest is easy. He assumes a shape and form which the people comprehends ; presently he answers to a familiar nickname ; and he dies in the glad con-

viction that he has won a lasting place in the history
of his country.

Some statesmen create their own legends, some
have legends thrust upon them. All are legendary
or forgotten. Even Pitt, the least vividly personal of
Ministers, survives in the general esteem as a model
of precocity and devotion. Of Fox, the pleasure-
loving gambler, who, in Landor's phrase, ' to the
principles of a Frenchman added the habits of a
Malay,' the world has preserved a very clear image.
His portly figure, his slovenly clothes, his amazing
hat, are more familiar to the present age than his lack
of principle and his hatred of his country. And as we
come down to our own time, the intensity of this
popular portraiture increases. The legend of Disraeli was most carefully prepared by the artist himself.
He understood the craft of life well enough to know
that unless he attracted attention his merits would
never be discussed. He was fighting a battle, as
none recognised more plainly than he, against a close
order and a suspicious class. A Jew without wealth,
he aspired to lead the nobles of England, and success
could never have been his had he not touched the
imagination and won the support of the people. For
this end the dandyism of his early years, the curled
locks, the chains in which he was hanged, were all
nicely calculated. When he was firmly seated in the
throne of power he contemptuously threw aside these
adjuncts of frivolity. But he never disdained the
common artifices of glory, and he reached the summit

of his ambition by a path which he understood better and despised more bitterly than most of his colleagues could despise or understand it.

Gladstone, never an artist like his rival, stumbled by accident upon a legend of universality. There was nothing he could not do, save make himself intelligible. And his very unintelligibility was a source of strength. There is a story told concerning him in Sir James Graham's *Life* so apt to my purpose that I make no scruple of using it to interpret my argument. Once upon a time—it was in 1845—Mr. Gladstone was minded to resign. Accordingly he wrote to Sir Robert Peel, marked the letter ' secret,' and by a characteristic perversity sent it *open* to the Minister. As Sir Robert said, ' it might have been read in every post office through which it had passed.' Graham's comment upon this adventure is wisely apposite. ' Gladstone's omission to seal such a letter,' says he, ' was most unfortunate ; but the enigmatical style has its advantages. I doubt whether there is a post-master in England who after reading the letter would understand one word of it.' Thus it was that Gladstone stood before the country for fifty years as an unanswered enigma. The fact that the enigma had no answer did not lessen its profundity in the public mind. The great statesman's eye rolled, his voice trembled, and though his speech corresponded in no respect to these expressions of emotion, his audience confessed with a frank delight that he was speaking over its head. The fact that he had said nothing which he had not qualified, that he had made no statement unguarded by ' ifs ' and ' ans,' eluded his perplexed admirers. They mistook their candour for his perspicuity, and believed that their failure to understand the unintelligible was a clear proof of their own inferiority.

But, well as this enigmatic reputation served Mr. Gladstone, it was the universality of his genius upon which his legend was based. He was an Admirable Crichton, to whom no enterprise came amiss. The most industrious man of his generation, he always sought leisure in doing something else. He could cut down trees and talk about Homer. He could discuss theology and turn English hymns into Latin. He was as many-sided as Cicero, and completely imbued with the spirit of journalism, though he was not, like the Roman orator, a man of letters. Thus the legend of Gladstone grew and prospered. He had become the hero of a fairy story long before his death—to these an ogre, to those a spirit of beneficence. His supporters worshipped him ; his colleagues feared him ; his opponents were conscious of the danger with which his legendary magnificence threatened the country. And his career illustrates the peculiar risk to which every democracy is exposed. The people adores not a man, but an idol which represents the man to its twisted intelligence. Unable to judge aright, it bows the knee to a nickname, an abstraction, or a bold advertisement. And the necessity of a legend increases with the increasing strength of the populace—for it is to the mob that a politician must make appeal. The hustings are his stage. His first business is not to serve his country, but to present himself in a fantastic shape to the democracy. The newspapers, which have wisely decided to suppress his speeches, eagerly chronicle the cut of his coat, his wife's tea-parties, and his success or failure at the sport which he affects. In other words, they treat him as they treat the actor; and it cannot be said that any of the demagogues who have pretended to govern the destinies of England got any worse treatment than they deserve.

These considerations help us to understand the eclipse of Sir James Graham. He was sternly incapable of inventing a legend or of awaking the fancy of the people. He appealed to the world as a plain man who did his duty, hoping for no other reward than the satisfaction of his conscience and the approval of his colleagues. A certain roughness in controversy was the only mark which might have distinguished him, but from the beginning to the end of a somewhat complicated career he rarely called attention to himself. At one moment—in 1844—he was involved in the scandal which, as I have said, comes very near to being fame. Knowing that Mazzini was the centre of a conspiracy against the Italian Government, Sir James Graham authorised the opening of his letters. He was instantly assailed with the utmost bitterness. It was proposed to prosecute him for usurping a power which, it was alleged, did not belong

to him. The Press espoused the cause of Mazzini
and his friends, and Graham was at last persuaded
to submit the question to secret committees of the
Lords and Commons. The committees approved
the practice of opening letters when the public peace
demanded it, declared that they would see the
authority abolished with the utmost reluctance, and
placed it on record that the power had been very
sparingly exercised, and never from personal or party
motives.

Graham, of course, had done no more than his duty ;
but he did not escape obloquy. The opinion of the
whole Radical party, which has a natural sympathy
with conspirators, was inflamed against him ; and
until the end he was forced to bear a heavy and undeserved burden of reproach. Ten years later he
again flashed vividly before the world. At a dinner
given to Sir Charles Napier in 1854 he made a speech,
as candid as it was indiscreet, for which he was called
gravely to account. ' My gallant friend Sir Charles
Napier '—thus spoke Graham—' says that when he
goes into the Baltic he will declare war. I, as First
Lord of the Admiralty, give my free consent to do so.
I hope that the war may be short and that it may be
sharp.' This incredibly foolish explosion was made
some weeks before the declaration of war, and most
men agreed with Greville in finding it ' marvellous
that a man of mature age, who had been nearly forty
years in public life, should be so rash and ill-judged
in his speeches.'

These are the two bright spots upon an industrious and uniform career. From one point of view Sir James Graham was a model Minister. None knew better than he how to transact business with promptitude and despatch. He filled many offices with credit, and though we may well question the wisdom of his actions, his loyalty and unselfishness are above reproach. A statesman who four times refused to govern India cannot be charged with mistaking private ambition for the service of his country. And Sir James Graham clearly embarked upon politics not for his own profit, but from a sense of duty. I have said that his career was uniform. Uniform it was in devotion, not in party. In the course of thirty years Sir James made acquaintance, so to say, with every corner of the House. He had combined in his single brain all the opinions. He helped Lord Grey to pass the Reform Bill of 1832. Lord John Russell's lack of respect for the Protestant Church drove him into the arms of Peel, whose lieutenant he was in the campaign against the Corn Laws. When the cry of Protection was no longer heard, he might have led the Conservatives to victory; and finally he became a Liberal of the official kind, though he distrusted Palmerston, and did not always look upon affairs with the eyes of Lord John Russell. As Mr. Parker puts it, ' he had been Conservative Liberal, Liberal Conservative, Conservative and Liberal.' We need not criticise the illogicality of the succession. After all, consistency is the least attractive of the virtues. But

Sir James Graham's progress from one opinion to another explains his unpopularity. Politicians dislike a renegade far more bitterly than an active foe, and at each change of party Graham created for himself a fresh band of enemies. He had sat on both sides of the House, above and below both gangways, and he vacated no seat without leaving behind some rancour and ill-feeling.

It is a popular superstition that the system of Parliamentary groups for the first time replaced the more stable system of party government in the twentieth century. It is a superstition, and no more. Precisely the same phenomenon may be observed wherever a revolution has taken place, or an ancient party has been shattered. The Reform Bill of 1832, changing the government of the country, was followed by a period of confusion, during which the old lines of division were blurred and new combinations were hastily formed. By a painful effort Peel put the Tory party together again, led it to victory, and in 1846 destroyed it suddenly and without warning. Again a series of hostile groups took the place of a solid party. Peelites opposed Protectionists with a fiercer rage than either group could simulate for the opponents of both. And it needed the genius of Disraeli to reconstruct the broken party out of its divergent elements. The truth is that there are always groups on either side the House, and it is of the best possible augury that, while the divisions on the Liberal benches grow wider as time goes on, the

Tories are knit together more closely in the bonds of unity.

Thus it is the action and interaction of Parliamentary groups that explain the manysidedness of Sir James Graham. There was always something in every coterie of which he could approve, and which was a sufficient excuse for a change. So he could turn through all the gradations of policy from Liberal to Tory and from Tory to Liberal without disloyalty or dishonour. From his own point of view he was, as has been said, a useful and high-minded statesman. From the Tory's point of view he was throughout the greater part of his career a malignant influence. That England is given over to a noisy demagogy, that our rulers have forgotten the duty which they owe to their country and their countrymen, that the land is deserted and the city packed with out-of-works, is largely the fault of Sir James Graham and of those to whom he lent his support. For in whatever camp Sir James fought, for the moment he was the constant champion of what are called ' progress ' and ' reform.' He advocated change with the carelessness of one playing at Blind Hookey. True, he reserved the Constitution and the Church from attack, therein differing from his successors, but, with these reservations, nothing daunted him. And, like all reformers, he saw the proximate effect of his action so clearly that he overlooked the ultimate.

Perhaps had he understood the logical conclusion of 1832, he might have paused before he gave his help

to the schemes of Lord Grey. Had he foreseen the
death of agriculture and the depopulation of the
countryside, he might not have urged Sir Robert
Peel so eagerly to abolish the Corn Laws. But the
reformer is the same all the world over. He is like
the Chinaman who burned his house down that he
might taste the delights of roast pork. To do a little
good, he will cheerfully countenance a great wrong.
Indeed, there is little else to praise in Sir James
Graham's long career than his good intentions. And
in politics, of what worth are good intentions ? If
politicians approached the government of their
country—the most difficult of the arts—with a tithe
of the preparation which they devote to law or agriculture, to sport or cookery, how much better would
it be for us all ! The contemplation of Sir James
Graham's honourable and dangerous career recalls
Burke's prudent warning, which should be written
in letters of gold above the door of the House
of Commons : ' Men little think how immorally
they act in rashly meddling with what they do
not understand. Their delusive good intention is
no sort of excuse for their presumption. Those who
truly mean well must be fearful of acting ill.'

THE CORN LAWS: A GROUP

*T*HE *Life of Lord George Bentinck* is in a sense the most serious of Disraeli's works. It was composed at a time when he had abandoned fiction for the more sternly engrossing pursuit of politics. During the years which had passed since the writing of his novels, he had devoted himself with all his inspired energy to the business of the House of Commons, and *Sybil* and *Tancred* were but interludes in a life of affairs. 'Literature he has abandoned for politics,' wrote Mrs. Disraeli to Peel as early as 1841, and when, in 1852, he essayed in *Lord George Bentinck* the portraiture of an English worthy, Disraeli was already better known as a statesman than as a novelist. His brilliant and pitiless campaign against Peel had overshadowed the victories won in another field; and his political biography was received with a respect not always shown to those who have practised successfully the art of fiction.

And it deserved all the respect accorded to its sound judgment and well-balanced style. Fashioned after the best models, it is embellished, like the works of Livy and Thucydides, with deftly drawn characters and authentic speeches. The biographer,

moreover, was writing of what he had seen and heard :
not merely were all the documents ready to his hand ;
he himself had taken a foremost part in the events
which he chronicled.   And nowhere in his book will
you find the taint of journalism.   On every page
there is a sense of great issues and lofty purposes.
Though Disraeli was removed but a year or two from
the battles of wit and reason, which are the matter
of his history, his imagination allowed him to see
the immediate past in a just perspective, and his one
defect, amiable and deliberate, is to underrate with
a true modesty the importance of his own part.   So
gravely does he consider the personages in his drama,
that they might have been ancient Romans, or the
subjects of a despotic doge.   And then how skilful is
the narrative, how right the feeling of proportion !
None but a master could interweave pages of *Hansard*,
' the *Dunciad* of Downing Street,' into the substance
of his book, and make every chapter interesting.
Sternly political though it be, the biography is always
dramatic, and the two chief actors in the drama,
Lord George Bentinck and Sir Robert Peel, are
brilliantly disengaged from the dingy background of
the House of Commons.   Of these he writes in the
true spirit of romance.   The picture of Peel sitting
unmoved and unconscious in the deserted House can
never be forgotten.   ' The benches had become
empty,' thus runs the passage, ' the lights were about
to be extinguished ; it is the duty of the clerk of the
House to examine the chamber before the doors are

closed, and to-night it was also the strange lot of this
gentleman to disturb the reverie of a statesman.'

And, while Disraeli saw even the arch-enemy
through the softening mist of imagination, Lord
George, as he drew him, seems to have stepped
straight out of the pages of fiction. ' One man alone
brooded over the unexampled scene,' says he at the
outset, and you are reminded straightway of *Henrietta
Temple* or *The Young Duke*. Again, he tells us that,
to make his first speech, ' Bentinck rose long past
the noon of night.' It is such touches as these that
make the book acceptable to those who do not regard
politics as the end of life, and his admirers will surprise
the true Disraeli upon every page. Like all great men,
he rises with the occasion, and the description of
Lord George's death is the work of a true artist.
With the noble extravagance, characteristic of his
style, he takes leave of his hero ' upon the *perron* of
Harcourt House, the last of the great hotels of an
age of stately manners, with its wings, and court-
yard, and carriage portal, and huge outward walls.'
And when he tells the last sad tale in a few pages of
admirable dignity, he is inspired to quote the *Ajax*
—Ὦ Θάνατε, Θάνατε, νῦν μ' ἐπίσκεψαι μολόν—though
Greek quotations seldom came from his pen. In
brief, the whole work is cast in the mould of fancy,
and, accurate and impartial though it be, it never
sinks to the arid prose of conventional biography.

Disraeli, moreover, being always sincere, does not
suppress his own qualities, even in so impersonal an

affair as biography. The narrative sparkles with humour, and is alive with wit. The Sugar question, not a lively one, is an excuse for a jest, that has not yet lost its point. ' Strange,' says he, ' that a manufacture which charms infancy and soothes old age, should so frequently occasion political disaster.' He gives free play to his wonderful gift of irony, and does not mitigate his stern convictions. Though he proclaims with enthusiasm the fortunate truth that ' the history of England is the history of reaction,' he admits that ' progress and reaction are but words to mystify the million. They mean nothing, they are nothing ; they are phrases, and not facts. All is race.' So he returns to the gospel preached with eloquent sincerity in his novels ; and it may be said of him, as of few men, that, whatever may be the subject of his discourse, he is always honestly and candidly himself. He conceals nothing, he attenuates nothing ; he does not hedge about his statements ; and thus he presents the strongest contrast to the politician who in after years was his fiercest opponent and most dangerous rival.

His *obiter dicta* are always ingenious. He is equally wise in the discussion of men and manners. Whether he writes of Hume, who ' never once lost his temper,' or of the aristocracy, which does not ' yield its confidence grudgingly,' he finds the right word for the sane thought. And it is Lord George Bentinck's loyal championship of religious equality, his stout advocacy of the admission of Jews to Parliament, that

excuses his longest and most eloquent digression.
This digression is an echo, subdued to a deeper note,
of the pæan sung to Judaism by Sidonia in the pages
of *Coningsby*. But it is something else than a pæan :
it is an argument as well, the argument of a Jew ;
and, though it was written by one happily unaccustomed to the theological jargon of the day, it is
closely reasoned and ingeniously conceived. Throughout this chapter Disraeli shows a genuine pride in
his race, and exults, like the aristocrat that he was,
in what he believed to be his ancient lineage. Having
declared that the dispersion of the Jewish people was
not a penalty incurred for the commission of a great
crime, that such an allegation is ' neither historically
true nor dogmatically sound,' he applauds the courage
and persistence which have survived the worst trials
ever put upon a wandering race. ' The Hebrew,' he
says, ' is sustained by a sublime religion.' ' The
trumpet of Sinai still sounds in his ear, and a Jew
is never seen upon the scaffold, unless it be at an
auto-da-fé.' Strengthened, moreover, by an inherited
virtue and energy, and justly proud of his blood, the
Hebrew despises the doctrine of human equality.
' Thus it will be seen,' says Disraeli, ' that all the
tendencies of the Jewish race are conservative. Their
bias is to religion, property, and natural aristocracy :
and it should be the interest of statesmen that this
bias of a great race should be encouraged, and their
energies and creative powers enlisted in the cause of
existing society.'

Even those, who believe that anti-Semitism is justified, can hardly read so loyal a defence of a once down-trodden people without sympathy. Natural as is the prejudice against the Jews—has not Disraeli himself told us ' that all is race ' ?—the most bigoted partisan may still be grateful for the genius that Jewry has sent us.   For genius transcends the common rules of life and blood.   And if it be true that every nation harbours the Jews, which it deserves, England may justly be proud of her forbearance. At least she may profess a grateful admiration for Disraeli, whose greatness lightened the chains of nationality, and made him, despite his race, an English patriot.   But, having established the conservatism of the Jewish race on a basis of pride and wealth, Disraeli goes a step further, and attempts to prove that Christianity is but perfected Judaism. To profess the whole Jewish faith is, in his eyes, to ' believe in Calvary as well as in Sinai.'   If some millions of Hebrews believe only in a part of their religion, that is an accident which he deplores, and which he attributes to the Romans.   And thus we arrive at the religious position of Disraeli himself. In his own phrase, he was ' on the side of the Angels.' He was a loyal and devout Jew, who held that the religion of his race was not petrified by Moses. ' Christians may continue to persecute Jews,' said he in his famous peroration, ' and Jews may persist in disbelieving Christians, but who can deny that Jesus of Nazareth, the Incarnate Son of the Most

High God, is the eternal glory of the Jewish race ? '
This is a digression, which, when it was written,
rightly estranged the most of Disraeli's colleagues,
and which to-day cannot be sustained.   The real
purpose of the book is to set forth the part which
Lord George Bentinck played in the drama of the
Corn Laws, and Disraeli has performed the delicate
and difficult task of writing contemporary history
with the quick humour and shrewd observation
expected of him.

II

In 1845 Sir Robert Peel, the leader of the Pro-
tectionist Party in the House of Commons, suddenly
changed his opinions.   Cobden's prophecy that
' three weeks of showery weather when the wheat
is in bloom or ripening would repeal the Corn Laws '
was amply fulfilled.   The autumn rain, which destroyed
much besides, rained away whatever scruples Peel
may still have cherished.   The failure of the potato
crop in Ireland drove him into a panic, and he saw
in that panic an excuse for legislation.   The symp-
toms of his change instantly showed themselves in his
letters.   ' The accounts of the state of the potato
crop in Ireland are becoming very alarming,' he wrote
to Sir James Graham in October 1845, and the correspondence which followed proves that Sir James
Graham was less master of himself even than the
Prime Minister.   As to Peel's excitement there is
no lack of evidence.   The Duke of Wellington told

Sir Edward Knatchbull that 'he never saw a man in such a state of alarm. He was hardly himself—the potato disease seemed to occupy his whole mind.' But, whatever alarm he may have felt, the illogicality of his ultimate action would have appealed to any one whose sense of humour was keener than Peel's. 'The Irish potato crop,' said he in effect, 'has failed in 1845. Therefore in 1849 I will admit corn free of duty into the ports of Great Britain.' The evil and its remedy had no sort of relation one to the other, except that, as the evil inspired the panic, so by the remedy the panic was allayed.

But there were other influences working upon the plastic mind of Peel. The Anti-Corn Law League, which had long been 'hiring theatres,' and making its 'tawdry speeches in tawdry places,' was not likely to lose its opportunity. As has been said, there was nothing better than a bad harvest for the success of its schemes. 'The Anti-Corn Law pressure,' wrote Sir James Graham, 'is about to commence, and it will be the most formidable movement in modern times.' Cobden, in truth, knew precisely what was his strength, and how to apply it. With perfect cynicism he acknowledged six months later that there were 'not a hundred men in the Commons, or twenty in the Lords, who at heart are anxious for total repeal,' and in October 1845 there were still fewer. But Peel was coerced by out-of-doors opinion. Like Sir James Graham, he feared the League, and bowed his head in horror before its 'forty shilling

bludgeons.' And what makes his position the
stranger is that he and the League were pursuing
opposite aims. If Peel may be said to have had any
clear object, it was to help the people. He asked
the Irish to tighten their belts until 1849, and then
he promised them the boon of cheap corn. Cobden
and Villiers, on the other hand, had little interest
in the masses. They were the champions of the
employers, and their end and aim was to reduce the
wages of the workmen.

Mr. Gladstone has told us that Villiers' argument
was as follows : ' Under the present Corn Laws, the
trade on which we depend is doomed, for our manufacturers cannot possibly contend with the manufacturers of the Continent, if they have to pay wages
regulated by the protection price of food, while their
rivals pay according to the natural or free trade price.'
And Cobden, frank as his colleague, does not hide the
truth. He confesses that the working-men have
neither attended his meetings nor signed his petitions,
that his agitation, in fact, has been ' eminently
middle-class.' ' We have carried it on by those
means,' says he, ' by which the middle-class usually
carries on its movements. We have had our meetings
of dissenting ministers ; we have obtained the co-
operation of the ladies ; we have resorted to tea-
parties, and taken these pacific means for carrying out
our views, which mark us rather as a middle-class set
of agitators.' This confession is candid enough, and
it increases our wonder that Sir Robert Peel, once

the leader of ' the gentlemen of England,' should have adopted the policy of Cobden on a false ground, and have ensured its triumph in a hostile House of Commons.

However, so strong was Peel's panic, that he could no longer endure the responsibility of office, and he resigned with a patient and loyal majority behind him. The many meetings of the Cabinet held in November 1845 arrived at no certain conclusion, and Lord John Russell, whose letter addressed from Edinburgh to his constituents had hastened the unnecessary crisis, was asked to form a Government. Having failed in this enterprise, he could do nothing else than ' hand back the poisoned chalice to Sir Robert,' who thus became Prime Minister for the third time. Bound by all the ties of custom and honour to protect the Corn Laws and to defend the agricultural interest, Peel re-assumed the duties of government with the firm purpose of opposing those who had sent him to Westminster. Yet so complete was his ascendancy, so easy was his management of the ministers, that in the shuffle of opinions he lost but a single colleague—Lord Stanley. One other minister —Lord Lincoln—had a glimmering whither the path of duty led him. In his eyes the ' manly and honourable course ' would be that ' in the session preceding the dissolution Peel should propound to the country his intention to propose to the new Parliament either a modification of the Corn Law, expressly framed with a view to its abolition within a given time, or a total repeal of the law.' He saw the ' manly course ' ; he did not follow it.

But Sir Robert was far too clever to expose his policy to the hazard of a dissolution. Though he knew as well as Cobden that the country and the House of Commons were both against him, he had made up his mind to carry through the measures of his opponents, and the sound advice of Lord Lincoln fell upon a deaf ear. Indeed, so accurately did Peel gauge the temper of the country that after an ominous defeat in Westminster and a pitiful collapse in North Notts, he resolved not to risk another bye-election, and two Cabinet Ministers—Mr. Gladstone and Lord Lincoln—remained during his last Parliament without seats in the House of Commons.

Now Peel's position is perfectly intelligible : he was an expert at the quick change. It is not so easy to explain the conduct of the Duke of Wellington and the rest. The Duke did not pretend that he had been converted to the doctrine of Free Trade ; he claimed it as a sort of virtue in himself that in not deserting Peel he was helping to govern the country. As Lord Stanley said, the Duke ' talked of supporting the Queen's Government in measures of which he dis-approves, as if he were not a member of the Government to be supported.' ' The principle laid down,' to cite Disraeli's words, ' may be an excellent principle, but it is not a principle of the English Constitution.' But the Duke with some reason believed his presence in the Cabinet essential to the public welfare, and by

staying in he hoped that he was keeping Cobden out.
Disraeli's attitude was more honest. ' For my part,'
said he, ' if we are to have Free Trade, I, who honour
genius, prefer that such measures should be proposed
by the member for Stockport, rather than by one
who by skilful parliamentary manœuvres has tampered
with the generous confidence of a great people and
a great party.' Peel, being an egoist, took another
view, and, while he adopted Cobden's opinions, he
suppressed Cobden's name until the hour of his
doubtful victory. ' The Manchester Confederates,'
wrote Disraeli, ' seemed to be least in favour with
Parliament and the country on the very eve of their
triumph.' The Front Bench might have sung with
one accord, ' Oh no, we never mention him, His name
is never heard ' ; and so sincere was it at first in its
suppression of the League and all its works that it
wore an air of martyrdom, as who should say, ' We
sacrifice our opinions to save the country from
Mr. Cobden.' But resignation was soon changed to
pride. That which Peel and his friends at first
defended as merely expedient, they presently boasted
to be virtuous.

III

Thus the contest was engaged, and the champions
on either side fought with a courage and pertinacity
worthy the occasion. First and foremost in the
attack upon the Corn Laws was Sir Robert Peel, whose
position alone made a sudden and complete change of

opinion possible. He had sat in the House of
Commons for five-and-thirty years. He had served
the Crown in many offices and under many administrations. A long experience, added to a natural
faculty for affairs, had given him a unique place, a
unique influence. 'In the Senate,' says Disraeli,
'he was the readiest, easiest, most flexible and adroit
of men. He played upon the House of Commons as
on an old fiddle.' And he played upon it because his
method of speech was perfectly adapted to its purpose.
He was neither eloquent nor impassioned. His was
not the art of oratory, which aroused sudden en-
thusiasms, or swayed vast multitudes. 'His flights,'
in Disraeli's words, 'were ponderous ; he soared
with the wing of the vulture rather than the plume
of the eagle ; and his perorations, when most elaborate,
were most unwieldy. In pathos he was quite deficient ; when he attempted to touch the tender
passions, it was painful. His face became distorted,
like that of a woman who wants to cry but cannot
succeed. Orators certainly should not shed tears,
but there are moments when, as the Italians say, the
voice should weep.' Peel's voice never wept ; there
was no taint of the histrion in his nature—that taint
which in later years made his pupil and successor,
Mr. Gladstone, a danger to the State.

On the other hand, his style was always clear, logical,
and persuasive. His command of facts was as rare
as his industry, and years of practice had made his
talent for speaking 'the most available that has ever

been brought to bear upon the House of Commons.'
Thus by the exercise of useful rather than brilliant
gifts, he had become by far the greatest political force
of his time. It had been his good fortune to rally,
even to recreate, the Tory Party, and for many years
he led the English aristocracy with a success which
was never repeated save by Disraeli. One would not
have thought that there was a strong bond of sympathy between the aristocracy and Sir Robert Peel,
yet Disraeli tells us it was complete. 'An aristocracy,'
he says, in a passage already cited, and with a prescience of his own career, ' hesitates before it yields its
confidence, but it never does so grudgingly'; and Peel
could not complain that his parliamentary followers
lacked either troth or cordiality. They followed him
wherever he led them in blind obedience, and he
accepted their allegiance without question, as a tribute
justly paid to his masterful intelligence. In Westminster, then, his supremacy was undisputed. He
managed the assembly, which registered his decrees,
with perfect tact and dignity, and he deserved the
compliment paid him by the fiercest of his opponents,
that he was ' the greatest member of Parliament that
ever lived.'

But Peel's ascendancy was bounded by the walls of
the House of Commons. A frigid and unsympathetic
manner destroyed whatever influence he might have
exercised in the world outside. If we may believe
Greville, he had ' no popular and ingratiating qualities,
and few intimate friends.' It was not his business to

argue with his colleagues or convince his party, but to impose his views upon the House, and through the House upon the country. 'The right honourable Baronet's horror of slavery,' exclaimed Disraeli in an immortal passage, ' extends to every place, except to the benches behind him. There the gang is still assembled, and there the thong of the whip still sounds.' And it was not only his avowed opponents who condemned his autocratic temper. He strained the forbearance of his loyal supporters to breaking point. Sir Edward Knatchbull,[1] a leader of the Country Party and the staunchest of Tories, has left a character of Peel, which in every point is an undesigned confirmation of Disraeli. The character was sketched in his *Political Journal* some three years before the repeal of the Corn Laws, and was thus unbiased by the violent passions aroused by the defection of 1846.

' I never in my time,' wrote Sir Edward, ' saw a minister who possessed more absolute power in the House of Commons than Peel. His influence and power are most extraordinary. In the House he is everything—but there his power ceases. If he was the same in Council, and in all his intercourse with mankind, he would exceed anything this country, or perhaps any other, ever saw, but I fear he is not equal

---

[1] The extracts here given from Sir Edward Knatchbull's *Political Journal* are printed for the first time, and my thanks are due to Lord Brabourne, who has permitted me to make use of a document as valuable as it is sincere.

to the situation he fills, and to the times in which he lives. By his power in the House of Commons alone does he keep his party together. Out of the House his conduct is well calculated to destroy it. Cold and uncourteous to every one—even to his colleagues in office, who appear to me to be afraid to differ from him—at times in manner he is almost insolent. It will be found when he dies that no minister ever possessed fewer friends, or would be personally less lamented. In his policy he is deficient in vigour and in courage. He rather looks too much to popularity, and if any great emergency were to arise . . . I feel that Peel would be found wanting.' Sir Edward's sketch of Peel does not merely justify his own distrust and consequent retirement from politics ; it explains Peel's sudden success in the conversion of his Cabinet, and his equally sudden defeat in what seemed the moment of victory.

Peel's influence gained in intensity from its very narrowness. He exacted obedience, and he got it. So stern a tyrant was he that he thought it a patent disloyalty if his party did not follow him in all the tortuous twists and turns of a changing policy. To-day it was treachery to support Free Trade ; to-morrow none but a traitor dare say a word in favour of Protection. In truth, Peel deemed himself far superior to the principles of his party. He demanded allegiance for himself alone, and he would, if he could, have forbidden his supporters the right of private judgment. So **stoutly** convinced was he of his supremacy, that he believed he would encounter no other than a fat-cattle opposition, and when a solid phalanx of Tories resolved to secede, he regarded their secession as a perfidy. ' I am fighting a desperate battle here,' he wrote to Hardinge in 1846 ; ' shall probably drive my opponents over the Sutlej ; but what is to come afterwards I know not.' Hardinge was fighting his country's foes ; Peel was fighting against his friends of yesterday ; so that his Sutlej was a very different river from that which Hardinge had recently crossed. And Peel was implacable. He put an end to a friendship with Croker, which had lasted for more than thirty years, because Croker did not change his views on the same day and in the same direction as himself, and it is not difficult to say which of the two men behaved with the truer faithfulness and the finer courtesy.[1] And as he treated Croker, so most unreasonably he treated all those who dared to preserve their ancient opinions. If Croker and his friends were ' convinced that the Corn Laws were essential,' as Greville said, ' not merely to the prosperity, but to the existence of the landed interest,' Peel had been mainly instrumental in confirming this conviction, and it was not for him to regard a conviction, which he had confirmed, as a rock of offence.

Moreover, Peel had already sacrificed his party once, and it was a monstrous indiscretion to repeat

[1] The last letters exchanged between Peel and Croker, printed in the *Croker Correspondence* (vol. iii. 96-97), leave no doubt as to Croker's loyal conduct and Peel's unjust resentment.

the manœuvre. What is done once may be an accident ; done twice, it wears the sad appearance of a
habit. Sir Robert was long an energetic and consistent enemy to Catholic Emancipation. He resisted
the arguments of colleagues and opponents alike.
Not even the persuasive eloquence of Canning availed
to move him. Nor had he formed his judgment
hastily and without experience. He had been Chief
Secretary in Ireland ; he was familiar with the facts
and prejudices of either side. And then, having remained upright for some seventeen years, he threw a
political somersault, turned his head in the air, and
landed on his feet a staunch supporter of the Catholic
claims. What argument and reason could not achieve
was achieved in a moment by Canning's death and
the Clare Election. For Peel, being first minister
of the Crown, might now claim the glory of all his
actions, and O'Connell's majority spoke with an
eloquence denied to Canning. But the minister
cannot be extricated from both horns of the dilemma.
Either his sincerity or his prudence was at fault. It was
he who had changed, not the situation ; and, leaving
out of the question the justice of the case, his party
had a perfect right to resent what seemed a betrayal.

Sir Edward Knatchbull declared that Sir Robert Peel
was ' deficient in vigour and courage.' Disraeli, with
a keener subtlety, noted that he was without imagination and without the creative faculty. In effect
the two critics agree. To want imagination is, as
Disraeli said, to want prescience ; to want prescience

is to want vigour. So Peel, not knowing what was to come, supinely accepted the views of his opponents, and made of necessity an ostentatious virtue. To a more energetic statesman there would have been no necessity. He would have fought for his own cause to the last ditch. Peel surrendered at the lightest hint of panic, and accused of treachery all those who did not throw down their arms with him.

But, if he lacked the creative faculty, he had, as Disraeli pointed out, ' a dangerous sympathy with the creations of others.' He was always learning, absorbing, appropriating, and so fierce was his egoism that whatever he appropriated he deemed his own exclusive possession. He followed many leaders ; he picked up his policies in many corners. ' In his sallet days,' says Disraeli, ' it was Mr. Horner or Sir Samuel Romilly ; in later and more important periods it was the Duke of Wellington, the King of the French, Mr. Jones Loyd—some others—and finally, Mr. Cobden.' How, then, could he lead his party with courage, when he knew not what lesson he would learn on the morrow, or what new influence was destined to turn his mind or shape his opinion ?

After his defeat in 1846 he made a bold attempt to prove that he had been a consistent Free Trader since 1841. And it is not surprising that this attempt to throw the responsibility of defection upon his Cabinet should have failed. If ever a statesman were pledged to a policy, Peel was pledged to the protection of the agricultural interest. ' I believe that the abolition of the Corn Laws,' said he in 1844, ' would produce great confusion and distress ' ; and again, ' I can say with truth I have not contemplated and do not contemplate an alteration in the present Corn Laws.' Politicians have short memories ; and not merely did Peel contemplate in 1845 the change that he had never contemplated in 1844, but in 1848, after the episode was closed, he asserted in a certain letter that the measures taken by his Cabinet in 1842 were preparatory to and intended to lead up to the Repeal of the Corn Laws.

To this statement Sir Edward Knatchbull, in the *Journal* from which I have already quoted, gives a plain denial. ' I cannot hesitate to say,' he writes, ' that as far as my recollection goes, it is entirely inconsistent with the truth. Whether my opinions have been right or wrong, wise or unwise, they have been deliberately formed, and acted upon with no other view than the public good. But I have always been in favour of the Corn Laws, in favour of protection to native industry, and opposed to what is called Free Trade. I never could then, in Cabinet in 1842, have consented to the measures, on which every member of the Cabinet, except that poor, silly, vain, and now ruined man, the Duke of Buckingham, entirely agreed, if they had been proposed with a view to the later measures of 1845. On this point my recollection is quite at variance with the assertion of Sir Robert Peel ; and I am quite certain that I am correct. To satisfy my mind, I have personally communicated with Lord Stanley, who admits at once that my statement of the case is correct; with Lord Lyndhurst, whose recollection agrees with mine; with the Duke of Wellington, who agrees. I had a long conversation with him. We felt it to be a very awkward question. The Duke said, that possibly we might both of us be called upon publicly to express our opinion on the matter. " You and I both know how the case is. All I shall say is that my recollection does not quite enable me to agree in the accuracy of the statement contained in that letter, and I advise you to say the same and no more." I have also seen Lord Hardinge since his return from India. He declared to me, that no such measures as those which were proposed in 1845, were spoken of or contemplated by the Cabinet in 1842. . . . If in 1842 Peel had hinted at any measures similar to those proposed in 1846, or if he had been suspected of entertaining any such opinions, his Cabinet I know would have fallen to pieces.'

Thus the evidence against Peel is overwhelming and irrefutable. Sir Edward Knatchbull is a sufficient witness, and his colleagues are unanimous in support. ' Either in 1842, and previously, Sir Robert was acting a deceitful part, or his mind was of that unstable, vacillating cast, as altogether to disqualify him for the position he held, as first minister of his country.' That is the conclusion, which cannot be evaded, and it is not very creditable to ' the greatest member of Parliament that ever lived.'

IV

And all the while behind Peel there loomed the figure of Richard Cobden. Peel was indeed no more than the shadow thrown by the impassioned Free Trader. Yet the two men were united by no bond of sympathy or friendship. Hitherto nothing had passed between them save hard words and bitter recriminations. If Cobden distrusted Peel, the dry, cold mind of Peel was never stirred by Cobden's hot-gospelling. On the one hand was a minister eager to come under a new influence. On the other was an agitator, willing for the moment to suppress himself, if only his measures were carried. What manner of man was it, then, whose influence in the theatre and lecture hall equalled that which Sir Robert wielded within the walls of the House of Commons ?

Sincere, indefatigable, and narrow-minded, a man of limited and pertinacious brain, who knew what he wanted, and meant to get it, though he did not realise its results—such was Richard Cobden. He was, moreover, an optimist, who believed devoutly in the perfectibility of man, and who was sanguine enough to be quite certain that he was himself incapable of error. So sure was he of his own position that in his eyes his opponents were either fools or knaves. He had a faith in the finality of his scheme which was almost touching, and since the future held as few secrets for him as the present, he professed to know, not only the cause of all existing evil, but its infallible

remedy. Therefore he did not hesitate to convert
what should have been a mere matter of expediency
into a sort of religious belief. Protesting all the
while that he was a business man, he declared that
Free Trade was a panacea for all the evils to which
humankind is subject. ' Free Trade ! what is it ? '
he asked. ' Why, breaking down the barriers that
separate nations ; those barriers, behind which nestle
the feelings of pride, revenge, hatred, and jealousy,
which every now and then burst their bounds, and
deluge whole countries with blood.'

Now, of course, there is no policy which could
gratify these loose, if noble, sentiments, and the
frequent recurrence in his speeches of such passages
as this is proof enough that Cobden did not take a
sternly practical view of his duties. Yet in one respect
he was sternly practical : he had a very shrewd notion
of what would profit him and his class. He entered
upon the struggle, not to benefit the whole community, but to enrich the manufacturers, of whom
none was more zealous than himself. If he could he
would have replaced the domination of the great
landowners, which in his eyes was an infamy, by the
far more disastrous domination of the capitalist. In
other words, he was supporting that new power
without responsibility which came into being in the
early years of the nineteenth century. As Enoch
Craggs says in *Endymion* : ' Master Thornberry is
the most inveterate capitalist of the whole lot, and
I always say, though they keep aloof from him at

present, they will all be sticking to his skirts before long. Master Thornberry is against the capitalist in land; but there are other capitalists nearer home, and I know more about them.' And Enoch Craggs proceeded to declare that he would 'sooner be ruled by gentlemen of estate, who have been long among us, than by persons who build big mills, who come from God knows where, and when they have worked their millions out of our flesh and bone, go God knows where.'

Cobden, who sat for Job Thornberry's portrait, did not share the scruples of Enoch Craggs. He believed that there was something sacred in profitable industry, that a mill-lord was invariably a nobler person than a landlord, that the dukes of England were criminals when they were not fools. And he had no fear of them. 'If the Duke of Richmond,' said he in a passage which clearly reveals his prejudice, 'sets up the Noodles and Doodles of the aristocracy, why, before we have done with them, they shall be as insignificant and more contemptible than the round-frocked peasantry upon his Grace's estate.' In spite of rhetoric, then, Cobden's agitation was conducted in the interests of a class. To buy in the cheapest market and sell in the dearest—this was his maxim: a maxim, said he, agreeable to the highest behests of Christianity, a mere paraphrase of the Christian doctrine, 'Do to all men as ye would they should do unto you.'

But it is when we consider the prophecies of Cobden

that we discover most clearly the recklessness of his argument. He was certain that if England adopted the principles of Free Trade, the rest of the world would instantly follow her example. On this point he had no doubt whatever. He reiterates his prophecy with a confident assurance, which to-day appears ridiculous. 'We have a principle established now,' said he in 1846, 'which is eternal in its truth, and universal in its application, and must be applied in all nations, and throughout all times, and applied not simply to commerce, but to every item in the tariffs of the world ; and if we are not mistaken in thinking that our principles are true, be assured that those results will follow, and at no very distant date.' No politician ever delivered himself more tightly bound hand and foot than did Cobden in this astounding pronouncement. Many years have passed, and ' those results ' have not followed. The inference, therefore, is clear : Cobden and his fellows were very much mistaken in thinking that their principles were true ; and we are still asked to put our faith in Free Trade on the mere word of an agitator.

Again and again did Cobden repeat this vain boast. ' I believe,' he exclaimed on another occasion, ' that if you abolish the Corn Law honestly and adopt Free Trade in its simplicity, there will not be a tariff in Europe that will not be changed in less than five years to follow your example.' And, vainest hope of all, it was to America that he looked for the speediest

adoption of his opinions. 'Well,' he declared after
his cheerful fashion in 1846, 'there is one other
quarter in which we have seen the progress of sound
principles—I allude to America'; and the America
to which he alluded with this reckless certainty has
resolutely supplied us with corn, and excluded our
manufactures by means of a tariff-wall.

Confident as he was that his example would be
followed, he was yet more confident that repeal would
not throw the land out of cultivation. ' Throw the
land out of cultivation by removing the Corn Law:
Who say that ? The worst farmers in the country
—the landlords, rather, of the worst-farmed land.'
Those prophets who dared to hint that the repeal
of the Corn Laws would restrict agriculture were
denounced by Cobden as ' selfish, ignorant beings.'
In the same spirit he boldly asserted that, while the
landowners 'had nothing pecuniarily, had nothing
ultimately to fear from Free Trade in corn,' if the
principles of Free Trade were fairly carried out, ' they
would give just as much stimulus to the demand for
labour in the agricultural as in the manufacturing
districts.' In brief, the bagman's millennium was to
be an age of gold for everybody ; wages would rise,
the landowners would increase their wealth, and,
above all, the tenant-farmers of England would reap
an enormous benefit. ' I believe,' said Cobden,
' when the future historian comes to write the history
of agriculture, he will have to state in such a year that
there was a stringent corn law passed for the pro-

tection of agriculture. From that time agriculture slumbered in England, and it was not until, by the aid of the Anti-Corn Law League, the Corn Law was utterly abolished, that agriculture sprang up to the full vigour of existence in England to become what it now is, like our manufactures, unrivalled in the world.'

So vain a pronouncement as this would be ludicrous if it were not tragic. But in Cobden's eyes repeal had no drawback. The importation of foreign corn would not, he was sure, lessen the sale of home-grown corn by a single bushel. With free commerce the energies of the people would be so vast that they would consume corn and provisions brought from abroad faster than the quantity imported could increase. And while we were to profit by throwing open our ports to the food of all the world, we should still preserve our independence intact. 'Dependence on foreigners!' he exclaimed in the House of Commons ; 'who in the world could have supposed that that long-buried ghost would come again to light.' In fact, the mere thought that Free Trade could inflict a hardship upon any single Englishman was met by Cobden with contemptuous derision. Even though Russia and America deluged our country with corn, the value of land could not possibly diminish. The value of silks, of cottons, or of woollens might be affected by competition ; but Cobden was perfectly assured that the taste for land, inherent in humankind, would never let its value decrease a shilling an acre. And while the value of our English acres would, in his fond imagination, never diminish, America would be diverted by the prospect of supplying us with corn from the development of her own manufactures. She would be content to dig and delve; she would devote her energies to a beneficent agriculture, and yet, by some miraculous process, would not prevent the sale of a single quarter grown in England.

So the Corn Laws were repealed, and, as every one knows, all Cobden's predictions were falsified. He was not one to be daunted by the failure of his hopes. Like most Radicals, he lived in a fool's paradise where facts are of no account, and where, if principles prove fallacious, it is not the fault of the optimist who frames them, but of some vile conspirator against the common good. For many years Cobden had declared that repeal would increase the wages of the labouring class ; nor was he abashed when he witnessed their speedy fall. It was enough for him to point out that the cost of living had decreased a little more than wages, and he was wholly indifferent to the fact that this argumentative jugglery was what he had been denouncing in his speeches for ten years. And he had a remedy ready. He told the landlords that they must abolish battue-shooting, and, to confront the depression of agriculture, which he had said would never be depressed, he urged the labourers ' to set gins and snares upon their allotments and in their gardens to catch all the hares and rabbits they could, and when they caught them, to be sure to put

them in their own pots and eat them themselves.'
This is a sad descent from the dreams of eternal peace,
the visions of disbanded armies and of swords beaten
into ploughshares, which were wont to decorate the
agitator's harangues.   The demagogue who once saw
in the principle of Free Trade ' that which will act
on the moral world as the principle of gravitation
in the universe ' was three years later forced to substitute for his multi-coloured visions a humble policy
of gins, snares, and boiled rabbits.

Now, if politics be anything better than a gamble,
the failure of Cobden's predictions should have shaken
his own opinion, and given a sharp warning to his
countrymen. No disaster could dim the Free
Trader's self-satisfaction. He had formulated a
doctrine which in his eye was wholly independent of
fact, a principle of moral gravitation, immovable by
events.   And the perfect trust, which he professed in
his own creed, has been reflected ever since in the
trust of others, to whom Cobden is but a name, and
who have never been at the trouble to test his statements.   Nor did Cobden limit his programme to
repeal—he held firm and definite opinions on all
matters of high politics ; and it is well that those
who cherish a blind faith in him should realise whither
his leadership would have carried them.   In the first
place, he was a stalwart opponent of the army and
navy. He held that the motto, *si vis pacem, bellum
para*, was a monstrous perversion of the truth; and, if
he did not see an immediate return for money spent,

he was convinced that the enterprise was bad. 'Buy
in the cheapest market, sell in the dearest'—this
Christian maxim was sufficient for him, and it made
no allowance for national dignity or a policy of empire.
The brain which refused to look beyond a monthly
balance-sheet could not take a large view, and assuredly
Cobden saw no empire beyond Manchester, no policy
beyond a 'full breeches pocket.'

Though by his own action England became de-
pendent upon foreign countries for her supply of food,
he saw no reason why a navy should be built to keep
open the seas. When he first travelled abroad he
was struck with what he thought the extravagance
of the navy. 'The cost of the Mediterranean
Squadron,' said he, with a thought of his own commerce, 'in proportion to the amount of trade it was
employed to protect, was as though a merchant should
find that his traveller's expenses for escort were to
amount to 6s. 8d. in the pound on his sales.' This
might be true enough if hostile countries stood to
one another merely in the relation of buyers and
sellers ; and if Cobden had had his way, we should
long ago have lost any trade of our own that was
worth protecting. Nevertheless, so candidly alien
were his sympathies that he believed disarmament
the natural corollary of Free Trade. When Sir
Robert Peel had at last passed his famous measure,
Bastiat, a French economist and Cobden's friend,
was gravely disappointed. It was not enough that
the markets of England were thrown wide open to

French commerce. ' What you have to show France
above all else,' said Bastiat in an astounding letter,
' is that freedom of exchange will cause the disappear-
ance of those military perils which France apprehends.
England ought seriously to disarm.' It would be
hard indeed to surpass the pedant *naïveté* of this
French Free Trader. It was not enough that England should surrender her markets—she must surrender herself as well, or France would not believe in
her sincerity !

And, while the policy which we should have pursued towards foreign countries demanded our disarmament, so also did our colonial policy. Cobden
denied that our dependencies oversea needed any
protection. Doubtless he would have let our colonies
go, in the same spirit in which he would have renounced India, or ' thanked his stars that America had
broke loose.' He indignantly repudiated the argument
that ships of war were necessary to protect our colonial
trade, and he had so little knowledge of mankind as
to believe that wealth and commerce were the real
test of a nation's power in the eyes of its enemies.
Which is to say that a traveller is safest from a high-
wayman when he carries most money in his pocket.
The disarmament which he advocated was, of course,
one-sided, like his free trade ; but happily the country
which followed him innocently in quest of that cost-
liest commodity, cheap food, was not prepared to
disband its army and break up its ships at the bidding
of a rival.

In truth, it was not his business to reason or to
doubt. His sanguine mind pictured the whole world
one vast Manchester, in which ' the stream of com-
modities was allowed to flow freely,' in which the
manufacturers, the true salt of the earth, might collect
mountains of gold, high beyond the dreams of avarice.
Had this famous ideal of ledger and balance-sheet
been realised, the working-man would have had as
short a shrift as the landowner. Now, when Cobden
wished to create a prejudice against the great landlords of England, he declared that high rents and
uncertain tenure were driving the farmers to emigrate,
and thus depriving the country of its noblest citizens.
What was sauce for the goose was not sauce for the
gander. While he thought that the farmer needed a
practical sympathy, he held that the millowner and
his workmen should be left to fight it out. He hated
Factory Acts as bitterly as he hated trades-unions.
He would have permitted nothing to come between
the manufacturer and his profit. If it were necessary
to restrict the hours of labour, the workmen should
rely, not upon Parliament, but upon their own efforts.
Combination being manifestly intolerable, the remedy
of each man was plain : he should save £20 and
emigrate to America. In other words, what was
tyranny in a landowner was enterprise in a manufacturer. And those eager Radicals who believe that
the teaching of Cobden is infallible would do well to
remember his famous pronouncement upon workmen's combinations. ' Depend upon it,' said he,

in the true accent of Manchester, ' nothing can be got by fraternising with trades-unions. They are founded upon principles of brutal tyranny and monopoly. I would rather live under a Dey of Algiers than a Trade Committee.'

V

In the war of wits, which was waged in the early months of 1846, Peel and Cobden met more than their match, and the opposition which they encountered was at once unexpected and well deserved. If Cobden's sincerity was less doubtful than his wisdom, Peel showed himself a politician rather than a statesman, and his devious past exposed him nakedly to the piercing shafts of his adversaries. His opponents, moreover, were marshalled by two leaders whose zeal was equal to their discretion, and whose honesty of purpose was as conspicuous as their prowess in debate. And of these one was the English worthy, whose life was afterwards written by Disraeli, ' the self-denying spirit, scorning rest,' who lived for a cause, and wore himself out in the service of his country.

When Lord George Bentinck rose to address the House on the 27th of February 1846, he began a career unparalleled in the history of our Parliament. Though in his youth he had served his kinsman, George Canning, in the post of secretary, though for eighteen years he had sat at Westminster as the representative of King's Lynn, he had hitherto taken little interest,

and no part, in the debates of the Commons.   Nor
was the hour of his speech less remarkable than the
fact that he should have spoken at all.   He stood up
at twelve o'clock to face a House already jaded by some
days of debate, and he spared his hearers no detail
of an elaborately studied case.   With an unsuspected
mastery he discussed the commerce of the country,
the trade in silk and wool, the price of corn and
cattle, and the many questions whose solution
establishes a policy, if they fatigue an audience of tired
legislators.   But Lord George did not hesitate.
' Diffident but determined,' he pursued his argument
to the bitter end.   With that facility of managing
figures which always distinguished him, he showed, at
two o'clock in the morning, how many hundredweight
of guano would produce an extra quarter of wheat,
and nicely calculated into how many pounds of
mutton a ton of swedes might be converted.   Never,
until his peroration, did he leave the arid field of reality,
and stately as his peroration was there was only one
phrase, in which he pictures the aristocracy of England ' proud in the chastity of its honour,' that
lingers in our memory.   And by this single speech,
Lord George Bentinck was changed from ' the Lord
Paramount of the Turf ' to a serious politician ;   by
this single speech he proved that there was one man
left to rally the broken forces of the Tories, and to
lead at least a single campaign against the minister
who had betrayed them.

His aspect and antecedents, moreover, alike afforded

a contrast to the high seriousness wherewith he pleaded the cause of Protection. A dandy after the manner of D'Orsay, he displayed in his attire and bearing something of the ' majestic frivolity' which distinguished his class. His vest was rolled back with as magnificent a sweep as that affected by his great exemplar ; his cravats, the envy of his contemporaries, rivalled those works of art which conferred imperishable fame upon George Brummell, and though, as we are told by an admirer, they cost a guinea apiece, he never wore the same twice. Such a fashion was perfectly adapted to the passion of his early life ; for until 1846 politics had been but an interlude in his pursuit of sport. He had attended the House as though by accident, and more than once he had gone into the lobby with the pink of the hunting-field concealed by a greatcoat of sombre hue.

Meanwhile, if he was little known at Westminster, his sway upon the turf was undisputed. For twenty years he had bred horses and backed them. He easily outstripped the most reckless of his contemporaries both in the magnificence of his stables and the splendour of his wagers. On more than one occasion he had stood to win £150,000, and yet he was always something better than a mere gambler. It pleased him to prove his confidence in the horses he bred, and he was a sportsman fine enough to subordinate his gain to his pride. He liked to win, not that he valued the money, but because money was ' the test and trophy of success.' As Greville says, ' he counted the thousands he won after a great race as a general would count his prisoners and his cannon after a great victory.' [1]   And his courage was equal to his generosity.   No disaster availed to turn his purpose, and however vast was the hazard, he never betrayed the smallest flutter of excitement.

Moreover, with the pertinacity and grasp of facts which he presently turned to excellent account in another field, he permitted no detail of the racecourse to escape him.   He watched over his stables at Goodwood with a tireless and intelligent zeal.   Everything which concerned the diet and care of his horses was of the highest interest to him.   The letters which he addressed to his trainer are so long and serious that they are comparable only to state papers, and they are a complete explanation of the eager policy which he pursued upon the turf.   Indeed, Lord George proved himself a statesman as well as a gambler so long as his colours were carried to victory, and, when at last he threw himself into the cock-pit of politics, he began the new fight strengthened by a vast experience gained in the old.   On the turf his triumphs had been great.   In 1845, for instance, he

[1] On this point Greville and Disraeli are in perfect agreement, and, strangely enough, they use the same phrase.   To whom the phrase belongs I do not know.   Greville's character of Lord George Bentinck purports to have been written before Disraeli's, and Greville declares that he read a part of his sketch to Disraeli.   But, of course, Disraeli's biography was published many years before Greville's death, and it is not easy to award the credit of an admirable judgment.

had won eighty-two races, and his profit in stakes alone amounted to £31,502; and he had gained a keen knowledge of the world in addition to the money. 'I don't pretend to know much,' said he, 'but I can judge men and horses'; and it was this judgment, combined with unwearied industry and a keen sense of honour, which enabled him after a few months' trial to lead a party in the House of Commons.

None knew better than he that politics were not his natural vocation, and nothing less than a crisis would have dragged him from his retirement; but he could not look on with equanimity while his principles were sacrificed and his party betrayed. For a second time, as has been said, Peel had surrendered his friends to his ambition; and he had made the surrender with so fine an adroitness, he had hoodwinked Parliament with so masterful a skill, that it seemed as if he would repeal the Corn Laws without opposition. It was then that Lord George Bentinck, goaded by a sense of duty, 'came out like a lion forced from his lair.' His opposition to the Manchester School was sincere and well grounded. Peel's sudden desertion of the party which had placed him in power was repugnant alike to Bentinck's sense of justice and feeling of sport. On the one hand, he held that it would have been easier 'to contend against Free Trade when completely and openly avowed, than when brought forward by one who had obtained power by professing his hostility to it.' On the other hand, he resented with all his sportsman's soul the suspicion of foul play. When Rogers, his jockey, lost a race for his own profit, Lord George was not happy until he proved the rider's guilt to the Jockey Club and got him disqualified. And he looked upon Peel as he looked upon Rogers. ' I keep horses in three counties,' said Lord George once to a Cobdenite, ' and they tell me that I shall save fifteen hundred a year by Free Trade. I don't care for that. What I cannot bear is being sold.'

He was inspired also by a deeper feeling than sportsmanship and the dislike of being sold. He honourably and devoutly believed that Free Trade would be the ruin not only of his class but of his country. His opinions were as strong and as wise as Disraeli's own. He was strenuously opposed to the Manchester School because he knew that, when once its tenets were accepted, our territorial constitution would be subverted, our freedom impaired, an irreparable injury done to Ireland, and our colonial empire weakened to dissolution. Unlike his opponents, he possessed the real gift of prophecy which comes of a knowing imagination. He foresaw at the very outset the danger incurred by our colonies ; he realised that one of the inevitable results of Free Trade would be to alienate the affection of Canada ; and, resolved to protect British capital wherever it might be invested, he fought against the measures of Peel, which should have been called the measures of Cobden, with all the energy and force of an indomitable temper.

Henceforth unto the day of his death he was Peel's bitterest opponent. He was at the House early and late. He worked harder than a slave, and lived like an anchorite. He ate no lunch, and dined at two in the morning. He overcame his natural defects of speech and gesture with a determined consciousness of his own shortcomings, and he atoned for a belated education by a superhuman industry. 'Virtually an uneducated man,' he wrote to Croker in 1847; 'never intended or attracted by taste for political life . . . I am well aware of my own incapacity properly to fill the station I have been thrust into.' A knowledge of incapacity is the first step towards its removal, and Lord George was presently pushed by sheer capacity into the leadership of a broken party.

When he exposed the fraud of Running Rein, the attorney who conducted the case declared that there was 'no sum he would not give to secure the professional assistance of such a coadjutor.' And Bentinck treated the sophistries of Peel with the same perseverance and ingenuity wherewith he baffled the supporters of Running Rein. He got up his case with a skill and energy that are beyond admiration. His speeches were incomparably superior in depth and compass to any others delivered during the campaign. He spared no trouble in amassing information. He was, so to say, a whole commission in himself. In his speeches he continually mentions a mysterious gentleman 'who had waited on him that morning,' and that gentleman was always a specialist

unrivalled in his own subject. There was no trade
whose battle he did not fight, and whose grievances
he did not master : the Irish graziers and butter-
merchants, the Leicestershire stockingers, the silk
manufacturers of Coventry, the hop-growers of Kent,
were all championed by this elegant and handsome
sportsman, who had sometimes seemed too lethargic
to make a match or lay a wager.

Though he proved an astonishing faculty of ac-
quisition, he was at first disinclined to make even his
own speech. For, despite a naturally arrogant
temper, he had not an atom of conceit, as friends and
foes agree.[1] He would, if he could, have remained,
like Latour d'Auvergne, in the rank and file. ' We
have had enough of leaders,' said he ; but here, as in
other points of policy, he allowed himself to be over-
persuaded, and with Disraeli's help he put together
again the broken pieces of the Country Party. Nor
could he have found a better colleague than Disraeli,
who was in all respects his complement. Lord George
had the command of dry, hard facts. Disraeli, on
the other hand, was distinguished by the dash and
brilliance which Lord George candidly owned himself
to lack. No sooner had Lord George shattered his

[1] Lord George Bentinck went so far as to take counsel with
a distinguished barrister, who recommended Serjeant Byles as
the proper man to plead the cause of Protection in the House of
Commons. But Serjeant Byles, though a convinced Protec-
tionist, remained loyal to his profession, and dedicated to
Political Economy no more than the leisure which sufficed for
the composition of his *Sophisms of Free Trade.*

opponents with the heavy artillery of argument, than
Disraeli rushed in with his light cavalry of taunt and
epigram to complete the rout.

When the Lords had passed the second reading of
the hated measure, its opponents did not relax their
efforts.   One battle was lost, yet, even in the moment
of victory, the triumphant general might be stripped
of his army, and with it of the power to win a second.
And so opposition not unworthily became vengeance.
Peel was a minister, in Lord George's eyes, whom
the country might not trust ; he had been coerced,
as Cobden confessed, by ' the out-of-doors opinion '
and the dread of the League ; and Lord George increased his ferocity as the chance of victory dis-
appeared.   He was always a good hand at damaging
an enemy, and he now employed his gift with a marvellous energy.   It has been justly said that Lord
George introduced a frankness of attack into parliamentary warfare that had been unknown before his
time.   That he had ample justification not even a
Peelite would deny.   Had Peel been an open and
avowed Free Trader there would have been no ground
for anger ; despite the certainty that the Bill would
pass, the Protectionists were confident that ultimately
they would triumph over their foe ; and the Country
Party, discomfited as it was, had something of the
satisfaction which comes of satisfied revenge.

For, by a stroke of unconscious drama, the Coercion
Bill was thrown out on the very night when the Corn
Bill became law, and Peel closed his public career in

what should have been the hour of victory. Lord
George Bentinck, though his first fight was fought, was
now fascinated by politics, and had no intention of
returning to his stables. If the Corn Bill was passed,
there was still work for him and his party to accomplish. And let it not be supposed that he was
eminent merely as a destructive critic. He was, in
truth, a statesman of exceedingly wise and moderate
views. He would have been satisfied with a duty of
four or five shillings on corn, which, he was sure,
would not sensibly raise the price in this country.
He was the unfailing friend of religious liberty, and
he urged that equal privileges should be given to Jews
and Catholics alike. He regarded Ireland never with
the eye of a partisan; he publicly proclaimed his
dislike of absentee landlords; he would have voted
for any measure designed to improve the relations of
landlord and tenant; and that he had always the
welfare of the Irish at heart is proved by his elaborate scheme of railway enterprise in Ireland, his most
ambitious attempt at constructive legislation. The
scheme was rejected, of course; the speech in which
it was advocated remains a masterpiece of accumu-
lated fact and serried argument.

Meanwhile he had discovered that the breeding of
horses was incompatible with a political career. He
was of those who do nothing by halves, and eighteen
hours devoted to hard work left him little leisure in
the day to attend to his stables. He therefore determined to renounce the sport of racing for ever, and

the episode of his renunciation is a dramatic episode even in a life packed with drama. It was on the evening of the third day's racing at Goodwood in 1846 that Lord George, appearing half asleep after dinner, suddenly put the question, ' Will any one of you give me £10,000 for all my lot, beginning with old Bay Middleton and ending with little Kitchener ? ' The question was not more startling than the method of putting it. And to keep the drama at a high level, George Payne instantly offered to pay a forfeit of £300 if he did not accept the offer by noon the following day. He paid his forfeit, and the ' lot ' presently became the property of Mr. Mostyn. This act of devotion, as Greville says, has never been sufficiently appreciated and applauded. Lord George did not put a trifling price upon his horses because he did not know their value. He was perfectly conscious that there were at that moment in his stable the best yearlings that ever he had bred. But expedition was important ; he had sacrificed his pleasure to what he deemed his duty ; and his only wish was to rid himself of his horses as quickly as possible.

Though the sale was inevitable, it cannot be said that he never regretted it. Two years later, Surplice, a horse that once had been his, won the Derby, to achieve which had for twenty years been the end of his ambition. The disappointment can be described only in Disraeli's magniloquent words. ' He had nothing to console him,' wrote the biographer, ' and

nothing to sustain him but his pride. Even that
deserted him before a heart which he knew at least
could yield him sympathy. He gave a sort of superb
groan : " All my life I have been trying for this, and
for what have I sacrificed it ! " he murmured. It was
in vain to offer solace. " You do not know what the
Derby is," he moaned out. " Yes, I do ; it is the blue
ribbon of the turf." " It is the blue ribbon of the
turf," he slowly repeated to himself, and sitting down
at the table, he buried himself in a folio of statistics.'
The passage is superb as Lord George's groan, and
nobly characteristic both of the biographer and his
hero.

The distinguishing mark of Lord George Bentinck's
character was a lofty seriousness. He was serious in
horse-racing, serious in Parliament, serious in gathering knowledge, most serious in attacking and worsting
his enemies. The truth is, this dignified debonair
sportsman could do nothing lightly. He must always
be at work, and the transport and diet of horses satisfied him until he found his true profession in politics.
His friend and biographer says of him in an admirable
passage : ' He never chattered. He never uttered a
sentence in the House of Commons which did not
convey a conviction or a fact.' He never chattered !
What man can hope to earn a better epitaph ? And
the compliment does more than many pages to light
up the doubtful corners of Lord George's character.
His sincerity was too deep for idle phrases, and his
sincerity won him a wide popularity, which not even

his arrogance and his talent of bitter speech could diminish.

Moreover, like all sincere men, he was both simple and courageous. Though he speedily mastered the mysteries of politics, he never concealed his designs, nor permitted intrigue to obscure the simplicity of his motive and action. And he was of so high a courage that he never shrank from the performance of an unpleasant duty. A shrewd observer of men and events, he possessed (or acquired) the gift of prophecy, in which Cobden was pitifully deficient. He was wont to say that ' the first who would wish again for Protection would be the manufacturing interest of Great Britain.' And at a time when Disraeli was either feared or disliked, even by his own side, he did not hesitate to proclaim his approaching triumph. ' His speeches this session have been first-rate,' he writes to Croker in 1848. ' His last speech, altogether burked in the *Times*, but pretty well given in the *Post*, was admirable. He cuts Cobden to ribbons, and Cobden writhes and quails under him just as Peel did in 1846. And, mark my words, spite of Lord Stanley, Major Beresford, and Mr. Phillips and the *Herald*, it will end, before two sessions are out, in Disraeli being the chosen leader of the party.' Here is a prescience founded upon judgment, which is very different from the facile predictions of uninformed optimism.

That he possessed certain faults which would have interfered with his ultimate success may be admitted.

He was prolix and insistent both in speech and on paper. He could give no touch of gaiety to his orations. Being a stern realist he could not and would not go an inch beyond the warrant of his facts. Perfectly decorative in himself, he had not a decorative style, and thus was a complete contrast to his great colleague. Moreover, he had not the power of selection. He was a late learner, and like all late learners, was sometimes overcome by the weight of his material. It was a passion with him to exhaust his subject, and when he took up his pen to write he was never content until he had covered many sheets of paper. Against this prolixity no constitution could battle with success, and Lord George Bentinck fell a victim to his own energy. To die of hard work is not the most picturesque of deaths ; yet, in his own despite, Lord George could not escape the touch of drama, even at the end.

He died suddenly on the 21st of September, between Welbeck and Thoresby—died when his work was un-accomplished, and when his hope of the future was at its highest. It was but for two brief years that he played the game of statesmanship with perfect gravity. Yet in those two years he made a place for himself in our history, and, though the silence of death over-took him in 1849, he seems to belong to our own time more intimately than any of our contemporaries save one. His speeches, purged of their acerbity, are as true to-day as when they were uttered, and they might be delivered again without losing their force

or impairing their argument. And when anxious
partisans still applaud the services of Mr. Cobden, it
is well to recall the strong resolution and splendid
achievement of Mr. Cobden's great adversary, who
with tireless loyalty sacrificed his pleasure and his life
to the cause whose triumph he believed essential to
his country's welfare.

VI

It has already been pointed out that, in writing the
life of Lord George Bentinck, Disraeli with a rare
modesty suppressed himself. Now and again he
declares that ' a friend ' said this, or that ' a friend '
counselled that, and though it is always evident who
the ' friend ' was, his exclusion from the history is a
conspicuous defect. For Lord George Bentinck could
not have achieved what he did without the aid of his
faithful and generous supporter. Never has there
appeared in the House of Commons a more brilliant
debater, a severer critic of inefficient policies, than
Disraeli. And as he won the attention, and aroused
the enthusiasm of the House, he had the added satisfaction that the arrogant prophecies of his youth had
one and all been fulfilled. He had stood upon his
head, and there was no head in England better worth
standing on. The time had come, indeed, when the
House should listen, and when, at his rising, a dropped
pin might be heard. One disappointment he had
suffered in that he got no office in 1841, but they who
pretend that a place in the ministry would have per-

suaded him to endure Peel's autocratic temper singularly misjudge him.   For the rest, he had an equal
confidence in his own abilities and in the justice of his
opinions.   Already famous as a man of letters, he did
not leave his splendid talents on the threshold of the
House.   He carried into politics his gift of literature,
and his speeches are quick with the wit and epigram
which sparkle in his novels.

The years, which had brought with them assurance
and respect, had but increased the vigour of his mind
and put a sharper edge upon the bitterness of his
tongue.   In spite of his achievements, and the place
he had conquered in what he called the Senate, he
was still the Young Disraeli, young in hope, young in
courage, young in resource.   His attitude towards
Protection and Free Trade was logical and consistent.
In 1842 he had voted for Peel's industrial measures,
because he believed that ' they were founded on sound
principles of commercial policy : principles which,
in abeyance during the Whig Government of seventy
years, were revived by that great Tory statesman,
Mr. Pitt.'   Moreover he objected that the term
Free Trade should ever have been usurped by Cobden
and his followers.   ' I am a Free Trader, not a Free
booter,' he said ;   and he pointed out again and again
that the policy of honest Free Trade was the invention of the Tory Party.   No man was ever less a
pedant than he.   ' What is Protection,' he asked,
' but an expedient ? '   And if it be an expedient, it
must depend on circumstances, and could not there-

fore be condemned or approved by the abstract
dogmas so dear to Mr. Cobden and his friends.[1]

Moreover, he saw clearly enough that the alternative offered to Protection was not Free Trade,
which was never possible, but Free Imports; and,
when Sir Robert Peel deserted his party, Disraeli's
course was clear. He was not one of the converts.
He was, as he said, ' a member of a fallen party, a
party which had nothing left on its side, except
the constituencies it had betrayed.' He supported
in Parliament the same policy which he advocated
with a greater deliberation in his *Lord George Bentinck*.
The views which he expressed in the one place were
identical with those which he expressed in the other,
and from the pages of *Hansard* it is possible to fill
the gaps which a too scrupulous modesty left in his
political biography. But there is a difference in style
and temper between the spoken and the written word
appropriate to the occasion. Disraeli wrote of his
friend when time and death had lessened the bitter-

---

[1] The followers of Cobden now, as then, mistake a problem
for a theorem. They speak as though the interchange of com-
modities obeyed an inexorable moral law. With a similar indiscretion they detect in cheapness an inherent virtue. How far
wiser was Coleridge ! ' You talk about making this article
cheaper,' he said, ' by reducing its price in the market from 8d.
to 6d. But suppose in so doing you have rendered your country
weaker against a foreign foe; suppose you have demoralised
thousands of your fellow-countrymen, and have sown discontent
between one class of society and another, your article is tolerably
dear, I take it, after all. Is not its real price enhanced to every
Christian and patriot a hundred-fold ? '

ness of the conflict; he made his speeches in the
House excited by debate, and aroused to indignation
by what seemed to him the perfidy of the minister.
Though he does not spare Peel in his book, he attacked
him face to face with a greater contempt and a more
savage irony.   And yet in his angriest invective there
is a spice of wit, which probably made it less galling
to bear than the serious indictment of Lord George
Bentinck.

The head and front of Peel's offence in Disraeli's
eyes was, of course, his disloyalty to his colleagues.
He had come into power on the strength of Tory
votes, and he relied for the permanence of his ministry
upon his political opponents.   'The right honourable gentleman,' said Disraeli in a memorable phrase,
'caught the Whigs bathing and walked away with their
clothes.'   He had surrendered his ancient ideals, and
trampled on his ancient prejudices.   'I remember
him making his Protection speeches,' said his pitiless
adversary.   'They were the best speeches I ever
heard.   It was a great thing to hear the right honourable gentleman say, " I would rather be the leader of
the gentlemen of England, than possess the confidence of sovereigns."   That was a grand thing.
We don't hear much of the gentlemen of England
now.   But what of that ?   They have the pleasures
of memory, the charms of reminiscence.'   And then,
in the firm conviction that a Conservative Government is an organised hypocrisy, he poured the acid
of his scorn upon Peel's egoism.   He reminded the

House that Peel had urged it to follow him on the ground that he had held high office under four sovereigns. ' Follow him ? ' asked Disraeli—' who is to follow him, or why is anybody to follow him, or where is anybody to follow him to ? ' He recalled the time when Peel delivered himself of the oracle, ' Register, register, register.' Why were they to register ? To save the Corn Laws, the Monarchy, or the Church ? For none of these things : when his supporters had registered enough, Peel ' showed them the sovereign passion—they were to register to make him a minister.'

In his biography Disraeli pictures Peel as always influenced by the opinions of others, as a man whose mind was always in process of education. In the House of Commons he made the same charge, but in more violent terms. ' For between forty and fifty years,' said he, ' from the days of Mr. Horner to those of the honourable member for Stockport, the right honourable gentleman has traded on the ideas and intelligence of others. His life has been one great appropriation clause. He is a burglar of others' intellect. Search the index of Beatson from the days of the Conqueror to the termination of the last reign, there has been no statesman who has committed political petty larceny on so great a scale.' Even more effective was the ridicule poured upon Popkins's plan. ' We know all about it,' said a Radical to Disraeli of Peel's plan ; ' it was offered to us. It is not his plan ; it 's Popkins's plan.' And, asks Disraeli in scorn, is

the England of Burleigh and Walsingham, of Bolingbroke and Walpole, of Chatham and Canning, to be
governed by Popkins's plan? Nor did he spare
the watcher of the atmosphere, the man who never
originated an idea, the minister who thought only of
posterity—of posterity which very few people reach.
And in his scorn he involved the whole of the Treasury
Bench.

' Throw your eyes over the Treasury Bench,' said
he, in his finest passage of contempt. ' See stamped
on each ingenuous front, " The last infirmity of noble
minds." They are all of them, as Spenser says, " Imps
of Fame!" They are just the men in the House
you would fix upon as thinking only of posterity.
The only thing is when one looks at them, seeing of
what they are composed, one is hardly certain whether
" the future " of which they are thinking is indeed
posterity, or only the coming quarter-day.' How
excellent is the unexpectedness of the ' coming
quarter-day'! How the ingenuous fronts of the
Treasury Bench must have blushed at the ridicule!
And Disraeli, tireless in scorn, gave them no peace
until Peel had led his ragged majority into the lobby,
and had himself fallen before a hostile vote.

Disraeli, in his opposition to Peel, was not content
with ridicule. He seldom made a speech which did
not lift the debate to a high plane of argument.
For some years before the Prime Minister had divided
his colleagues, Disraeli had been the leader of the
Young England Party, and though after his speech

on the Maynooth Grant he ceased to act with it, the views of Young England had a profound and lasting influence on him ; and nowhere can this influence be more clearly detected than in the speeches which were inspired by the debates on the Corn Law. A pride in England, a love of the people, the championship of labour—these are the substance of his most eloquent perorations. He taught in his speeches the same lessons of devotion and honour which he had taught in *Sybil*. When he said that he wished to secure a preponderance of the landed interest, he was thinking of the welfare, not of a single class, but of the whole country. With Lord John Manners and George Smythe he regretted the decay of the feudal system. He pointed out that the Conqueror did not distribute the land without exacting responsibility. 'You shall have that estate,' said he, ' but you shall do something for it : you shall feed the poor ; you shall endow the Church ; you shall defend the land in case of war ; and you shall execute justice and maintain truth to the poor for nothing.' This, at any rate, was a better ideal than the ideal of Manchester, to buy in the cheapest and sell in the dearest market, to become rich and ever richer without the interference of industry and toil. So Disraeli's ambition was to see not a ' spinning-Jenny machine kind of nation,' but an England which once more possessed a free Monarchy and a privileged and prosperous People. A very different hope from that of Richard Cobden, who cared as little for the people

as he cared for the landed gentry, and who was strain-
ing every nerve to transfer the power to the middle
class, to create the most dangerous of all things—
wealth without responsibility.

And already Disraeli had struck the note of Imperialism which, familiar to-day, was then rarely
heard. ' I for one,' said he in 1843, ' am not prepared
to sit under the power of a third-class, if I can be a
citizen of a first-class empire.' Moreover, he saw
clearly that Peel and his supporters were losing the
chance of binding the Colonies to the mother country.
' You turn up your noses at East India cotton,' said
he to the House, ' as you have done at everything
Colonial or Imperial.' And it is the fashion to say
that Disraeli had no interest in our empire oversea.
The detractors who bring this charge rely on a hasty
phrase in a private letter, as though a statesman were
on oath if he aired a grievance to a friend.[1] Not only
in his speeches but in his policy, he was a consistent
champion of Colonial interests. In 1863 he already
prophesied that Canada would become the Russia
of the New World, and he declared that, if we were
to quit the possessions that we occupied in North
America, ' we might then prepare for the invasion of
our country and the subjection of the people.'

[1] The sentence may be found in a letter addressed on August
13, 1852, to Lord Malmesbury. ' These wretched colonies,' he
wrote, ' will be independent in a few years, and are a millstone
round our necks.' Against this one petulant expression, not
meant to be published, may be set the constant policy of many
years.

In 1872 he was still more definite in his opinion, still nearer to the policy of to-day. ' The two great objects of the Tory Party,' he declared, ' are to maintain the institutions of the country and to uphold the empire of England.' In the same speech he advocated an imperial tariff, he insisted that the people of England should enjoy unappropriated lands, which belonged to the sovereign as their trustee, he urged that a military code should define precisely the means by which the Colonies should be defended, and by which the country should call for aid from the Colonies themselves. Thus he anticipated all that a generation, keenly alive to the importance of our Empire, has hoped or thought, and thus he takes his place in the long line of patriotic ministers who since the time of Bolingbroke, his master, have guided the destinies of England.

When once the Corn Laws were abolished, Disraeli took the only course that was open to him : he accepted the accomplished fact. His speeches on agricultural distress, delivered within five years after Peel's measure was passed, sufficiently prove that he had not changed his opinion ; and when, having gathered together the *disjecta membra* of the old Tory Party, he assumed the leadership of the House, the question was closed. Whatever distress assailed the country, the remedy of protection had passed for the moment beyond the range of practical policy, in spite of Disraeli's opposition, and with the reiterated approval of the people. ' Under these

circumstances,' as Disraeli said in 1879, ' it was impossible for a public man, whatever had been his
opinions upon these great commercial questions, when
these important changes were first introduced, to have
had an open controversy for a quarter of a century.
The government of the country could not have been
carried on.' Nor, when reciprocity was suggested as
a cure for the evils which beset the State, did reciprocity seem possible. We had nothing to reciprocate. We had given up the means by which an
honourable system of commercial treaties could be
established. But they err who assert that Disraeli
renounced in his old age the principles for which he
fought so valiantly in 1846 ; and, though it is idle to
vaticinate what course he would have followed in
another age, the consistent policy of his whole life is
an eloquent proof that he would never have surrendered the commercial supremacy of England for the
sake of a dogma.

VII

With such combatants engaged on either side, the
contest could not but be dramatic, and Disraeli has
described it with all the resources of a literary crafts-
man. And most finely dramatic of all is the closing
scene when triumph and defeat overtook Sir Robert in
the same hour. The passage in which Disraeli describes
this last act of the tragedy has an epic touch. He
marshals the ' men of metal and large-acred squires,
the Manners, the Somersets, the Bentincks, the

Lowthers, and the Lennoxes,' in the same spirit wherewith Homer numbers the ships of the Greeks. Sir Robert was beaten by 73. ' He looked very grave, and extended his chin as was his habit when he was annoyed and cared not to speak. He began to comprehend his position, and that the emperor was without his army.' Nor did the emperor ever reassemble his shattered forces. And losing his army, he had lost his influence. ' Peel can never be at the head of any party,' said the Duke of Wellington to Sir Edward Knatchbull—' that is, of any considerable party. He will keep his seat in the House of Commons, and will endeavour to act as a sort of umpire between parties. He will not be disposed himself again to take office. The country will not trust him again.'

Nor did the last speech which he delivered as a minister tend to recover his lost friends. For the first time he mentioned Cobden by name, and paid an unexpected tribute to the agitator. Even Mr. Gladstone was outraged by this indiscretion. ' Mr. Cobden,' said Mr. Gladstone, ' has throughout argued the Corn Question on the principle of holding up the landlords of England to the people as plunderers and as knaves for maintaining the Corn Law to save their rents, and as fools because it was not necessary for that purpose. This was passed by, while he was praised for sincerity, eloquence, indefatigable zeal.' Thus politics also has its ironies, and it is strange to find Mr. Gladstone in public supporting the sad, lost cause of the landlords. The reception of the Corn Bill by the country emphasised the truth that it was passed not for the people, but for the manufacturers. The news, we are told by the *Annual Register*, caused much rejoicing in the manufacturing districts of England and France. ' Bells were rung ; flags and banners, bearing appropriate inscriptions, were displayed from factories or carried in procession about the streets. . . . In many places arrangements were made by employers to give their workmen a holiday and an entertainment.' To the bald eloquence of this statement no word need be added.

THE EIGHTH DUKE OF DEVONSHIRE

THE career of the Eighth Duke of Devonshire has an interest which is already archæological. If he were a statesman, we know not what they are who have presumed to carry on the traditions of his craft. Between him and his successors there is no binding link of purpose or ambition. When he had been dead less than four years, he seemed already as remote as the heroes of Plutarch's world. So fast have we travelled down the inclined plane of lawlessness, that we can hardly realise that this staunch champion of law and order ever lived and spoke in our midst. But the wanton revolutions which have taken place since his death in the conduct of affairs increases the worth of his achievement, and we can wish our politicians no better fate than that they should keep before them the high example of this wise and patriotic Duke.

For fifty years, as Lord Cavendish, the Marquis of Hartington, and the Duke of Devonshire, he took part in the government of his country, and never for a moment did he loosen his hold upon the faith and

respect of the people. There was none, either friend
or foe, who did not trust his high sense of honour and
his profound knowledge of affairs. His countrymen
always recognised that he brought far more to the
task of government than he expected to get out of it.
For him politics was no adventure. He was not
forced by necessity or a false ambition to trim the
sails of his bark to the popular breeze. The son of a
noble and distinguished house, he inherited the best
traditions of English policy, and he hoped to serve
England, not to compel England to serve him. A
sense of duty sent him into the House of Commons,
and a sense of duty kept him there. There is a vast
deal of evidence in Mr. Holland's volumes [1] to prove
that, if he could, he would early have retired to the
private life of an English gentleman. 'We are in
again, I am sorry to say,' he wrote in 1873, ' not without an attempt on my part to get free.' Though he
would not put his colleagues to any inconvenience,
he had already ' come to detest office.' When
Mr. Gladstone had discovered prematurely that he
was arriving at ' the closing of his days,' Lord Hartington hoped against hope that he might not be forced
to succeed that eminent man. ' It will really be a
great relief to be out of it,' he wrote ; ' and not only
on idle grounds. I should never have liked it ; but
I don't think I could endure the toleration I should
have to put up with.' When he saw that he could

[1] See *The Life of Spencer Compton, Eighth Duke of Devonshire*,
by Bernard Holland.

no longer escape the leadership, he assumed it with a strong hand. Yet the reluctance to lead never left him. 'It is extraordinary,' he wrote to Lord Salisbury many years later, 'what an attraction office seems to have for some people.' It had none for him, and he boasts the unique distinction of having refused three times to be Prime Minister.

This is the first secret of his profound influence : the whole world knew him to be disinterested. And not merely was he disinterested ; he had an unconcealed dislike for cant of every sort. When Mr. Gladstone was rushing up and down the country denouncing what he called 'Bulgarian atrocities,' Lord Hartington deplored the summoning of a Conference. 'I see no great harm,' he wrote to Lord Granville, 'if it is a failure, so long as the moderate men of the party are not mixed up in it. They cannot talk more nonsense than has already been talked at the meetings ; but why should we encourage any respectable member of the party to go and listen to, and be in some sense perhaps committed by the speeches of men like Freeman, Canon Liddon, Jenkins, Maxse, Lyulph Stanley, etc., etc., and innumerable parsons ? The number of the latter on the list is quite enough for me.'

It was this same hatred of cant that made him take a modest view of his parliamentary services. He did not believe that because he was returned to the House of Commons by an enthusiastic constituency he was the saviour of his country. The vice of pomposity was impossible to him. 'I have seen much of the shorthorn world,' he wrote, when men's minds were inflamed by the Eastern Question, 'who do not appear to be wiser than other people.' Once upon a time when an orator in the House of Lords said, 'this is the proudest moment of my life,' the Duke murmured to his neighbour, 'the proudest moment of my life was when my pig won the first prize at Skipton Fair.' It was his great virtue never to put false values upon things, nor to disguise his preferences. He firmly believed that his birth and destiny called him to the political field. The obligation of honour did not leave him a free man. Had he been free, perhaps he would have given to sport not his leisure but his life. 'Sometimes I dream that I am leading in the winner of the Derby,' he said, 'but I am afraid it will never be anything but a dream.' It is certain that he never dreamed that he was Prime Minister.

With this nonchalance were bound up a transparent honesty, and a perfect sense of truth. He made no sacrifice to the exigence of the moment. By a happy fate he was spared the disgrace of rhetoric. Such words as he had, and they were persuasive rather than many, he employed not to cloak but to reveal his mind. As Mr Holland says, 'the witch, Imagination, had no power over him.' It was his constant endeavour to strip falsehood of her trappings. A magnificently ingenuous passage in a letter of Mr. Gladstone lucidly explains the difference between the two men. ' I have been a good deal distressed,' wrote Mr. Gladstone in 1883, ' by a passage as reported in Hartington's very strong and able speech, for which I am at a loss to account, so far does it travel out into the open, and so awkward are the intimations it seems to convey.' It would be impossible to surpass the unconscious humour of these observations. Candour is always ' awkward ' in the eyes of the politician, and to travel out into the open ways of truth is inexcusable when it might cost a vote.

And the Duke of Devonshire was always in the open. ' He cared only to state things as they were.' His opinions were plain for all men to approve or discuss. If his colleagues did not share his opinions, then he resigned ; and the fact that he and others resigned at certain crises of our history reminds us that politics, even Radical politics, were once the pursuit of honourable men. I can imagine few differences of opinion so great that they would have persuaded a single member of any subsequent Government to resign. The Duke himself noted this pitiful falling off in public morality. ' I take a very gloomy view of the prospect,' he wrote in 1908. ' Campbell-Bannerman seems prepared to go to any lengths, and Asquith, Haldane and Co. will do nothing effectual to stop him.' He, of course, in such a case would have resigned instantly. For the limpets of office there is no resignation, but a wicked responsibility in the misdeeds of others.

When Lord Hartington severed the last link which bound him to Gladstone, Auberon Herbert, who disagreed with him in politics, wrote him a letter which it were well for politicians of either side to remember. I make no apology for printing here these sentences of honest wisdom. ' I think we may go right or wrong about Ireland, or almost any great matter,' wrote Auberon Herbert, ' and, if wrong, recover from our mistake; but the one thing from which I think there is no salvation is when men begin to have no confidence in themselves and their own opinion, and to become the mere instruments of party. I have long hoped to see you break with what I have believed to be a false position, and I think your having done so will give a new sense of duty and a new power of action to hundreds of men throughout the country. Every man who consents to action of which he is believed to disapprove helps to lower the sense of individual responsibility in all others whom he influences, and the moment he refuses to do so any longer he wakes others from a mental and moral sleep.' There, expressed by another, is the Duke of Devonshire's creed of politics—a creed long since trodden under foot by ambitious adventurers, not one of whom will ever wake himself or others from the torpor of self-interest.

In the common sense of the word the Duke was not nimble-witted. ' All through life,' he said, ' I have had to work with men who thought three times as quick as I did, and have found this a great disadvantage.' The disadvantage was not as great as he thought. The very slowness of his reasoning added enormously to his tenacity. When once he had determined upon a course of action, he was not easily driven from his course. The ample simplicity of his mind enabled him to discard all that was not essential to the policy in hand. He could not juggle with right and wrong. He would have scorned to assume the facile omniscience dear to some of his colleagues. He gladly acknowledged an ignorance of what he did not know, and thus discovered another reason why all men should trust him. His attitude towards the Fiscal question was straightforward and character-istic. He had been brought up in the school of Free Trade, and his Conservative instincts persuaded him not to change his view. It is clear that he did not understand the arguments of Mr. Balfour and Mr. Chamberlain. And, not understanding them, he very rightly left the Government. The uncertainty of his position he explained to a friend with his own dry humour. 'The politics of the family are rather mixed,' he said. 'Victor is a Balfourian, Dick is an out-and-out free-trader, and God knows what I am.' There is no jugglery here.

The deliberation of his thought saved him from the worst pitfall which yawns for public men. He was never the victim of a discursive cleverness. He could not chatter idly of Shakespeare and Shelley. The light which came from his brain was intense, not diffused. He regarded art and literature with the same candour wherewith he looked upon life and politics. It is recorded that he once picked up

Paradise Lost and began to read it aloud. Then stopping for a moment he said, ' How fine this is ! I had forgotten how fine it was.' Try to imagine what Mr. Gladstone would have said on a like occasion, and you may measure roughly the contrast between the two men. It is indeed this contrast which most forcibly seizes the mind of him who reads the annals of the time. For many years Mr. Gladstone and the Duke were colleagues or adversaries. They represented two sides of English politics. They were incompatible always in method and ambition, and the wonder is that they worked together as long as they did. It was unfortunate for Mr. Gladstone that they were at last disparted. For if the influence of Mr. Gladstone upon Lord Hartington was inappreciable, the influence of Lord Hartington upon Mr. Gladstone was always salutary.

Mr. Gladstone was an actor, protean and irresponsible. For him words were a thousand times more important than deeds ; and by a cruel irony, even the words which he spoke were almost meaningless, if unaccompanied by his massive gesture and the flashing of his vulturine eye. His mind was in a constant state of fluidity. The heresy of yesterday was converted by opportunity into the gospel of to-day. The past was nothing to him ; the future immaterial. He vaunted only with persuasive eloquence the advantage of the present. In all things the Duke was his antithesis. He was far too honest and sincere ever to act a part. So securely anchored was he to the traditions of his race and time, that he could not separate the present from the past. Unchanging as the rocks of his native Derbyshire, he was loyal always to himself and to others. The story that he yawned in the middle of his own speech is true in essence, if not in fact. He cultivated a plain, even a dull, presentation, partly because plainness was natural to him, partly because he had a wise distrust of rhetoric. He had that quality which the French call *morgue*, and this prevented him from displaying an enthusiasm which he did not feel.

He was a first-rate administrator, with a vast power of work, and he could get the heart out of a blue-book with astonishing speed and accuracy. As Mr. Holland has said in precisely the right words, ' his work was done with a weary, or bored thoroughness.' His attitude was that of a man ' refusing to be hurried.' He could never have been described, like Mr. Gladstone, as ' an old man in a hurry.' His character, as summed up by Mr. Holland, wholly justifies his influence. ' Hartington,' writes Mr. Holland, ' as Lord Granville once told him, resembled a certain diplomat of the day, who says that his head is so constructed that it can take in very little of what is not perfectly clear. He was, as the French say, of a *caractère très uni*, or, as we say, " all of a piece," *unum hominem*. . . . His speeches only succeeded, so far as they did succeed, because of the weight and sincerity of his character. His word was known to be one with himself ; he was, as the saying goes, " as

good as his word." He was averse to speaking, nor
was he flattered by the applause of the crowd. Had
he evoked any loud applause, he would probably have
felt like the Greek aristocrat who, hearing plaudits,
turned to a friend near him and asked, "Have I said
anything very foolish ? " ' A far different statesman
from the noisy rhetoricians who since his time have
usurped the reins of power, and who have thought
the Empire well lost if only the raucous voices of
the mob echoed in their ears.

Such was the man who was appointed by providence to be a watch-dog upon the actions of Mr.
Gladstone. How faithfully he performed his office
is known to us all. It was particularly in Ireland
that he dogged the footsteps of his great chief and
opponent. His qualifications to speak of Ireland
were many. He was an Irish landlord who liked and
understood the people of the country. He had been
Irish Secretary, and was familiar with all the tricks
and deceits of the agitators. His clear sense of reality
convinced him that you could not solve a difficult
problem of government by such empty phrases as
' a nation struggling to be free.' He believed in reform, in land reform especially, and he believed in law.
He was therefore at the opposite pole from Mr. Gladstone, whose sentimentality assured him that you
could staunch the blood of dying men and relieve
the persecuted from boycotting by murmuring such
empty words as ' the union of hearts.' The diver-
gency between the two showed itself early. In 1870,

when the sanguine Mr. Gladstone was confident that the disestablishment of the Church had created a new Ireland, Lord Hartington poured a cold douche upon his colleague. ' It would be the height of insanity,' said he, ' to suppose that the establishment of religious equality or the passing of a law regulating the tenure of land would put a stop to the Ribbon conspiracy. I cannot see on what possible ground it could be imagined that the establishment of equal and just legislation should have any effect on the minds of men who have a system of laws of their own— not just laws, but the most unjust, the most arbitrary, the most tyrannical, the most barbarous. I cannot see what sympathy such men could have with good legislation.' These words were spoken in 1870, and they are the prelude of as wise and consistent a policy as ever was followed by a wise and consistent statesman.

Henceforth he exposed, with all the force of sincerity that was his, the lightest suspicion of Home Rule. ' I said that I believed, and I believe it fully now '—thus he spoke in 1880—' that it would be fatal to all hopes the Liberal party might ever have of getting a majority and of regaining power in this country, if they were to show any complicity with those who agitated for the separation of Ireland from the Empire.' It was not mere expediency which moved him ; his resolution was based upon reverence for law, a reverence far deeper than any desire he might have cherished of getting a majority. ' Whatever may be the fate of our efforts,' he said a year later,

' to improve the law, we hold now, as we have always done, that it is our duty to carry out the existing law as it stands, and not to surrender the powers, ordinary or extraordinary, which Parliament has confided in us into the hands of the Land League or any other body.' How strangely antiquated sounds this public respect for the law in the ears of those who have not forgotten the contempt of the Duke's successors and the condoning of the Irish rebellion !

It was in 1885 that the real struggle against Home Rule began, and the value of the letters which Lord Hartington wrote and the speeches that he made then and in the following years cannot be overrated. The revolution of time has brought England back since to precisely the same situation she was in then, and Lord Hartington still speaks with all his ancient force and cogency. Truly he forged an armoury of weapons, which those who come after him may wield. Some are still left, we trust, who can draw the bow of Achilles and scatter, with aim unerring as his, the enemies that gather about us on every side. The first clear note of warning was struck in December 1885, in a letter to Lord Granville. ' From all I can hear,' wrote Lord Hartington, ' Gladstone appears to be acting in a most extraordinary manner, and I should think will utterly smash up the party. I don't know who is going to support him in proposing a Home Rule policy for Ireland. Chamberlain and Dilke, as at present advised, are, I hear, entirely opposed to it ; but they may come round.'

Meanwhile Gladstone had no counsel to give his followers, except that they should not ' commit themselves.' By this he meant not to commit themselves *against* Home Rule. In favour of Home Rule he said and wrote what seemed good to him. Lord Hartington at once pounced upon this discrepancy. ' Mr. Gladstone,' he wrote, ' may say as much as he likes about our not committing ourselves ; but he has committed himself up to his chin.' There was a vast deal of clamour and discussion on all sides. Chamberlain and Harcourt were as much opposed to Home Rule as Lord Hartington, though, as we all know, Harcourt presently found it convenient to swallow his views. Lord Hartington never wavered. His course was clear at the outset. In January 1886 Gladstone offered him office, which he declined. ' He was very civil,' says Lord Hartington, ' and we parted apparently good friends.' But the severance was now final and complete, nor did Lord Hartington delay in making clear his position to the House of Commons. The first speech which he made after the parting left no room for doubt. Its peroration has lost none of its meaning in the years which have elapsed since its delivery. ' I believe that now, at all events,' said Lord Hartington, ' the people of this country will require that their representatives shall, in relation to Irish affairs, agree to sink all minor differences, and to unite as one man for the maintenance of this great Empire, to hand it down to our successors compact as we have received it from our forefathers, and at the same time to maintain throughout its length and breadth the undisputed supremacy of the law.' Even if Lord Hartington's views appeared contemptible in the eyes of Mr. Gladstone's successors they will still be cherished unto the end of time by the sane majority of his countrymen.

It was, indeed, the sanctity of the law which came first in Lord Hartington's esteem. When Sir William Harcourt defended the Plan of Campaign by citing the lawless and rebellious habit of the Whigs, Lord Hartington was cold in his contempt. ' It is extremely difficult,' said he, ' to argue with opponents who avow there is a moral justification for defiance of the law. I believe we are here in this House to amend the law, if necessary ; but to support the Government in the enforcement of the law. We are not here for preaching or condoning resistance to the law, either passive or overt.' While his general principles of law and order were perfectly sound, he covered in detail the whole field of the controversy, and it is this thoroughness which makes his speeches about Ireland of the utmost importance. He spoke of Ulster in a tone which flippant Ministers might still regard as serious were they not the kept puppets of self-interest. ' The people of Ulster,' said he, ' tell you they will not willingly submit to the form of government which it is proposed to impose upon them. I have never attempted to say whether you are to believe that the people of Ulster say what they mean or not, but I will say that it is a very ill-

advised action, at all events, on the part of the supporters of the Bill, to treat the manifestations of
Ulster as mere bluster.' Ill-advised was the action
of the Home-Rulers then, ill-advised is it likely to
prove always, and not ill-advised merely, but un-
supported by a shred of argument. If Ireland were
right to resent the rule of England, then would Ulster
be doubly right to refuse to bear the yoke which her
enemies would lay upon her.

In one other respect the situation has remained
constant. In 1885 Home Rule was a policy which, as
Lord Hartington said, 'emanated from the brain and
will of a single man.' As in 1885 so in 1893. 'It
is not a policy,' said the Duke of Devonshire, 'which
has proceeded from a political party; it is not a
policy advocated by a political party and then adopted
by its leaders. It is a policy which has been imposed
upon his followers by the single will of one man.'
Every word spoken those many years ago is still true.
Home Rule has never been the policy of the nation;
it has never been the policy of a party. Ireland,
secure in her prosperity has never wanted it. It
has meant always a career for this or that adventurer,
not a national aspiration. And whenever it has
seemed near to be realised, the leaders have shrunk
back, because they would not have their occupation
gone.

Another argument, the confusion and fallacy of
which remains to be exposed, was countered again
and again by the Duke of Devonshire. The advo-

cates of Home Rule could never make up their mind
whether Ireland was to stand in the same relation to
England as Canada, or whether henceforth England
and Ireland should be related one to the other as
the separate provinces of Canada are related. The
Duke demanded a clear answer to his question:
'When the Government speak of the measure sometimes as one preserving the unity of the United
Kingdom, and sometimes the unity of the British
Empire, are we to read these terms in the sense in
which they are now applied to the United Kingdom,
or only as they are now applied to the British Empire?'
To this question the Duke received no answer. The
world since has fared no better than he. And yet on
the answer will always depend the fate, not only of the
United Kingdom, but of the British Empire. Thus
the unending battle is fought, and we fight it with
a better courage, because we have before us the
shining example of those who defended the Union
under the auspices of this staunch upholder of the
law. Nothing contributed to win the battle then so
much as the wisdom and moderation of the Duke of
Devonshire, and we can imagine no better preparation
for the fray which will repeat itself interminably
than a deep and faithful study of his orderly and
honest career.